By the same author

SEVEN MEN AT DAYBREAK

THE LOVELY SERGEANT

WORD FOR LOVE

THE SMALL WOMAN
made into the movie
The Inn of the Sixth Happiness

DAYLIGHT
MUST
COME

DAYLIGHT MUST COME

The Story of a Courageous Woman Doctor in the Congo

ALAN BURGESS

DELACORTE PRESS / NEW YORK

Originally published in slightly different form
by Michael Joseph Ltd., London

Designed by Deborah Speed

Library of Congress Cataloging in Publication Data

Burgess, Alan.
Daylight must come; the story of a courageous
woman doctor in the Congo.
"Originally published in Great Britain . . . in
different form."
1. Roseveare, Helen. I. Title.
BV3625.C63R633   1974   266′.023′0924 [B]
ISBN 0-440-03365-9   74-5479

🌿 FOREWORD

My most sincere thanks are due first of all to Dr. Helen Roseveare for allowing me access to her letters, diaries, and other material, and for putting me in touch with Norman Grubb in the U.S.A., who lent me Helen's invaluable correspondence with him, dating as far back as 1953.

I am also deeply indebted to Helen for those splendid weeks in Congo when she introduced me so patiently and explicitly to the locations and people pertinent to this story, and for the long days we spent together while she talked about her experiences, hopes, beliefs, and philosophies.

I am also very grateful to Jack and Jessie Scholes, Frank and Mrs. Cripps, Florence Stebbing, Daisy Kingdon, Agnes Chansler and Marjorie Cheverton, Amy, both Elaines, Pat, Gladys, John Mangadima, Brian Cripps, the Worldwide Evangelization Crusade in general, and many others for their absorbing reminiscences, recounted in the hot sunlight or starlit darkness of that most original and dramatic background: the tropical rain forest of equatorial Congo. Thanks also to Stuart Rising, the young mercenary soldier, for the graphic details of the incredibly heroic rescue foray of 54 Commando.

Finally, my sincere thanks to Dr. Carl Becker and his staff at Nyankunde, not forgetting Bud and Marie Mac-

Dougal, whose hospitality and kindness during that period I shall always remember with gratitude and affection.

Place names create a small problem—Congo is now Zaire; Leopoldville, Kinshasa; Stanleyville, Kisingani; and Paulis, Isiro—but for the benefit of what I believe is clarity, I have used the old names.

Photographs follow page 152

DAYLIGHT
MUST
COME

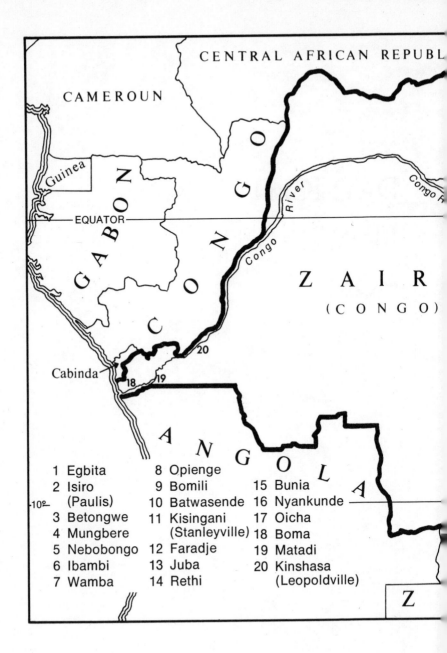

CENTRAL AFRICAN REPUBL

CAMEROUN

Guinea

GABON

CONGO

Congo River

Congo R

EQUATOR

Congo

ZAIR

(CONGO)

20

Cabinda

18 19

ANGOLA

-10°

Z

1 Egbita	8 Opienge	
2 Isiro	9 Bomili	15 Bunia
(Paulis)	10 Batwasende	16 Nyankunde
3 Betongwe	11 Kisingani	17 Oicha
4 Mungbere	(Stanleyville)	18 Boma
5 Nebobongo	12 Faradje	19 Matadi
6 Ibambi	13 Juba	20 Kinshasa
7 Wamba	14 Rethi	(Leopoldville)

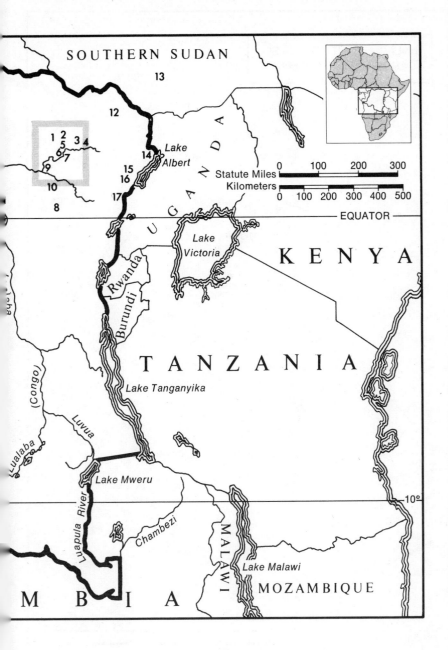

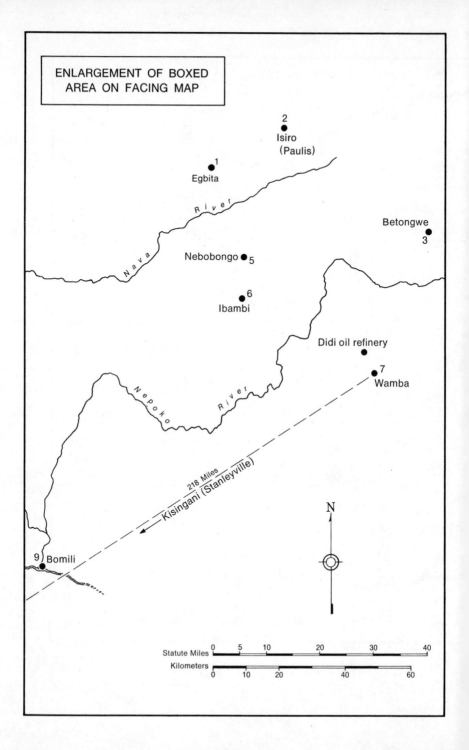

ENLARGEMENT OF BOXED
AREA ON FACING MAP

Egbita 1

Isiro
(Paulis) 2

Betongwe 3

Nava River

Nebobongo 5

Ibambi 6

Didi oil refinery

Wamba 7

Nepoko River

218 Miles
Kisingani (Stanleyville)

Bomili 9

N

Statute Miles
0 5 10 20 30 40

Kilometers
0 10 20 40 60

PART ONE

PART ONE

🌿 CHAPTER 1

The truck door slammed. The driver, placid, docile, and, so far as they knew, disinterested in their future, pumped the accelerator pedal, to produce a series of staccato roars. The crowd of Congolese cheered derisively as the truck grated into gear and slowly labored away from the dilapidated store which acted as rebel headquarters in the tiny tropical rain-forest village of Ibambi.

It was Saturday, mid-morning, November 28, 1964. They might have been off for a day out, the annual picnic, a visit to market; a casual spectator could never have guessed the purpose of the journey from the noise, the excitement, the jeering laughter. But Helen and all the others, trapped in this ferocious Congo uprising, were well aware of where they were going.

She was certain—she knew with total conviction—that they were on their way to execution, that death was inevitable and only a few hours away—the time, in fact, it took them to drive to the settlement of Wamba, some fifty miles to the east. And it was certain to be a hideously cruel death.

The fear which consumed her was numbing. So many others had been tortured and killed, and it was obvious that their end had merely been fortuitously delayed, and thereby made more terrifying. Indeed, she wondered why her captors were wasting so much time taking them to Wamba when they could execute them immediately. But perhaps they thought that the sight of seven Christian missionaries on their way to slaughter would provide a thought-provoking and cautionary spectacle for the public. Certainly, it would endorse the fact that the new Simba regime was implacable in its vengeance.

From her perch high up on the truck, she looked down at her colleagues. Seven little missionaries in sun helmets, khaki shirts and shorts, or print dresses and openwork sandals, the suitcases neatly packed, the Bibles to hand, the noses sunburned. Their years of endeavor, hymns, sermons, and pious exhortations were soon to be concluded on the blood-stained grass at Wamba. So silly. So absolutely ridiculous. A long Congo road to Calvary, marked not by carrying a cross but by riding on a bunch of bananas.

Despite her fear, Helen could still recognize with one detached part of her mind how ludicrous their situation was. Who but the Congolese would cart off prisoners to execution in such a manner? Who else would think of piling them up on the back of an old truck which was also encumbered with suitcases, boxes and bales, chickens, goats, bicycles, stalks of green plaintains, and a dozen Africans hitching a lift to various villages along the route? Even the French aristocrats jolting in their tumbrels toward that eighteenth-century guillotine must have retained a shred of dignity. For Helen and her friends there was no dignity at all.

Dr. Helen Roseveare, Cambridge graduate, thirty-nine years old, skinny from a lack of interest in food and a total commitment to work, wore a loose, crumpled print dress which maintained coolness, comfort, and modesty and avoided any known fashion trend that might ever have existed. Her hair was trimmed short, and the gray-green eyes behind the glasses were attractive and eager. As family and friends had readily admitted over the years, she was not "the pretty one" of the four Roseveare daughters; she was the one with "the brains." Helen had never been very excited by having "the brains," but she was quite reconciled to hearing about her own shortcomings, always prepared to own up to them and even, occasionally, to admit to some she did not possess. Helen thrived on a steady sense of humility.

She was aware that she was diligent but headstrong, and that for the past eleven years she'd been driven by a sense of urgent purpose. It was a characteristic which, in a country marking time by moons, seasons, births, deaths, and harvests, rather than hours or minutes, drove everybody to the edge of distraction. She couldn't help it. It was the way that God had made her. On a utilitarian level she thought of herself as a serious, dedicated employee in the service of God; she gave Him her entire love, belief, and loyalty, and was therefore His complete responsibility. Because of that philosophy, she had accepted the present situation as inevitable, written her last letters, concealed her diary, hoping that it would eventually reach her mother, and in her prayers tried to impress upon her Maker that her impending arrival was near. However, it was just possible that at the very back of her mind two mental fingers were firmly crossed in case a miracle did happen, for she did not—most certainly did not—think that this was much of a way to end her life.

Stuck up on a black-japanned steel truck, its sharp edges sticking into her legs, she could see that the faces of all her friends—Amy and Elaine; Brian Cripps, dark-haired, cheerful, and twenty-seven; Stebby, veteran nurse-midwife; and Jack and Jessie Scholes, who led the mission at Ibambi, both in their sixties and graying—were tight and drawn, and she guessed her own must look the same. Fear prohibited conversation. And even though quite recently Amy had declared, "Helen, you'll still be chattering when they lead you out in front of the firing squad," she dared not exchange even a whispered remark.

As the truck rumbled up the red clay road past the twin rows of ramshackle wooden houses which identified this village in the middle of Congo's tropical rain forest, her lips shaped the words "Good-bye, Ibambi."

In this district she had worked for eleven years building her own hospital, delivering babies, laboring over the sick, grieving for the dying, and for the past four years—since the Belgians had granted independence to the new Congo state and most of the members of the country's professional classes had left, as quickly as possible—she had been the only doctor for hundreds of miles around for much of the time. "And a fat lot of good that is going to do me now!" she thought.

They crawled up through the avenue of trees; the fierce Congo sunlight probed the dark green of the branches. The bright blossoms of geraniums, bougainvillea, and marigold grew wild and unattended in patches of garden, against wooden fences, and wherever else they could take root.

Color, Helen reflected, was synonymous with Congo: deep blue sky, vivid green grass, red earth—red as rich as the blood which had spilled so liberally in these last few weeks. Blues, greens, oranges, purples, heliotropes—colors as strident and awesome as the passions released in this bewildering Simba rebellion which had so recently swept across Congo.

On her first arrival, eleven years before, in 1953, she had been inclined to compare these Congo landscapes with the pastel rain-washed scenery of the English countryside. She compared them, but not because she missed the latter. She did not even regret leaving that scenery, for she had deliberately abandoned her past. Congo was home. Those tides running in through the morning mists over the hard-packed sand of Cornish beaches, those scarlet buses moving serenely through London's traffic were the nostalgic memories of childhood and adolescence. This Congo village from which she was being taken for execution was home.

It was ironic perhaps, that these black people with skins dark and smooth as purple grapes—whom after a few weeks she hadn't even seen as "black"—who had been her friends, neighbors, colleagues, and pupils, were soon to be her executioners. But on reflection she knew that this also was only a half truth. All decent people were stunned by this sudden Simba uprising. They called themselves the People's Army of Liberation, but so far all they had done was torture, slaughter, and destroy in a particularly bestial manner.

The lorry reached the top of the hill, the driver changing up into second as they passed the cotton factory. One of the three Simba guards, dangling his legs over the tailboard, turned to brandish a hand grenade in her direction. "If the mercenaries come, we'll kill them," he shouted exultantly.

Half naked, wearing khaki shorts, his body decorated with sprigs of green and bits of animal fur, he might have looked ridiculous in a different situation. Harsh and bitter experience had proven that the Simbas were dangerous and vicious. From the very first moment a few weeks ago when the first group had driven up to the hospital at Nebobongo, she had been conscious of their definite aura of evil; they were barbaric and terrifying because of their intimidating power over life and death.

The Simba now mimed the action of wrenching out the grenade's firing pin with his teeth and tossing it into the cloud of red dust billowing behind them. "That'll be the end of the mercenaries," he yelled, imitating the noise of the explosion: "Boom! Boom!"

Helen had never seen a mercenary. Indeed, she was not quite sure what the word really meant. She had heard over the BBC that a force of white volunteers had been raised to help the National Congolese Army fight the Simbas, but these people were as far removed from her life as lunar astronauts.

More to the point, however, she was a little surprised that, with the insatiable curiosity of all Congolese, the Simba hadn't already pulled the firing pin of his grenade, just to see if it worked.

At this particular moment it seemed to Helen that all was madness. Her world, and its day-to-day sequence of events, had slipped out of focus into nightmare unreality. Even motherly Jessie Scholes, wife of the mission leader, a champion of conservative prudence and common sense, was at that moment hatching a plot which seemed totally insane to Helen.

Under that blanket draped across her knees was a large flag. A Union Jack! In the unlikely—indeed, near miraculous—eventuality of one of these legendary columns of jeep-borne mercenaries closing in behind them, she intended to leap to her feet and wave it boldly to attract their attention, thus proving that she and her captive colleagues were British and in desperate need of rescue.

Having experienced the pathological fury of the Simbas when opposed, Helen knew that if they discovered the flag they would react with predictable and lethal rage. They would not know whose flag it was; they would believe it was the flag of either the U.S.A. or some other equally hostile country, and in their anger they would almost certainly execute them all on the spot. At that moment, several groups were hated enemies: Belgians, because of their recent colonial ownership; all Catholics, because they were an official part of that regime; and all Americans, who were said to be helping the Belgians.

Helen, however, did not argue or even protest to Jessie. Civilized thought and rationality had disappeared in the jungle weeks ago. Indeed, she looked with a new interest and respect at the innocent Jessie clutching her Union Jack under the blanket with the same dedication as the Simba brandishing his hand grenade. The contiguity of death, it seemed, made conspirators of them all.

The truck swerved around a corner, and the hot blue sky framed between dark segments of forest wheeled across Helen's vision; centrifugal force heaved chickens, goats, and people to one side, the animals bleating or clucking disconsolately, the Africans squealing with glee.

From any hilltop, she knew from long experience, they would look like a small black bug dragging a trail of scarlet foam in its wake along a light brown pencil line. Similar pencil lines drawn wire-straight across a vast, dark-green landscape would represent dirt roads stretching for hundreds of miles through sparsely populated country.

Flying in eastwards for a thousand miles from Leopoldville, all you saw was a vast, empty green landscape. You stared down on a surface so tightly forested that it resembled the texture of an endless cauliflower or the exposed membrane of some gigantic brain stripped from its skull, stained green, mottled brown, and veined with the shining streaks of black and turbulent rivers. This wilderness of tropical rain forest sometimes opened to reveal a huge swamp of bright, iridescent color, like a freshly spilled pool from a lime-green paint pot.

The first mutinies and troubles at the declaration of Congo's independence in 1960 had not greatly disturbed the Protestant missionaries at Ibambi. Indeed, even when the

Simba rebellion broke out, late in 1964, they were allowed to continue their work, and were told, "It has nothing to do with you. This is a People's Liberation Army dedicated to overthrowing the corrupt regime in Leopoldville. Carry on with your work, you will not be harmed."

But a week before their arrest on that Saturday of November 21, 1964, all seven of them had gathered around the radio and listened with grave concern to the bland English voice reading with firm assurance and total lack of awareness the news item which spelled out a death sentence for hundreds of white civilians in northeastern Congo.

"It is reported," the voice said, "that a thousand Belgian parachutists have arrived at Ascension Island, flown in by American transport planes. They are waiting there for permission from the Congo Government in Leopoldville to drop on the town of Stanleyville and rescue the many hundreds of white civilians held hostage by the Simba rebels."

Helen had stared in disbelief at Jack Scholes. So fatuous an announcement was beyond comprehension. She could barely stutter out her protest. "Don't they understand that the rebels listen to the radio too? Why tell them what's going to happen? Why tell them?"

Jack had looked round at the stunned faces of the others, aware of the importance of maintaining morale but unable to conceal his own anxiety. "I don't understand it," he said. "I really don't understand it at all."

"They must be mad," continued Helen angrily. "Why give away the plan? Do they have to tell the whole world they're mounting a rescue operation which is supposed to be a surprise? Don't they realize we're all front-line hostages?"

The voice—and there were dozens of such radio voices, beamed from all over Africa—continued:

"A rebel statement claims that all white civilians have been removed out of Stanleyville. Other reports from Nairobi, where talks about the safety of white civilians trapped in the northeastern provinces are still continuing, claim that negotiators are horrified by this move on the part of Belgian and American authorities. They declare it sets Africa back, with a violent slap in the face, four years, to the worst moment in Congo's history."

They sat dumbfounded in Jack Scholes's living room. There was little anyone wanted to say, or could think of to say. There was nothing they could do. Stanleyville was a two-day journey to the southwest over a terrible road. At Ibambi, they were hundreds of miles behind the front lines (if there were any such things as lines at all in these countless thousands of square miles of rain forest). They were locked in Simba territory with the Belgians about to mount a well-advertised rescue attempt which would result, inevitably, in angry rebel retaliation against hundreds of white civilians.

On Tuesday the radio told them that Stanleyville was surrounded by the National Congolese Army. A little later they heard that the paratroopers had dropped, and that they had rescued a hundred hostages and were waiting to fly them out.

"The Belgian and American authorities have agreed with Tshombe's Central Government in Leopoldville," the endless radio voice droned on, "that the paratroopers have only been used as a humanitarian gesture. They will withdraw as soon as all desiring to leave have been removed."

Later in the day came the real and horrifying news. As soon as the parachutists closed in, scores of white men, women, and children had been herded out of their Stanleyville hotel and massacred by machine-gun and rifle fire from the angry Simbas.

Within hours, the announcers were reading their scripts in tones of well-bred gloom which added to Helen's anger: "Very little hope can now be held out for white missionaries or civilians in the northeastern territories still in rebel hands."

It was this broadcast which angered her more than anything else. The radio networks had scandalously broken security about the Belgian and American parachute operation and had thus precipitated the massacres. Now they had the impertinence to anticipate her own death and those of her friends; their opinions could only serve to alarm her mother and family, back in England, and the others' relatives all over the world.

The lorry coasted down a long slope, its engine sputtering, and they stopped in the shade of some trees. Helen knew that if you put only two or three pints of petrol into an engine the size of theirs, you would speedily run out of power. This did not seem obvious, however, to the three Simba guards, the dozen African villagers hitching a lift, or even the driver himself. Not that it mattered. Why should she fume over the length of a journey likely to be her last?

All she needed now was patience while they fiddled with the engine, adding another few pints of petrol, and as they labored away again she stared up at the blue sky and at the great ironwoods and mahoganies thrusting up towards a high tent top of leaves.

The engine was already sputtering again as they passed Mbandi. The sun in its afternoon loop across the sky was now very hot. The shade beneath the thick-leaved banana plants at the roadside gathered in small dark pools around the roots; farther back, beyond the spiky, bright green grass which fringed the twisting red road, the temperature in the deep shade of the big trees was that of an oven on medium heat.

Of the other women on the lorry, Amy Grant was a secretary, Florence Stebbing and Elaine de Rusett were qualified nurse-midwives. Elaine, self-possessed and cheerful, with a dry, laconic sense of humor, was Australian. Like Amy and Stebby, she enjoyed working in Congo; it gave point and purpose to their Christianity, and their commitment was total.

The youngest member of the Protestant group apparently destined for execution was Brian Cripps. Both his mother and father were zealous mission workers at Ibambi, and both were away in England on leave at this time. Frank Cripps, his father, was in charge of the printing works at Ibambi, and he affably demonstrated to visitors the complexity of his machines and explained how the typeset word of the New Testament printed in Swahili had helped the spread of Christianity to this remote part of Africa.

Helen understood how Brian must feel now, facing an agonizing death. He was the only young man in the party. "Things" were expected of him. What legacy of "good behavior" would he leave behind? Or would he crack under the stress?

Since the mass killings at Stanleyville four days earlier, on Tuesday, November 24, they had expected attack or at least arrest. For safety's sake, a month previously Jack Scholes had ordered Helen, Stebby, and Elaine to leave the mission hospital at Nebobongo, seven miles away, and join them at the main mission center at Ibambi. Reluctantly Helen had complied, for even though in John Mangadima, her assistant, she had a worthy African deputy, somehow she intuited that she might never again see the hospital she had helped to create.

On that crucial Saturday morning of November 28,

although their own instincts and common sense told them otherwise, they allowed the senior African members of the mission to dictate their actions. When the inevitable moment of Simba reprisal arrived, and news reached them that lorries were rumbling out from Ibambi village, two miles away, the African evangelists insisted that all seven white missionaries hide in Jack Scholes's study, behind locked doors, with the shutters closed. The Africans would deceive the Simbas with the news that the missionaries had fled and the house was deserted.

Hindsight proved that the plan was far too naive to stand even the remotest chance of success. Crouching down in Jack's office in silent tension, they heard the front door smashed open, the heavy footsteps approaching, the doorknob rattled, the panels banged with a violent fist, the protesting voices of the mission Africans vainly trying to head off the invaders. Jack and Brian braced their shoulders against the door as the Simbas shouted threats. The woodwork bulged, and it was Jack who realized that this stupid resistance was tantamount to suicide. He motioned Brian to stand back, and unlocked the door. But it was Brian who stepped boldly forward into the Simbas' path, ready to take the first blow or bullet that might come.

Helen had, only with difficulty, prevented herself from saying, "Don't do it, Brian. Don't be rash just to prove your manhood."

But she knew that if she did say this, he would simply look at her with his dark, serious eyes, a smile would appear, and he would make some light-hearted remark to dismiss the matter.

The calmest member of the party perched on the back of the lorry undoubtedly was Jessie Scholes. Jessie and Helen had many things in common. The first was a total and uncompromising belief in God. Jessie, with her blunt Lancas-

trian honesty—the echoes of the northern shires still hobnail-
ing through her speech—was constantly puzzled that people
could not or did not seem able to grasp the simple, essential,
and eternal truth that if you believed, really *believed,* then
nothing could ever really harm you. You might grieve, yes.
You might suffer pain, be hungry and miserable, experience
all the frailties and despairs inherent in the human condition. But life led irrevocably to death. For the individual,
life was a transitory moment in eternity, a quick journey
you undertook, protected and guided by God, to a far
more joyous and eternal kingdom. Jessie's philosophy was
both comforting and formidable. Therefore, jolting towards
execution, her hair already rimed with the red dust swirling
about them, Jessie Scholes was undiminished and unafraid.

To Helen's continuing irritation, the truck driver was
making innumerable stops and idiotic detours. He halted at
every roadside shack where drinks were sold. He made
interminable journeys up endless tracks to deserted or near-
deserted cotton plantations, ostensibly to look for whites,
when everyone knew there was not a white within miles.
He stalled his engine with incredible incompetence, decided
that mechanical repairs had to be performed every five
miles or so, and then stood in absorbed contemplation
looking down under the open bonnet for what seemed like
hours.

Helen knew that he was not a Simba, merely a hanger-on.
All right, he was probably afraid, as they were all afraid.
He knew, as they all knew, that if you were not *with* them,
then you must be against them, and that assumption invited
a quick and cruel death.

Indeed, the farther they moved from Ibambi, the more
threatening became the mobs which surrounded the truck at
every roadblock. At the last one before the Nepoko River,

the mob gathered, shaking their fists, yelling that they wanted the prisoners to torture, kill, and eat. Helen, they indicated, they would flay alive, and her state of mind was so peculiarly lucid at this point that she spent the next few minutes trying to figure out how you could possibly skin a person from head to toe. It was here also that one of the Simba guards decided to have his fun with Jack Scholes.

He reached up and flipped off Jack's sun helmet. Jack said nothing, merely turning around to pick it up and replace it. The guard knocked it off again. And, as if this was the signal for violence, one of the Africans in the crowd thrust a spear forward so that the point pricked Jack's throat.

Baiting him, the guard mockingly held the sun helmet aloft. "We don't have hats. Why do you have hats? It's because you think you're better than us, don't you?"

The guard tossed the topee back into Jack's lap. "Now it's your turn to take off your hats to us."

Helen found it hard to control her anger. It was sickening that they should treat this brave and honorable man in such a manner. Jack Scholes had taught Africans to find love in place of evil and superstition. He had given direction and purpose to hundreds of people who had had none before. He had abandoned his own home and friends and lived on a few tins of bully beef and a handful of vegetables; he had labored at Ibambi giving all he had to give, and now they piled him into the back of an old truck and stuck a spear at his throat and led him off to death like an animal. They should be ashamed . . . ashamed!

The guard threatening Jack's life decided against carrying out his intent. With a rough joke he knocked the spear point away. The driver got back into his cab and restarted the engine. "Come to Wamba tomorrow," the Simba invited the

crowd as they moved off. "You can see all of them executed, a free show for all!"

They drove on towards Obongoni, and when they reached
the crossroads Helen realized that once again the driver
had made a wrong turn, and that it would be dark by the
time they crossed on the ferry and got to Wamba.

It rained heavily before they reached the Nepoko River,
and they were all soaked, but as they crawled down the
incline the black clouds rolled back and the sun balanced
itself precisely on the crown of the road behind them. The
beauty of the river crossing had always fascinated Helen.
Now, even in their situation, the sight of the deep, fast-flow-
ing river, its polished black surface reflecting the vibrant
sunset and the sweep of trees on the opposite bank, lightened her heart.

The Simbas yelled for the boatmen to bring across the
pontoon. Everyone was ordered off the truck. Helen took
a few steps along the bank to stretch her legs, and breathed
in the peace and stillness, thankful that the pounding roar
of the engine had been silenced. Suddenly it was cool in
this short interval between day and night; the deepening
shadows brought tranquillity. Voices were softer; the bark
of a dog in the distant village, the ripple of water, even
the laughter of the ferrymen coming towards them, were
muted and restrained.

The truck drove on to the pontoon, and they were
ordered back into their places again. When they reached the
opposite bank, the sense of peace and serenity still persisted
as darkness closed in and a thin mist seeped across the road.
But at Didi Oil Refinery, six miles from Wamba, the crowd
gathered at the roadblock was infinitely more menacing and
evil than the last. Helen had a feeling that this crowd had
already—and probably literally—tasted blood.

As soon as the mob realized there were European prisoners aboard the truck, they pressed in. There were mainly brutish and angry old men here, threatening with clubs, spears, and knives. There was no laughter from the crowd this time, only waves of vicious hatred flowing up at them. The mob hammered on the side of the truck, rocking it from side to side. *"Mateka!"* they screamed, *"Mateka!* Dead flesh! Give them to us! We'll rape them, mutilate them, eat them!"

Helen sat paralyzed. She knew that Amy's and Elaine's ignorance of the Bangala language prevented them from understanding most of the obscene threats, but they could not miss the crude gestures of castration directed at the men and of equivalent atrocities intended for the women.

For a few terrible moments it looked as if the guards had lost control, but fortunately the authority of the senior Simba guard prevented their journey from ending fatally at Didi. Holding his rifle ready, he shouted, "You can't have them. We're responsible for them. They're Simba prisoners. Come to Wamba tomorrow, they'll be publicly executed. You can see it all then. We shall flay the women alive. You can do what you like with the remains."

The scene was unbelievably nightmarish; the sheer physical intensity of feeling shocked Helen more deeply than she had ever been before. The dark, glaring faces and bloodshot eyes expressed hatred for *her! Her* personally! Before this moment she had had no conception that such strength and ferocity of group animosity existed. They hated *her!*

This was an assault upon her brain and spirit which sickened her soul. As the truck edged away from the angry crowd, on its final lap to Wamba, she sat shaken, trembling from the experience. She came from a world where verbal anger and aggression—the sharp retort, the argument, the slanging match, the hard-fought debate—were natural corollaries to reason and rationality. But that mob left in the darkness behind them represented the personification of evil to her. Those people had returned to the jungle. They represented the primeval terror, the simian bestiality, the barbaric fear that walks in the night.

Jung observed that man is the origin of all impending evil. Sheltered inside the mass hysteria of the group, man absolves himself from all responsibility. Jung added that the signs of God as well as those of the devil exist inside every man. But it was difficult to accept his credo after the experience they had just endured. Time would be needed for Helen's mind to reestablish the belief that those people were God's creatures at all. Now she understood completely why so many hundreds of simple Africans had fled into the forest.

None of the Protestant missionaries understood why their world had blown up like a land mine in their faces; why, blackened and bewildered, they stood in the debris trying to disbelieve the evidence of their own eyes. Perhaps it was all a mirage: the love and gentleness they had seen, the belief of their converts, the continuity provided by the pastoral and spiritual peace in their isolated mission station with its printing shop and its small bungalows set among quiet acres of grass and shady trees. But now they doubted the effects of the life they had established. Were they any more real than those pastel-colored illustrations in holy textbooks manufactured by Christians to comfort their own souls? Perhaps the ugly, distorted faces of the men who had threatened to flay her alive and eat her—and she knew such dreadful deaths had been inflicted on many during the last few weeks—were the real faces of Africa?

She sat high up on her black box, her arms clutched tightly across her body, in great despair. To die before one's time in a world which is sane and secure is hard enough.

To die when one's personal universe has disintegrated is bewildering, and to die in terror makes a mockery of life itself.
No matter what words sprang to her mind, she could not
stifle her fear. She decided she could resign herself intellectually to the approach of death, but somewhere inside her
vulnerable body a pulse of terror as regular as her own
heart plagued her, and although she appealed to God to excuse this ridiculous female manifestation, there seemed nothing she could do to lessen it.

Wamba is an attractive town of wide red-earth streets.
The pretty bungalows hide behind low white railings and
flowering hedges. Everywhere there are bushes and trees,
green lawns, flower beds, trellises dripping purple- or cycla-
men-colored bougainvillea. The shops sit under wooden
colonnades. There is an air of rural colonial peace about
the little town. Like the British and French colonists, the
Belgians built their villages thousands of miles from home
to remind them of their own summer countryside.

Now Wamba was shuttered and dark, and no one moved
on the streets. They stopped outside a large bungalow set
well back from the roadside, and one of the guards went
up the path to fetch the commandant. A few moments later,
he strolled down towards them, apparently disinterested,
followed by a young lieutenant in khaki uniform.

The lieutenant took over. "Your passports," he demanded.

The prisoners handed them over, and Helen was conscious that hers was out of date and contained no Congo
visas. It didn't seem to matter.

"Your nationality is British?"

"Yes."

"What is your occupation?"

"We are Protestant missionaries."

The passports were snapped shut and handed back. The
commandant and the lieutenant talked together for a few

moments. They seemed bored, or perhaps the attitude was uncertainty. But Helen plainly heard the last order, which was given in French.

"Drive the women to the convent. Take the men to the priests' dormitory. They will be shot tomorrow."

CHAPTER 2

As they drove around to the huge Roman Catholic mission station, a series of handsome red-brick buildings scattered over a wide area of lawn, Helen did not dare to look at Jessie Scholes, or consider the fact that Brian would achieve his martyrdom after all.

The main building was dark and silent. The five women were ordered down at its front door. Jack and Brian helped them with their suitcases. They had only a few seconds to say good-bye to the men. They clung together. There were tears in Helen's eyes. She wanted to say, "God bless you!" but couldn't get the words out. At that moment it seemed unfair to her that no intimate language existed with which to confide her real and agonized feelings. It was too dreadful a thought for her to either contemplate or accept that Jack and Brian would be killed in the morning. She felt that Jessie Scholes was behaving magnificently. Only much later did she discover that neither Mrs. Scholes nor any of the others had understood the commandant's final order, given in rapid French.

One of the guards climbed the steps and pressed the bell. They heard its penetrating buzz deep within the building. There was a long delay; then the lock was turned and the door half opened. A face framed in the gray headdress of a nun peered around. She seemed quite small in stature, but she barred the way as she asked in French, "What do you want?"

Helen answered, "We're the Protestant missionaries from Ibambi. They've brought us here."

Immediately the door was opened wide, and Helen saw that the Mother Superior wore the simple gray robe and headdress of the Belgian teaching order of the Community of the Infant Jesus. She smiled at them. "Please come in. You are very welcome."

As they filed through, carrying their blankets, boxes, and suitcases, Helen thought what a strange invasion this must have seemed: five sweaty, dirty women, their hair tangled, their faces pale and strained.

There were several more guards inside, who crowded around them. Other nuns—there was a great number—sat on benches facing an inner courtyard. They appeared cowed and desperate, their heads bent. Few even glanced up to look at them, and Helen guessed it was fear rather than inhospitality which dictated their behavior. The heavy door was closed. They heard the truck which held such terrible memories grind away into the darkness. The sense of relief was so overwhelming that they were almost in tears. The Mother Superior, sensing their distress, was gentle and comforting.

"Now, would you like to sleep with us in our large communal dormitory, or would you sooner have a smaller room to yourself?"

Helen translated, and Amy, Elaine, Stebby, and Jessie Scholes looked at each other in bewilderment. Lately they had only been *given* orders. Now they had to make a decision, and it seemed an enormous problem to solve. Eventually Mrs. Scholes made the choice. "We'd sooner stick together—a small room to ourselves, perhaps?"

The Mother Superior smiled understandingly. "Of course. Now, if you'll come with me . . ." But before they could move off, a guard intervened. He was pugnacious and offensive, and he carried a rifle over his shoulder as his symbol of authority. He pointed at their baggage.

"This will have to be searched."

They froze. Their eyes flicked from one another to the luggage; the sudden memory of what the blanket draped over Mrs. Scholes's suitcase concealed terrified them all. To the guards, that strange, unknown flag would mean only one thing: They were enemies. And enemies must be executed.

Helen began to argue. "But we've been examined already. Four times we've been examined."

The guard glared at her angrily. "The luggage must be searched."

"But it's been searched already." She was too exhausted, too frightened to sound convincing. The Mother Superior, seeing their hesitation and sensing danger, stepped in to rescue them.

"You can search it tomorrow, then," she said placatingly. "They will still be here." Her reasonableness and quick action overruled his indecision. "Now, if you come this way . . ." She started off along the veranda, and they trailed after her with their luggage. The guard followed, surly and suspicious, but, sure of his power to intervene, he let them go.

Halfway along, the Mother Superior stopped at a door. She opened it and walked through into a small room, turning rapidly on her heel to speak quickly in an undertone to Helen before the guard had time to get closer.

"Be careful. Don't undress at night. You'll be watched. Be careful."

Immediately Helen felt the fear and terror flood back. The immediate danger was confirmed. The convent was not a refuge. It was a prison. She turned, to see the others crowding in after her. They realized that the Mother Superior had said something important, and they knew instinctively that it was a warning. There was fear again in all their eyes.

It was Jessie who now lifted their spirits a little, by pointing out that the strange and apparently inexplicable behavior of the truck driver had probably saved their lives. He was not a Christian, in their terms. A casual appraisal might be that he was an ordinary mortal with the usual male appetite for women and strong drink; he was probably more often inclined to sleep in the sun than do a heavy day's work.

Nevertheless, it seemed that, while wishing to pursue his own uncomplicated life, he still desired to play no part in ending theirs; there was evidence, in fact, that he admired them. He had witnessed the blood lust in Wamba; he knew that it had reached a crescendo of mob hysteria, with executions and tortures occurring as daily spectacles. He knew that if he brought the hostages to Wamba in daylight, before the hour of the strictly enforced curfew, they would inevitably be snatched down from the lorry and killed—as had almost happened at Didi. No Simba authority would have been able to protect them there; in fact, whoever was in charge would probably have facilitated having them torn apart by the mob.

So this was the reason for the long diversions, the Buddhalike contemplation of his truck's engine, the slow conversations, the sips of petrol he added to the tank. These were all stratagems he had employed, at considerable risk to himself.

No one would ever give the little driver a medal for his part in aiding their survival. It was certain that neither Helen nor any of her friends would ever feel like buying him a meal. But, reflecting on this information about him afterwards, she wished she could have thanked him and murmured her apologies for her impatience.

The Mother Superior was in her early fifties, small and

straight-backed, and she moved with an air of quiet assurance and dignity. Framed by the white surround of her headdress, her face was clear and unblemished, her mouth firm, the eyes candid and often amused in even the most desperate situations. But they were eyes which indicated a woman who gave orders, accepted responsibility, and expected obedience. Like the other sisters in her order, she had left her friends and relatives in Belgium many years before and dedicated her life to Congo. For those Catholic sisters there had been no "home leave," no eventual retirement to a small town on the South Coast; they worked until they died and then were buried under the warm tropical soil.

Now, by a bitter turn of political history, these good, saintly, and simple women had been declared enemies of the People's Liberation Army. They were repaid by rape, torture, imprisonment, and often by a hideous death. The sight of a nun stripped naked, hanging upside down between stakes and cleaved down the middle like an animal carcass, sent many cynical professional mercenaries into wild orgies of reprisal killing.

In the past few weeks the Mother Superior had been forced to watch many bestial executions. They were intended to humiliate and shock her, and they did both. But they did not intimidate her. The Simbas might kill her. They might rape her. But at her age—with so many of her younger charges already violated and still available, and with the African novices' quarters next door—this was unlikely. Whatever pain or humiliation they inflicted upon her, she would not be silenced nor intimidated. She would speak up; she would seek to protect those in her charge.

On that first occasion, when the angry Simbas had raided the convent, she'd been attacked. The warriors, furious at being stalled for even a few seconds while she unlocked the door, charged in, and might have killed her. But Sister Marie Frances, a giant peasant woman of Flemish farming stock, whose work for God was done in the kitchen and the laundry, had anticipated violence and had been close at hand. Her Breughel face contorted with determination, she had bashed her way into the brawling mob of soldiers, grabbed her Mother Superior like a doll, gathered her to her breast, and pushed through to the wall. Jamming the Mother Superior beneath her, she had arched her own body into a protective shield until the vicious blows with rifle butts and rubber truncheons had smashed her down to her knees. Almost unconscious but unyielding, she had protected her Mother Superior until the violence and fury ended. Helen had heard of the incident even before the Mother Superior inquired gently if she would mind examining Sister Marie Frances. Helen dressed the bruised, lacerated back, legs, and body, the injuries sufficient to kill some women and certainly put most in bed for a month. But not Sister Marie Frances. Her broad, beaming smile of victory and bland assurance that she was in perfect health told Helen of a most extraordinary and courageous woman.

The first attack did not for one moment dissuade the Mother Superior from fulfilling what on the face of things seemed a humble and commonplace task, but which was, in reality, a most hazardous operation: opening the front door when the bell rang. The sound of the electric bell was usually followed by a fist hammering on the panels. Everyone reacted instinctively to the sound. It curled a spring of terror in their stomachs, dried their throats, made them pause in mid-stride and mid-sentence, seeking for a place to run and hide.

Each of the seventy women in the convent realized that her life hung by a spider strand. Practically all of them had witnessed or endured the most terrible experiences, and knew that the sound of that doorbell might presage the end of dignity, or of life itself: a brutal beating up, selection for rape or as the target of a firing squad.

The Mother Superior always answered the bell when it rang. If she was away in a distant part of the convent, she would be fetched. That fact was symbolic of how much the morale in the convent depended upon her. It was the Mother Superior who in the matter of the hidden flag, on that very first night, came to the new hostages' rescue.

After a subdued supper in the refectory, Helen took her aside and told her what Jessie Scholes was hiding. When she suggested that they might burn it, the Mother Superior led her to the kitchen and indicated the guard. "You see. Far too risky. If he caught you destroying such a thing . . ." She shook her head at the enormity of the offense. "Couldn't you cut it up?"

Helen remembered that she and Jessie each had a pair of nail scissors. "I suppose we could unpick one of our pillows and stuff the bits inside," she said thoughtfully.

They settled on this method, even though it turned out to be laborious. With a sentry posted at the door to warn of the approach of a guard, all of them took turns snipping the Union Jack into confetti fragments and stuffing them in with the down in a pillowcase. It was wasted effort. Next morning the guard never made an attempt to search the luggage. Like the commandant's unfulfilled threat that Jack and Jim were to be shot, this was another example of the rebels' indifference. Undoubtedly, the guard went back to his bed and forgot all about it. The Mother Superior, who was in touch with the priests and male civilians held prisoner in another part of the convent, assured Helen that Jack and Jim were both quite safe and, as yet, in no danger of execution.

A few days later, the Mother Superior sought Helen out and took her to the quiet seclusion of the chapel.

"I need your help," she said.

"Of course," replied Helen.

"Mrs. Scholes tells me that you are a doctor."

"Yes."

"You have heard that many of the sisters have suffered terribly last week?"

"Yes." The rumors were prevalent, although no one wanted to go into detail.

"It was quite dreadful. It all began when the Belgian parachutists attacked Stanleyville."

Helen nodded. The tragic dimensions of that well-publicized and ill-fated expedition would probably take months to be revealed in their entirety.

"The commandant in Wamba is a decent man," continued the Mother Superior, "but the Simba colonel in charge of the troops here is a fiend. When the news reached him, he ordered his men to drive out to all the convents within fifty miles of Wamba, arrest the sisters, and bring them into the hotel in Wamba. "

Helen looked at her solemnly as the nun told her story in a flat, impassive voice.

"Two of the younger girls, Sister Dominique, an Italian, and Sister Clothilde, who is Belgian, suffered dreadfully. Sister Dominique, even after many men, was taken to the colonel to be used for his purposes."

Outside Congo the word "rape" could still generate whole series of jokes. In Congo no one was amused. The reality of the situation here quelled any laughter. It had become a shock word, incendiary and intimidating, as violent in implication as the explosion of a mortar shell. In practically every white society in equatorial Africa it triggered off immediate panic-stricken reactions and suggestions for possible quick getaways.

Helen heard the Mother Superior pause in her story and sigh—a long, lonely exhalation of breath.

"Sister Dominique is young. Very pretty. This colonel wants her as his property—as his wife, so he says."

Her eyes met Helen's. "Will you speak to her?"

Helen was surprised. "Speak to her?"

"You are a doctor."

"You mean she has been injured physically?"

The Mother Superior paused. "No."

"But what can I say to her?" Helen asked in bewilderment. Indeed, she was a doctor, but at such a moment it seemed to Helen that consolation of the soul was the major treatment Sister Dominique would need.

The Mother Superior guessed what Helen was thinking. She said sadly, "I have tried to reach out to her spiritually. I cannot get through to the poor child."

"But I'm not of the same faith."

"Does that matter?"

Helen drew in her breath. She had no experience consoling girls who had been raped. This girl was a Catholic nun from a vastly different background and philosophy; her faith and her life were so different.

The Mother Superior said quietly, "If I had not failed myself, I would not turn to you." She hesitated, and then she made the appeal which left Helen no alternative. "I think she is on the edge of madness. I fear she is turning towards insanity because she cannot attain death."

Helen took a deep breath. "Of course I'll talk to her, Mother Superior. It's just that I don't think I'll know what to say . . ."

"You are a doctor, you are also a missionary . . ."

Helen considered the practical aspects. "Won't it be difficult . . . the guards? If we're seen talking? Where can I meet her?" No matter where you were, you had to be careful. Occasionally the guards were cheerful, even helpful, but usually they were brutal and domineering, and to be seen chattering or whispering usually brought a brutal blow from a rifle butt and the possibility of serious injury.

"I shall arrange for you to meet her in the laundry. You could both be working there. We can post a lookout."

"It will take some time. We'll have to get to know each other. I'll need to gain her confidence."

"We will arrange several meetings." The Mother Superior hesitated. "Besides . . ."

"Yes?"

"This colonel is a very wicked man. And this girl is quite beautiful . . ."

"You mean he'll come for her again?"

The Mother Superior nodded, and Helen sensed that she carried many burdens aside from this one.

"There is so much tragedy, and we must do what we can to help," she said, and then added, "I will instruct Sister Dominique to come and see you at once."

The laundry was large and cool. No one was washing there at that moment. Helen looked around at the concrete tubs, which in their time had frayed a thousand pairs of hands and scoured ten times as many surplices. She ran her finger along the top of one of them and sighed. She did not relish this impending talk with Sister Dominique. Her own emotions were confused and tumultuous; how, therefore, could she talk logically or console anyone else? She looked up at the sunlight slanting down through the high windows and sighed again. Only one thing seemed to be on her side: She knew that it was often easier to point out a path for others, even when you found the path difficult for yourself.

There was a movement at the door and Helen turned, to see the young woman standing there.

"Sister Dominique?" she asked gently.

The girl nodded and came closer, and now Helen could

understand the Mother Superior's concern. Sister Dominique wore the long white robe—small red buttons dotted down the front—and the simple white headdress of her Italian order. She was tall, her face oval, her features classical, and she was very beautiful. Helen did not really know how to begin the conversation, and it was obvious she was not going to get much help from Sister Dominique.

"The Mother Superior asked me to talk to you," she said lamely.

The girl nodded again. She looked straight ahead, twisting and untwisting the tiny handkerchief clenched between her fingers, and Helen wondered how she was ever going to get the girl to unbend. Yet she should have known that to pour out your grief, to confess your sin, to talk to someone of your deepest need is a therapeutic remedy as old as the human condition, understood by priest, physician, and psychiatrist alike. And very often a stranger is the best recipient of such confidences.

She decided she must be blunt. "You must tell me what happened," she said plainly. "We are all in this together, and I am a doctor." She saw the girl's eyes fill with tears, and Helen, at once softening, put her arm around her shoulders.

"It's all right," she murmured consolingly. "Tell me something about yourself. All I know is that you're Italian, and I'm English. You believe in God as I do. How did you enter the Church?"

Slowly, hesitantly, Sister Dominique began to tell her story. She came from the north of Italy, from a poor but prolific family; the custom of one son for the priesthood and one daughter for the convent was a tradition which went back many generations. She had embraced the faith gladly. She had found joy in Africa; she taught and played with the children. In many ways, Helen realized later, she was no more than a child herself. She was "a bride of

Christ." She had forsaken the sensual earthly pleasures, relinquished her potential role as wife and mother, and given herself entirely to God. And now, in her mind she had betrayed that trust. She had been forcibly grabbed, her robes torn away: she had been paraded naked and ridiculed, her flesh had been molested. All she had lived for had been destroyed—and here there was no doubt that the Mother Superior was right: Her senses were taking refuge from hideous reality by fumbling towards the absolute release of insanity.

She said in a despairing voice, "There is no point in my living any more. I have no purity left."

Helen quickly replied, "That is simply not true."

Sister Dominique was insistent. "It *is* true. You know it is true. I have betrayed my trust. I have no purity!"

Helen said forcefully, "If you belong to Christ, if you know of Christ living in you, no one can touch your *inner* purity. Don't you understand that?"

The girl was crying now, still whispering, "I have no purity—no purity."

"No living man can touch or destroy or harm that real purity *inside* you. Believe me."

Helen sighed, and thought how ironical it was that in a Western society where virginity often meant so little these days, where a great part of the world watched beatings, shootings, and murders on television in the safety of their warm sitting rooms, with no power to halt them and little will to intervene, she should be sitting here trying to console this broken-hearted girl. If she could only convince her that her plight was not all that desperate, and that her salvation rested simply in the hands of the God in whom she believed.

"You have not lost your purity," repeated Helen severely. "If anything, you have *gained* purity in the eyes of God."

To Sister Dominique this was so outrageous a statement

that she had to stop crying to consider it. "I do not understand."

"Do you understand, then, that the world in which the Virgin Mary lived must have been quite certain she had lost *her* purity?"

The dark, tear-filled eyes turning towards her were suddenly hostile.

"That is not true."

"Of course it is true. They would have jeered at her and called her adulteress."

The eyes were still disbelieving.

"Joseph was not the father of Jesus Christ. Your religion tells you it was a virgin birth. Joseph knew that. But his neighbors would never believe such an absurd story. They would sneer behind her back, rumor that she was an adulteress. Yet you know that God said she was blessed amongst women . . ."

The girl's eyes were still puzzled, and Helen went on:

"Jesus Christ suffered for us. Now you have suffered for others."

Again, there was confusion in the girl's eyes as Helen reiterated the point. "You suffered. Many of you suffered. But the Mother Superior tells me that you and a Belgian sister suffered most because you were the youngest and most desirable. So you saved others from the same shame. God will not judge you harshly for that, will He?"

Helen knew by the touch of the girl's shoulder against her own that she had made some progress. She was not convinced, but she was ready to consider the thought.

"It was Tuesday, in the night," the young nun said. "They came for us in a lorry. They were like savages. They shoved us aboard as if we were cattle. Then they drove us to a hotel in the center of Wamba. They were all drunk. They jeered at us and struck us. Then they began to tear off our robes. They threw our crucifixes down into the dirt and trampled on them. We were naked. They drove us out into the street so everybody could jeer at us . . . spit at us . . ."

"Go on," said Helen quietly.

"Seven of us, the younger ones, in front of everybody . . ." This was really too much for her to recount.

"Go on."

"They forced us. Afterwards, after I had been used many times by the soldiers, they took me to this colonel. He is little and wicked. He too . . ."

There was now no stopping the outpouring of her grief and outrage. "He is such a wicked man. He had murdered the bishop and now he lives in his house. The soldiers took all the priests and laid them down naked in a path and then they danced over their bodies, screaming with joy." Her hands touched her mouth; the memory was vivid and painful. "They killed them all; they slaughtered them; they made us watch."

"I know," said Helen gently. "I know."

The remembered agony of the hideous cruelties inflicted on the priests who had believed, as she did, in the goodness of God and the certainty of salvation was almost more than Sister Dominique could bear. She covered her eyes with her hands.

"Now do you understand why I say there is no point in living any more, that I have no purity left?"

"I understand what you say, but I know you're wrong," Helen replied.

"But you don't understand. You can't understand. Unless it has happened to you, how can you—?"

"But it has," intervened Helen gently. "It has happened to me."

The girl's head lifted slowly. The large eyes widened with disbelief, and then clouded with pity. Strange, really, Helen thought. No longer did Sister Dominique consider her a funny English doctor-lady in spectacles, offering motherly advice of no practical value. Now she understood. Now she was a comrade. Perhaps she should have told her earlier, but she had hesitated because of her own reluctance to bring up painful memories.

"You," whispered Sister Dominique. "You also?"

# CHAPTER 3

Helen regarded the young nun with solemn eyes. If confession was good for the soul of Sister Dominique, perhaps it might also benefit Helen.

"Yes," she replied. "To me also. More than a month ago, now, when the Simbas really began to cause trouble."

The events of that terrible night of Thursday, October 29, had started in her house in the hospital compound at Nebobongo. And Helen could never have anticipated that by the end of it she would be left hurt and bewildered, her clothing torn, her face smashed, forced by brutal experience into an arena where her philosophy and her faith were in jeopardy.

"I heard the banging and shouting at the front door somewhere between one and two thirty A.M." she said, and she paused to remember.

The noise woke her from a sleep which, those nights, was never far from the edge of wakefulness. She sat up fumbling for her dressing gown, mentally noting where her slippers lay. The dryness was in her throat again, the queasy sickness stirring in her stomach.

The hurricane lamp by her bedside filled the room with a soft glow; you kept your light burning all night in times like these. The noise at the front door grew more violent. She heard the drunken command, "Open up for the Armée Populaire. Open up or we smash down the door."

"It's just a house inspection," she told herself in the calm voice she affected to rationalize her fears. "Just a normal house inspection. Now don't panic. It's happened before. It will happen again."

But the other inner voice, the one she didn't want to hear, was insisting querulously, "A house inspection after midnight? Don't be absurd."

"All right," she shouted. "I'm coming."

Elaine de Rusett and Florence Stebbing slept in a cottage too far away to hear the disturbance, as did John Mangadima, Helen's assistant, but in the living room Hugh and Francis, the two young male student nurses appointed as official bodyguards, were watching the bulging door apprehensively. They had strict orders not to open any door until Helen arrived.

Helen turned the key and the men burst in—six of them, drunk, coarse, and angry at being kept waiting. They were army—she knew that at once. Not *jeunesse,* or the young hangers-on, the ones who shouted and waved sticks and spears and went along for the ride; this lot was hard-core army, and therefore was dangerous and ruthless. Only one wore a complete uniform. He was a youngish lieutenant, well-built and truculent, his authority emphasized by a gun belt, cartridges, and a revolver in a thick black holster which hung at his hip. He turned on her.

"Where's your husband? Where's he hiding?"

The question put Helen immediately on the defensive. "I haven't got a husband."

"Don't lie to us. Fetch him. Where is he?"

Helen shook her head. "I haven't got a husband. I'm a missionary. This is a hospital and school."

They all cursed at her, seemingly incensed at her lack of a husband.

"He's somewhere here. We'll search the house and find him."

Helen felt numbed by their filthy language, the jostling and hostility. She didn't know what to say, and was frightened and confused. Search the house? All right, let them search the house. She had no husband; she had nothing to hide. Let them get on with it. So the soldiers stamped around, and it was now clear that the search was going to be cruder and more violent than anything that had taken place before.

"What's in here? What are you hiding? Where are the keys?" They knocked things over, they smashed glasses, they deliberately broke up her home. As in earlier searches, they were looking for tape recorders, record players, radio sets, typewriters—all to be "liberated" in the sacrosanct name of the revolution.

In the first room they made her unlock the huge cupboard where she kept many of the glass utensils used for school and hospital teaching, and they jeered like hooligans as they smashed them on the floor and against the walls.

She began to protest but stopped, realizing it was useless. They took the money for buying plantains she had set out on the table; they took her watch, uniforms, and berets for the students and the primary-school children; they took the gramophone and records. Anything they fancied they filched, and they piled the articles up in a heap in the living room.

It took them what for Helen was a long, tiring, destructive hour. Then they ordered the two students, Francis and Hugh, to carry the loot out to the lorry.

"Now," thought Helen in relief, "at last they're going. Thank God they're going. It's all over. We're safe. We can go back to bed. We can sleep."

The two soldiers and the two students were carrying stuff down the path when she heard the lieutenant call her from the narrow corridor which led to the bathroom and her bedroom. No real fear came to her, simply a feeling of irritation, of "Oh Lord, what's he found that he wants now?" She went to investigate. Since the inspection was over and there was nothing else really left for them to steal, she wondered, "Why doesn't the beastly man join his friends on the lorry and go away?"

It was dark in the corridor, but she still carried the hurricane lamp. He was standing in the darkness. He indicated the bedroom. His voice was harsh.

"Go in there and get undressed," he said.

Whether this fear, this threat, had lurked at the back of her mind from the moment the banging on the door woke her up, she would never—even in the future—be able to resolve.

But her reaction was immediate and spontaneous.

"No!" she cried. She turned on her heel and ran. She scuttled along the corridor, through the living room and out onto the veranda, almost bumping into Hugh, who was just coming back to the house for a second load of booty.

"Go, Hugh, go!" she shouted, realizing at that second how idiotic she was to be flying through the night in bare feet, thin dressing gown, and flimsy nightgown, still carrying a hurricane lantern. She threw the lamp at Hugh and raced around the back of the house like an animal seeking the shelter of darkness. A terrible fear had suddenly engulfed her and, hearing the shouts of pursuit starting behind her, there was a sort of wild madness about her confusion.

Suddenly the blackness was impenetrable. Branches slapped her face. It had poured with rain only an hour or two before, and her feet skidded in the mud. She had never run away from anything or anybody in her life before—she didn't know how to run away. She had no experience of escape, and already nagging at the back of her mind was the dreadful thought that now *she* had precipitated violence. Now, if they didn't catch her, they would take it out on the Africans. All this flashed through her brain, and her reason kept protesting weakly: "Why hadn't they gone? They'd stolen all there was to steal. They'd got all they wanted. Why hadn't they gone? They should have gone. It is all so unfair."

She could hear them yelling and screeching all around her. Obviously, they thought her plan was to race past the hospital some seventy yards away and hide in the bush beyond. To forestall this, they had spread out in a half circle at an even greater radius and were now moving back towards the house to flush her out.

She didn't consciously choose a place to hide; instead, she instinctively threw herself down under a small hedge which would hardly have concealed a cat, let alone a human being. She could see their flashlights cutting bright swathes through the darkness as they came nearer, swearing and threatening.

Among the leaves and mud she scrabbled the dressing gown down around her feet, trying to conceal her white skin. She curled herself into a ball, holding her head in her hands. Her terror was blind, primeval, paralyzing; she'd never dreamed that such a primitive agony of fear could exist. Of course, it was useless. Within seconds she was fixed in the beams of six powerful flashlights, which revealed her cowering in the mud, entangled in the thin stems of the hedge like a small terrified animal.

She never knew who jerked her to her feet, only that he was huge and brutal. His breath stank of drink; she could smell his sweat. Then the lieutenant grabbed her, blazingly angry, furious, she supposed, because she must have made him look foolish in front of his subordinates. He gripped her shoulder with one hand and struck her hard across the face, then backhanded her with such violence that he knocked her to the ground. The bully who had first found her completed the treatment, hauling her to her feet again and striking her viciously across the face with his rubber truncheon. She felt a great impact; there was no immediate sensation of agony, even though later that night her exploring tongue discovered three smashed and aching back teeth. All around her she was aware of confused jostling, screaming voices, and vicious hatred.

There were bright lights in her eyes, and she heard coarse laughter. The blows had smashed both sidepieces of her glasses. The glasses were lost in the tramped mud. A gash had opened down the side of her nose. Blood poured down her chin and onto her night clothes. She was almost blind, and absolutely helpless. In all this mixed confusion and violence, she thought imploringly: "The end must come soon. It must be soon." She would have welcomed it. But no! Someone found her spectacles and thrust them back at her. Trembling, she cleaned them on her nightgown, then popped them back on her nose, as if the act might somehow bring her back from a preposterous world in which no grain of sanity remained.

Now they were pushing her back towards the house. She couldn't bear to feel them touch her, so she tried to keep one step ahead. That was as far as thought went: to keep one step ahead, just to keep one step ahead and keep their hands away from her.

Reaching the small, square, brick-floored veranda, the lieutenant shoved her up against the main pillar, his revolver in her face. She fell back against it, feeling the rough brickwork against her shoulders. Oh, why didn't they finish it? She was too exhausted and defeated to stand any more; she could feel the blood running down her face. She felt the hard muzzle of the lieutenant's revolver against her forehead.

"I'm going to kill you. I'm going to pull this trigger and blow your brains out." His voice was hysterical.

"Thank God," she thought. Anything was better than this terrible, blinding, all-pervasive terror.

She heard other strident voices arguing and protesting.

"Pull the trigger," she thought. "Quickly! Get it over with."

Whether in his drunken and drugged state the lieutenant would have killed her, she will never know. But Hugh, the young student nurse, tried to save her. The other male nurse, Francis, had fled into the night, and Helen did not blame him. But Hugh had waited on the veranda until she was captured. With terror-filled eyes he had watched them brutalize his doctor, seen the gun shoved against her temple, known they were about to murder her. It was more than he could stand. Yelling, "Leave her alone!" he threw himself between the lieutenant and Helen, and his head struck the revolver and knocked it aside. It was an act of instinctive and devoted courage, and it was precisely the action to serve the purposes of the lieutenant and his men. Killing a white woman could create a lot of trouble for them; even in their crazy, drunken condition, that realization still penetrated. But this attack upon Simba authority had come from an African, a servile creature of this white woman, a miserable student daring to intervene against the invulnerable Simba power, which had already given the warriors control of four-fifths of Congo, and which, they were certain, would sweep away the National Congolese Army, the hated whites, and all those who disbelieved in the divinity of Lumumba in a sea of blood and revenge.

Now they had something satisfying: a black body to punish. The heavy rubber truncheons, which inflict agonizing pain and physical damage, crashed against Hugh's head and body, knocking him to the ground. He uttered one sharp cry and then was silent. The boots kicked the bruised body; the sound they made and the crack of truncheons flailing against flesh made Helen vomit.

Outside, the night sky flared with stars above the darker outline of trees and palms. Cicadas shrilled with their insistent pitch, fireflies moved in the dark recesses of the banks, moths fluttered across the gravel roads, and deeper in the rain forest animals, with eyes like little yellow lamps in the trees, hunted their prey, killing in the primitive pattern of jungle law with quick and merciless efficiency.

On the veranda, however, so-called civilized man was beyond mercy. The soldiers kicked and beat the inert body with vicious ferocity, until Helen knew Hugh must be dead. They kicked him down the shallow step of the veranda and outside onto the gravel. Their flashlights formed a pool of light, in which he lay like some poor dying fish, the impact of boot on flesh sounding like the slap of angry waves.

With a brusque order, the lieutenant stopped the game. Hugh did not move. "Get back to the lorry," the lieutenant shouted at his men. Then, gesturing to Helen with his revolver, he said, "You. We're taking you back to town. You're under arrest. Get dressed."

He shone the torch into the living room and down the corridor, showing her the way, following her with heavy strides. He kicked open the door and with the point of his gun motioned her in.

"Go in and put your clothes on." Helen went in, stood hesitantly, then took off her dressing gown. She hardly knew what she was doing, and yet instinctively she knew what was about to happen. The ruthless beam of the flashlight robbed her of all privacy.

"Get dressed," he snapped again, and she was conscious

that he was moving towards her. Of course, there was no
question of getting dressed. Hardly before she had time to
get out of her nightdress, he was on her in savage, crude
attack. He forced her backwards on the bed, falling on top
of her. She scarcely knew whether she struggled or fought.
The will to resist and fight had been knocked out of her.
But she screamed over and over again, and no doubt the
pitiful screams reached the ears of the soldiers laughing and
joking at the truck.

The brutal act of rape was accomplished with animal
vigor and without mercy. On the veranda a few minutes
before, Helen had been certain that her God had deserted
her. The pitiful cry which she knew by heart but which she
had never before understood in its deepest significance now
rang in her mind with tragic clarity: *"My God, my God,
why hast thou forsaken me?"*

If God had indeed forsaken her, as well as Hugh, now
lying dead on the veranda, then the entire edifice of her
life had collapsed. Her belief, her faith, her work were all
a sham and a hoax. How could she believe there was a
God? All the training, all the long years of teaching, all
the joys, the prayers meant nothing. There was nothing . . .
nothing.

This was the desperate sickness of spirit she carried like
an iron weight down the corridor to the bedroom. *This*
knowledge as she lay pinioned and spread-eagled under the
rapist was the real horror. God had deserted her. The evil
that lived in man had surfaced, and she had been chosen
for rape and death, not for life. God had refused to answer
her prayers, and simply watched her reach this ultimate
abyss without answers and without hope. There was nothing in life, and, therefore, nothing beyond death.

She was conscious that she was filled with pain. His
breathing was stertorous in her ear. She could feel the car-

tridge belt and revolver holster pressing into her flesh; in his haste he had not bothered to remove it. And then, in the middle of the bewilderment, the hideousness, agony, misery, shame, and physical pain, suddenly a feeling of peace flowed into her mind.

It was an awakening of such clarity, something she had never experienced before, that the relief was overwhelming. The answers she wanted formed themselves in simple, logical sentences on the mental retina of her brain. To Helen, this was Christ's simple answer to her suffering. "They are not persecuting you as you. You are only My representative here. This is My eternal Calvary, My age-old, never-ending death for all mankind. I ask you only for your body. The perpetual suffering is Mine, not yours. Stand with Me. I accept responsibility for all this evil. It is being done to you because of Me. Because I am in you. And I have not forsaken you."

She was crying as the lieutenant clambered off her body and her rickety single bed. But the tears—of relief—were not because her ordeal was over, but because she had found her faith again.

The lieutenant, satiated now, was gentle; his was a possessive gentleness that women with some sexual experience would have understood, but which Helen did not.

"You are my wife now," he told her. "We are going in the truck. Get dressed."

And even though she had received a spiritual reawakening in her own terms, the physical pain, terror, and numbed misery remained. She felt desperately unhappy.

She reached for the worn work dress which hung over the back of the chair.

"No," he said. "Not that one. Get a clean one out of the cupboard. You're my wife. I want you to look smart so the others will admire you."

In retrospect, his solicitude at the conclusion of the act of rape was laughable. But Helen did not feel like laughing now. She obeyed orders. Opening the cupboard door, she extracted a clean dress and put it on. Obediently she walked by his side to the truck and let him help her into the cab. He gave a curt instruction to the driver and they rumbled off into the darkness, their headlights illuminating the gravel path and probing the bushes.

"My name," he said amiably, "is George. Lieutenant George." Even his tone of voice indicated how his attitude towards her had changed. He was her protector; he owned her; no one else was going to touch her. He put his arm around her shoulders, and as they drove through the night Helen wondered what life in a Simba army camp was going to be like. She was now his wife, a trophy, a spoil of war. There was no government, police, or magistrate of any authority who could intervene or to whom she could turn. No one in her mission could assert any physical or moral pressure. In any case, no one would know where she was. Like thousands of others during this lawless period, she would simply "disappear."

She stared numbly through the window of the cab, watching the truck lights flicker past familiar landmarks. She was faintly surprised when they turned right, taking the narrow road which led from Nebobongo to Ibambi, seven miles away. Delayed shock made her feel exhausted and physically ill. She couldn't understand why he kept asking her questions about the Ibambi missionaries. How many lived in that village, he wanted to know; how many were Americans? Did she know any Americans?

In Ibambi they stopped outside the store owned by Mr. Mitsingas. Mitsingas was a portly, middle-aged Greek with greased dark hair, olive skin, a triple chin, and eyes which glinted through creases of fat. To Helen, his throaty chuckle

always seemed to betray his glee as he extracted his exorbi-
tant margin of profit from the transaction at hand. Her
reactions towards Mitsingas specifically and the local Greek
community in general were always based on the suspicion
that she was being "done."

In her terms, they were wealthy and exploited the poor.
Her allowance of just over seven pounds a month, most of
which she gave away, put her among the rank of the poor.
The Greeks made a profit from all of them, including her
African assistants. She had come for God; the Greek mer-
chants had come for money. They were polarized on either
side of ten thousand miles of philosophical space. To add
to her doubts about these people's motives, there were
strong rumors that the Greeks kept themselves out of trouble by paying the Simbas to leave them alone. Helen did not
approve of that practice either. However, she had attempted
to do all she could for them; she had intimate friendships
with many wives and children. She brought the women's
babies into the world and attended to their aches and
pains. She was their doctor and observed her responsibility
as such.

But she did not have much chance to tend to their souls,
for if they had any religion—and she was inclined to think
they'd left such luxuries behind in Greece—it was carefully hidden and allied to Catholicism, although the sect was
called Greek Orthodox. Helen's main feeling of disapproval,
however, concerned the fact that they all seemed to function because of and for the sake of the profit motive. It
was often difficult for her to remember the social and
economic hardships which had brought the Greeks to Congo
in the first place. They had left their native villages because
of a lifestyle of poverty which Africans born in the fertile,
lush rain forest could never even comprehend. To a Greek
peasant unfortunate enough to be condemned to scratching
a living from such barren soil, Congo was better than home.

So Mr. Mitsingas and his compatriots had emigrated. They opened little stores in areas of equatorial Africa where no one else wanted to exist, and "exist" was exactly all they could do here. Colonial history in Africa confirms that most other European powers had parceled out the land to suit themselves. They had imported their own civilizations, laid down their laws, installed their communications, and made worthy efforts to educate the blacks. They had extracted fortunes from the top of the profit margin— a practice which Helen instinctively distrusted—and departed swiftly when they found they were not wanted or the going got too hot. Usually they had homes and countries to go to. Mr. Mitsingas, his countrymen, and vast communities of Arabs and Indians scattered about Africa had had nowhere to go throughout a hundred years of commercial endeavor. Africa was their home.

They made profits, yes. Some made large fortunes. But many only survived; they made a living from the sale of half a cigarette, two pounds of dried coconut, a handful of coffee beans. Helen, however, never saw them as pioneers. But perhaps God could calculate what margin of profit was honorable—or when it was.

Helen could see at a glance that Mr. Mitsingas had recently lost a large proportion not only of his profit but of his very livelihood. Her captors walked her around the back and into the huge, dark store, and she stared at the bare shelves. The shop had been looted. She wondered where the owner was. Scattered about the large table were mugs and empty beer bottles. A dozen or so soldiers slumped in chairs or were sprawled out on the floor. A smoky oil lamp lit the scene.

Lieutenant George led her into a bedroom beyond this large room, and her heart sank. The room was practically filled by a large double bed, and a man and woman were sprawled on the dirty sheets.

Lieutenant George swore at them angrily, and they sheepishly scrambled away back into the store. He turned to Helen.

"These are my quarters. You can lie down there." Helen glanced at the bed and closed her eyes in despair. Had he brought her here to use her for his own purposes, or possibly for the use of those other men next door? She couldn't bear to think about it.

A voice called: "Lieutenant George?" and he said to her authoritatively, "I've more work to do. Stay here. I shan't be long."

With a sense of intense relief, she watched him leave. The last thing in the world she wanted to do was stay in this filthy bedroom. She peered out the door. In one corner she saw an unoccupied rickety wooden chair. She crept out of the bedroom and sat down with the others. Once seated, her strength and will seemed to ebb away. Hunched there, arms clutched around her body, bent half forward to try to diminish the physical pain in her stomach, she clung to this small oasis of stillness, separated from the dark threat of these men and their intention. She did not move; she just sat there rigidly.

The hours seemed endless. Men hurried in and out from the street. Trucks constantly arrived and roared away again. Occasionally someone came close and peered at her and then moved on. Perhaps Lieutenant George had made it clear that she was his property.

She wondered whether the Simbas had gone back to Nebobongo to search for Stebby and Elaine. Lieutenant George must surely have known they were there. And poor Hugh? Surely Francis would raise the alarm and they would go and find him. The thought of his battered body lying in front of her house filled her with pain.

Another thought plagued her insistently. She had been

raped. Supposing she was pregnant? What would she do if she had a baby? Her life would be finished. Where would she go? Who would have her?

Then, far away, she heard the first cockcrow: an evocative cry ringing through the stillness. Almost immediately it was repeated by other birds. She knew then it must be four thirty, close to dawn, because in that part of Congo the cocks are as reliable as alarm clocks. Somehow their raucous calls brought a glimmer of relief. Daylight must come soon, and with it at least some partial respite from the horrors of the night. She longed for a return to the things she found sane and believable.

A few minutes later there was a great commotion as they herded a new batch of prisoners into the store and pushed them into one corner. When she dared look across, Helen recognized five Roman Catholic sisters, three priests, and a young layman from the Ibambi cotton factory. She longed to be able to join them, but she simply could not summon up the physical strength and courage to leave her chair. It seemed absurd to her; she felt almost as if she were tied to the chair. All she had to do was get up, walk towards them, and sit down again. But she couldn't, and she prayed that the Lord would give her His strength and faith, for hers was quite used up.

Half an hour later four local Greeks were pushed in among them and roughly ordered not to talk. Helen realized that one of the Greeks was Mitsingas, and he had seen her. He smiled—no one was going to stop Mr. Mitsingas from smiling—and patted the empty chair next to him.

Perhaps it was the smile, perhaps it was simply the courage needed to smile, which made the vital difference. Like someone recovering from a long illness, she managed to stand up; then, slowly, she edged across and sat down. She saw the concern in his eyes and realized that with her broken glasses and blood-spattered face she must look a mess.

"Are you all right?" he whispered.

She nodded. She didn't dare try out her voice. Even this man's first small gesture of friendship almost brought tears.

Light was flooding in through the windows now, revealing the sordidness of the room, when Lieutenant George returned with a new audience of cowed Europeans to bully. He bristled with official authoritativeness.

"You have all been arrested by order of the government. You will be taken to prison in Paulis." He glared at Helen with disfavor; obviously he felt she should still have been in the bedroom. "Radio instructions to this effect reached me at midday yesterday. All aliens to be arrested and transferred to prison."

This was a surprise to Helen. So last night's episode hadn't been merely a random house search. Her arrest was part of a larger pattern.

His harsh voice continued. "I've just returned from Wamba. All whites there are in prison. The arrest of all whites in the Babonde and Ibambi areas is continuing."

He stomped out of the room. Five seconds later a Simba came in to collect Helen. The lieutenant wanted to see her.

On the veranda Lieutenant George glared at her. Last night's display of affection had plainly been a one-time thing. The man who had put his arm around her in the truck had changed his attitude. Daylight had made her an enemy again, but Helen preferred it that way.

"I have heard," he said threateningly, "that there is another 'miss' at Nebobongo. Is this true?"

So they hadn't found Stebby and Elaine yet? Well, there was no point in telling lies; the two women would be safer with the main group of captives.

"There are two girls in the house near mine," she admitted. "Two other misses."

His face stiffened. Obviously, he had failed in his job, and
blamed her. He was so furious that for a second she thought
he was going to strike her. Instead, he turned on his heel
and marched across to his lorry. Seconds later it went roaring back towards Nebo.

His departure removed much of the tension. Everyone
was tired; no one seemed very interested in guarding anyone any more. Helen asked one of the nuns if she thought
they might leave the store. Then Mr. Mitsingas intervened.
"Come to my house," he said. "It's only just across the
street; they know we can't escape, so the guards won't
really be angry if we leave their headquarters." He was
right. Only a "cub" Simba, a boy of about fourteen, bothered to follow them.

Mrs. Mitsingas, plump and motherly, took one look at
Helen's bruised and swollen face and instinctively seemed
to know what had happened, and that in itself was an
enormous relief to Helen. She was gentle. She put her arm
around Helen's shoulders and ordered her husband, "You
go away and make the coffee." As he turned away she
added, "There's bread and cheese in the pantry." To Helen
she said, "Come on, my dear, we'll go to the bathroom and
clean you up."

In the bathroom, Helen looked wryly at herself in the
mirror. Blood coated her face and was clogged in her hair.
Her lips were swollen. There was a gash down her nose.
With her tongue she could feel the three aching broken
teeth at the back of her jaw. Mrs. Mitsingas bustled about
her, wiping blood away, tenderly dabbing bruises, and asking no questions.

Lorries still roared up and accelerated away, and more
white prisoners were being brought in. A little later Helen
overheard someone saying, "Yes, the Protestants are here."

That was all she needed. She rushed out to meet them.
There were her friends. She wanted to kiss all of them, but

immediately the questions started, "Helen . . . your face! What happened?"

Later she realized she should have kept quiet. But she could not. The relief of seeing her friends again, of being able to confide, was too much for her. So she babbled; she chattered in a great rush of relief, and suddenly she realized from the stony, horrified faces around her that they didn't want to hear. They didn't want this horror to be real, and now she was making it real.

She saw the look on Amy's face, and she let her voice dwindle away. Why should Amy understand, and why should she shock and horrify her in this way? How could Amy understand the cruel reality of rape? How could she be sympathetic to a situation so totally beyond the bounds of her comprehension?

Helen decided to bear this herself, but then Jessie Scholes, who'd been lagging behind the party, came into view, and everything changed. Jessie ran forward to hug her. "Oh Helen!" she said, and by her voice Helen knew she understood everything. "Oh Helen!" This was the sympathy she needed. Jessie had been like a mother to her for all her years in Africa. She was the person to whom Helen could pour out her story, the one who could assuage her grief.

Soon afterwards, Stebby and Elaine were brought in by car, and they transmitted one piece of news which gave Helen immense relief: Hugh was not dead. He had recovered consciousness, managed to stagger off for help, and warned Stebby and Elaine of events.

It was midday by the time the Simbas decided to convoy their prisoners to Paulis. All the Europeans were piled into lorries and driven away. They were told they were going to be shot. They arrived at two o'clock and were assembled in three groups: Catholic sisters, Helen and the other Protestants, priests and civilians. All were lined up in the shade of the lavender-blossomed jacaranda trees.

The commander of Simba troops at Paulis drove up. He
was a smart young African modeled on a long line of
Belgian officers, and he was furious. Who in the name of
Lumumba had ordered the arrest of all these people? The
authorities at Wamba? He had heard of no such orders
emanating from Wamba. He had received no authority for
their arrest. They must be returned to their stations and
homes at once. No one dared question his authority, and
Lieutenant George did not seem to be around to try to
refute it.

Chattering and singing, the lorryload of Christians just
delivered, as someone jokingly remarked, "literally from the
lions" drove back along the forest roads.

Helen simply could not stop talking. She talked about
anything, to anybody who listened. The intense feeling of
relief welled up like a spring bubbling out of the earth. The
wind battered her skin; the heat of the sun and the lurch
of the lorry were so strong that she had to brace her muscles to hang on. She felt marvelous. To be able to smile at
people for no reason and receive a smile back in return,
this was the very bread of life. You could not savor its
flavor until you had encountered the mindless violence and
proximity to death of last night. No one knew this but
Helen. Now she understood more about that small element
of continuity, perplexity, and agony which is the sum of
one human being than she had ever understood before.

Sister Dominique, listening to Helen's words as she sat
beside her in the laundry, sighed deeply. Helen could sense
her confusion about her own attitude. How could a woman
after such a deep and fundamental humiliation as rape find
sustenance in the world again? How could she, a missionary,
a "bride of Christ," in Catholic terms, ever face people
with a smile in her mind or on her lips? How could the
brutal possession of her body by a rapist ever be forgotten?

She found it hard to explain that it could not be forgotten, but that she could rationalize the ordeal; that her education and faith allowed her to set it where it belonged, in the past. More to the point, she instructed Sister Dominique: "You must trust in God and know absolutely that the shame is not yours. You must believe that ultimately you carry no responsibility. You may carry the hurt of it but not the shame. The shame is the man's. You must believe that."

 CHAPTER 4

Life at the convent settled quickly into a routine as each group of women decided on their individual pattern of existence. The Protestants shared the same language, faith, and communal bedroom. The Spanish nuns kept very much to themselves. They were large, indomitable women, mainly of peasant stock, and they wore long cascading robes. Their faces under the huge white wimples and trailing veils were sharply defined, hollow-eyed, tight-lipped, seemingly chiseled out of walnut. Strong, independent women, they muttered prayers which sounded to Helen more like threats than entreaties for God's mercy as they walked around the convent. Five hundred years of Jesuitical fanaticism had helped to fashion their faith, and certainly it had given them courage.

The Italians were very different. Practically all were good-looking; several were beautiful. In their snowy white robes enhanced by five crimson buttons, crucifixes hanging on long scarlet cords, they touched their rosaries with quiet gentleness. Helen thought of them as stunned children unable to believe what was happening to them. They made friends so quickly and embraced so easily; their love was so outgoing.

There were children at the convent who belonged to the civilian Belgian women also held captive there. Many more were still held at the hotel in Wamba, and quite early on Helen learned how deeply the Mother Superior was concerned with their welfare. Helen learned, through her, of other tragic occurrences that affected the women.

"The Belgians simply refuse to believe that their husbands are already dead," said the Mother Superior, shaking her head in concern. Helen found this a little hard to follow. "Perhaps it's better they should still hope," she reasoned.

The Belgian civilian women were the most difficult to get on with; they were used to attention, servants, a life of cocktail parties and "sundowners" (the nannies who looked after the children), and they made little effort to help with chores in the convent. Most of them were good-looking women in their early thirties. They had little faith or philosophy to fall back on now that their rather easy existence in Congo had come to an end. The Mother Superior was concerned about their facing up to reality, however.

"There is no hope. I was forced to witness." She paused, glancing at Helen as if wondering whether she should continue, and then she added, "Five days ago they took us down to the town. They paraded the prisoners in two lines —the priests, the Belgians, and the Americans in one line, the other nationalities in the other. Then they killed the priests, Belgians, and Americans very cruelly, very vilely, making us watch and threatening that it would happen to us all very soon."

Helen's throat was dry. "*All* the Belgians and Americans were murdered?"

"All of them."

"Not the English?"

The Mother Superior looked at her. "You are asking about the two boys from your Protestant mission?"

"Yes. Bill and Jim."

Helen saw the expression on the Mother Superior's face and wished she had not asked. She tried to go on gabbling, to avoid the truth she knew she now had to hear.

"Bill McChesney was American. I brought him out from England when I came back from my last leave. From Arizona . . . such a nice young man . . . twenty-four." Helen closed her eyes, her chatter dwindling away.

Bill was American. They would not spare him. "But Jim as well?" she managed. The Mother Superior nodded. "But Jim was English, not American," Helen whispered.

Jim Rodger was slim, dark, quiet, and deeply religious. In the early days in Congo he had once asked Helen to marry him, but she had been too full of the Lord, her plans, and the excitement of a new country even to consider accepting.

"The young American, Bill, had been badly beaten up in the prison," continued the Mother Superior. "When they divided the prisoners into two lines—one for execution and one to be marched back to prison—he was too ill to walk, so the Englishman put his arm around him and held him up. They called the roll and made the Americans and the other Belgians stand on one side. They ordered all the other nationalities in the other line. But the Englishman would not leave his friend. He would have dropped to the ground, this young American, had Jim not supported him."

"But didn't anyone call out?" Helen demanded in agony. "Didn't they tell the Simbas he was English?"

"Yes, they did. But the Simbas did not understand or care. And Jim would not step out of that line and release his friend. So they took him away, and he was murdered with the others."

Helen wanted to be sick. Here was the nightmare back again. How could she stand hearing of the murder of two of her dearest friends without declaring her grief, exhibiting her desperation? Weeping was not enough. Poor Jim, who had so often doubted the quality and depth of his own belief, who had been so shy and humble, so deeply worried about his own contribution to the missionary world. His concern was not even with the mark he might leave on a world full of zealous Christians and pioneer workers for God, but only whether he would even be able to keep abreast of his colleagues. Now he would worry and doubt no more. His Christian God had suddenly faced him with a view of Calvary. Common sense would have said, "Put your friend down and step away to safety. No one will judge you harshly for this. You cannot save this American. If you die you will receive no medals; your own death will not alter or soften his. No one will think you a coward. In this arena of brutish killing, no one will remember your isolated action. Many people will think you are stupid. Step away to life."

Helen could guess how these voices of reason and logic would have whispered to Jim. But she knew he would not have listened. Bill McChesney was his friend. To stand by a friend was a fundamental Christian precept. How could he step away? It would be stepping away from Christ, and from everything that had enriched his life and made it real and worthwhile. How could he live with himself if he failed at this challenge, even though he knew that this vital decision would be his last? Helen knew that he must have gripped Bill's waist tighter. And he had not moved.

Helen stood there with tears on her cheeks as she listened to Mother Superior describe how the Simbas killed all their prisoners. Sparing Helen nothing, she explained their use of the terrible "commande" torture. They bent their victims backwards, tying their wrists to their ankles, forcing them into agonizing positions. They kicked them about as if they were footballs, laid heavy planks across their bodies to make seesaws, mutilated and murdered them eventually with their heavy machete knives.

Helen felt that the Mother Superior was deliberately putting her to the test. It was essential that they, the strong ones, know what had happened and what might happen to them so that perhaps they could help the weaker survive in a future which was bleak and intimidating. "We must have strength," she declared, "and God will help us. Besides, only the living matter now. They have need of our counsel and advice."

The red brick buildings of the convent, the attached schoolrooms and dormitories, sprawled over a wide area of grassland hacked out of the tropical rain forest. The grass was lush and green. The whole setting recalled the gentle orderliness of the French or Belgian countrysides. Only the heat, the blaze of the sun in the sky, and, in normal times, the hundreds of noisy, laughing little black girls with kinky hair and pretty gingham uniforms told you that this must be Africa.

The main convent building was built around an open-ended square. A stone-paved veranda lined the inner sides, enclosing the flower beds and lawn, and beyond them, falling away down a steep hillside, lay the vegetable garden, chicken coops, the place for chopping wood. At the very bottom of the hill was the stream.

On December 2, not long after their capture, Helen noted in her diary, "Just been sitting in the cloisters after a fairly savage time, new guards on patrol, in silence, nothing to do . . . one dared not move . . . a move or sound could engender a savage blow from a gun. I was between a twelve-year-old girl and a nine-year-old boy. The guards passed down the cloister and I nudged the boy . . . we'd have two minutes before the guard returned . . . and I showed him how I could wriggle my ears. For twenty minutes he kept quiet, straining his facial muscles into every grotesque position imaginable, trying to do the same. The guards passed again . . . I nudged the girl and showed her how I could turn my tongue over—to right or left—and screw it up into a tube or flatten it out like a plate: for twenty minutes she laboriously practiced and twisted and curled in hope of training her tongue. Meanwhile with a hairpin I unpicked ten inches of the hem of my dress, and after the guards passed for a third time, showed the lad how to make a cat's cradle, and we kept quietly amused for another hour. We got cramped, the low cement wall we were sitting on was getting chilly as the sun passed away from the courtyard, and evening came.

"We had kept silent and still for several hours—and so, suddenly, with the inexplicable change of mood of our captors, they brought out some large unripe pawpaw fruit and called the children to join them in a ball game."

During this period, Helen and the others found that keeping the younger children quiet was difficult enough, but once they were given an inch—like playful kittens or puppies—it was simply impossible, since they sprang instinctively into action. Any Congolese guard was likely to turn a corner and find himself ambushed by a pugnacious six-year-old plus smaller sister, leaping from cover to point a toy gun and mow him down with a machine-gun rattle of burping noises. Some of the guards were not amused, and these antics kept Helen in a state of perpetual nervousness. If familiarity with the more genial guards had not been quickly established, it would have been unlikely that any child would have survived. But then again, many of the guards reacted with a childlike simplicity of their own; they were always likely to roll an orange in the path of the same desperado six-year-olds and engage in a quick five minutes of football. There was no rhyme, reason, or intelligent continuity about their behavior. But even when the prisoners were allowed to move about more freely, to get books out of the library, write, sew, tend the garden, teach the children songs, it was always necessary to be on the alert for an unpredictable outburst of violence.

On many occasions Helen had to creep secretly into the laundry to console the two stricken nuns, Sisters Dominique and Clothilde, and make her own philosophy plain to them. How ironical that, in a convent dedicated to God, to contemplation, to religious instruction and saintly introspection, these two women were only now coming to grips with the meaning of violence in their lives.

Practically every day during that December of 1964 was one of sustained terror. In the second week, after breakfast Helen set off down the hill carrying her two buckets, to fulfill her morning task of fetching water. A Simba guard, belligerent and suspicious as usual, trailed after her, and as they walked through the gardens and over the brow of the hill, Helen heard the sound of lorries arriving at the front door of the convent.

The noise made her feel anxious, and she turned, trying to influence the guard. "Can't we go back? It might be important."

"No," he said sharply. "You go on."

They followed the track behind the convent, past the African sisters' dormitory, which the Simbas invaded practically every night, and turned down the narrow path of beaten earth between the vegetable gardens and the wire-netted run for the chickens and ducks. Helen was already conscious of the weight of her two big buckets. They were quite heavy even when empty. She looked across the valley, hazy in the sunlight, towards the Protestant mission compound, glimpsing the top of the church and near it the roof of the mission house itself. She wondered how the three Protestant missionaries remaining there—Daisy Kingdon and the two younger ones, Pat and Elaine—were getting on, and why they had not been allowed to join the others in the convent.

At the bottom of the hill she slithered down the last four yards of muddy bank of the water hole. It was no longer clean, for the dry season had arrived and animals both wild and domesticated drank there. She used an enamel mug as a ladle to fill both buckets, then tried to struggle back up the bank.

Slipping and sliding, it was at this moment that the humiliation, pointlessness, and sheer physical ache from what she was doing and how little she was achieving suddenly struck her. She felt tears welling in her eyes and despised herself for being such a weak-kneed, cowardly female. She slipped again, and the water sloshed over the bucket's rim. Then she saw the hand reaching down to help her. "Here. Give me one," said the guard, grabbing a bucket from her. His quick, generous action undid her even more. As her face turned up, he must have seen the shine of tears in her eyes, for not only did he carry that bucket to the top of the bank but he returned to collect the second one. On the return journey he carried one bucket, Helen struggling behind with the second. She was sniffing and weeping to herself, this gruff and unexpected kindness unsettling her far more than she had thought possible.

She reflected on how often she made inner resolutions never to trust these people again. Then, just as the pain in her chest, the exhaustion, the giddiness and sickness almost overwhelmed her, one of them did something so unexpected—protected her from a blow, stretched down a hand —that she was left uncertain and unbearably moved.

At the top of the hill the guard commented that her ankles were puffy, her sandals torn, and she didn't look well at all. She said she didn't feel very well.

"All right," he answered, "you can sit down on that tree trunk and rest for ten minutes."

He carried both buckets up the next incline, but a hundred yards from the convent, as she had expected, he assumed his professional face and abruptly banged them down, snapping brusquely, "You carry them now."

With that he marched on ahead, reasserting his tough Simba image. His poise was abruptly shattered when a young boy came racing towards them, gabbling in a mixture of French and Swahili. He was the child of one of the Belgian mothers. Helen stopped him and told him, "Now calm down. What's the matter?"

"They've gone! They've gone!" he howled.

Helen put down the buckets as if their handles were suddenly red hot.

"Who've gone? Gone where?"

"My mother, the sisters, all your ladies. I was playing behind the woodshed and they've left me behind. Everybody's gone."

Filled with overwhelming terror and distress, Helen began to run, the guard and the boy at her heels. "Please, God," she gasped as she ran, "please, God, don't leave me behind. I couldn't stand it alone."

The courtyard was silent and empty, the message of those droning lorry engines clear in the distance.

"I've got to find them," she cried, turning to the guard. "I've got to find them, d'you hear? If they're going to shoot them, they've got to shoot me too. I can't be separated from them. I can't."

Her overwhelming feeling of hysteria was frightening. Since the beginning of the rebellion, she had repressed this fear of being alone; now some mental sluice gate had shattered and uncontrollable panic flooded her mind. She raced out of the front door, heading towards Wamba and, preferably, the first firing squad she might encounter. Two hundred yards from the convent, with the puzzled but distraught Simba pounding along behind her, she saw a lorry driving up the gravel road towards them. She stopped and stood to one side to watch it pass. She gaped at its passengers in disbelief, her face crumpling like that of a small child, tears blinding her as she saw Jessie, Elaine, Amy, Stebby, all her friends . . . all safe . . . oh, thank God they were safe!

She began to chase back after the lorry, running and not catching up, in a sort of Kafkaesque nightmare experience. At last she reached the lorry, outside the convent door, but only Amy was sitting there.

"Amy?" she cried, "Amy, what's happening? Where are the others?"

The guard had now caught up with her again. He grabbed her arm.

"They're inside," he said angrily. "They've been taken inside. You've got to come inside too."

Amy sat in the back of the lorry, her shoulders hunched, utterly dejected. She said despairingly, "They asked me if I was the doctor and I said, 'No,' but they wouldn't believe me; they've told me to stay here."

Helen tried to pull away from the guard. "But that's absurd!" she cried. Her voice was shrill, and she couldn't bear to see her friend so distressed and frightened. "I'm the doctor. I'll stay with you here. I'm the doctor. If they want me they can have me. But you can't suffer in my place. I'll stay here."

The Simba guard, realizing that this rebelliousness was tantamount to mutiny, grabbed Helen by the shoulders, spun her around, and propelled her towards the door. "Inside!" he roared. "You are to go inside!"

In the cloisters, Jessie, Elaine, and Stebby were sitting huddled together. Plainly, they were terrified by what they had gone through recently and by what they feared for the future.

"Pray!" whispered Jessie urgently. "Pray!" Helen bent her

head. She didn't want to pray; she wanted to know what they were doing with Amy outside. They knew as well as she did that Amy wasn't the doctor. "Amy?" she whispered, unable to control herself any longer. "What are they doing with Amy?"

As if in reply to her urgent question, the main door opened, and Amy came through and walked towards them.

"They just let me go," she announced in a dazed voice, "they just let me go."

It was half an hour before Elaine felt it safe to tell Helen the whole story. "They took us all down to the jail. It was awful. They were pushing and jostling and hitting us. That dreadful little colonel arrived in his car, leaped out, and knocked down several of the nuns, just punched them to the ground with his fists. That acted as a sort of signal. All the Simbas turned on the nuns, tearing off their veils and rosaries and screaming obscenities at them. The violence was terrible, absolutely horrifying . . ."

"What about you and your group?"

"We were collected together in a little bunch; one of the Simbas pushed us to one side."

"What happened then?"

"The colonel knocked down Sister Marie Frances with his fists. He was just like a savage animal. Then he saw us and his entire attitude changed. 'Who are you?' he asked, and when the guard told him we were the Protestants he was almost gracious and said, 'You can go back to the convent. This is nothing to do with you.' So they brought us back. But we were so frightened."

"But what were they doing with Amy?"

"I think the colonel was trying to tell us we should say we were medical workers, doctors, and then we wouldn't get beaten up."

"And one of the Simbas got the message wrong?"

"I expect so."

"Sister Marie Frances?" demanded Helen. "D'you think she was badly hurt?"

"He knocked her down, but I think she's all right. She's tough. Those poor sisters, they've still got them down there."

At lunchtime Sister Dominique and Sister Clothilde returned, followed during the next few hours by the others. It was now plain that while Sister Dominique was still fighting for her own mental survival, Sister Clothilde, who was also more abused by the men than most of the other young nuns, had come to terms with her situation. This young Belgian nun, forced to endure humiliation she would never have imagined in her worst fantasies, had by now adopted a very different course from that of her colleagues.

It was the Mother Superior who first told Helen about her, but the inclinations of Sister Clothilde had also been observed by the other nuns; they saw what was happening, and as gossip—even among women as saintly as sisters of the Church—was not uncommon, tongues were beginning to clamor.

It was clear that Sister Clothilde had taken Helen's philosophy at face value: that, by suffering herself, she could, quite literally, save her sisters from rape. But there was more to it than that. The other nuns had perceived that hers was no saintly sacrifice but, rather, an indulgence in carnal pleasure.

The introspective, silent young nun of no rare beauty or outstanding zeal had discovered the fierce attraction inherent in the physical excitement of her body. Although she had made a choice early in life for the path of saintly contemplation and introspection, events had now revealed a different facet of her personality. She had discovered that the flesh, indeed, could be more, much more, than merely a housing for the contemplation of God in all His infinite mystery.

The rebellion had brought her sexual experience, and somewhere in the unobtrusive shy female, desire and the need for fulfillment had awakened. A deep sensuality could now masquerade—for she had not enough self-knowledge to understand her discovery—as a defense of her fellows. She offered herself and therefore she was not abused or forced. And this offering was to men who were rapists and enemies. It was a situation outside Helen's comprehension and beyond any advice she could offer, as it was, indeed, outside that of the Mother Superior's and the other nuns'. They said she must be mad. These dreadful events, which were destructive enough, God knows, to breed insanity in any woman, must have driven her mad. But reluctantly, perhaps subconsciously, they sensed the betrayal latent in their own bodies. This was disturbing, for their preservation appeared to rest entirely on their willingness to survive together. Should they divide on matters of principle or morality, they were doomed.

During the next few days the nuns were allowed to return to the convent in small groups, but, through December, 1964, sudden raids took place, with increasing frequency.

Perhaps the most terrifying one started at nine minutes past eight one Tuesday in December, a time recorded exactly by Helen in her diary. The atmosphere in the convent was quiet and sane. As usual after supper, the nuns were walking or sitting on the veranda, the Belgian mothers were getting their children ready for bed, and even though darkness had brought the inevitable apprehension and fear, a sense of peace and security existed inside those red brick walls.

There was no warning bell this time; the front-door bolts were shot back by a guard, obviously at a prearranged signal. The door banged open and Simbas came bellowing into the convent, screaming and capering like madmen.

The abrupt, noisy attack was clearly calculated to spread maximum alarm, confusion, and terror, and it did. The panic was heart-stopping; women screamed, children began to wail.

The Simbas, a few in uniform, most half naked and sprigged with the usual oddments of animal fur and green leaves, seemed both drunken and drugged. In a mass hysteria of rage, they lashed out with rifle butts, spears, and clubs, their motive apparently being to slaughter everyone in sight. The nuns cowered; the other women sheltered their children in their arms and waited for death. Helen, sitting next to Amy, could only gape in fear.

"Stand up, stand up all of you!" Helen was grabbed by a wild-eyed Simba and thrust against the wall.

"Over there, you! And you too!" Another grabbed Amy and thrust her in the same direction. The nuns were pushed to the opposite side. The soldiers' plan was now becoming clear: a roundup of all the Catholic sisters. Kicking, striking them with rifle butts, tugging at their clothes, the Simbas forced them into line. Helen caught the despairing eyes of Sister Dominique, but could do nothing to help.

Within minutes they had swept through the convent and assembled the Mother Superior and her charges into a long file along the veranda. Some were bleeding, many weeping. The sight of the line of broken women, many elderly and gray-haired, seemed to delight the Simbas. To Helen their jubilation was sickening. "You are to be shot!" they shouted. "D'you understand? You are to be executed!"

Hitting and jostling them, they herded them out into the night. The nuns looked so piteous that Helen and the other Protestants, as well as the Belgian women, stood transfixed, weeping and unable to help.

Were they to be taken too? No, it was only the sisters who were to be executed. The door banged shut again, and it was all over. Only two of their usual guards were left behind, and they appeared not to know what this raid was all about. Fortunately, these were two of the friendlier ones, and they conferred together for some minutes before the older spoke up.

"We think it would be better if the five Protestants moved into the main dormitory with the Belgian women and the children. There are plenty of mattresses and we can guard you more easily if you're all together."

Helen glanced from Jessie Scholes to Amy, Elaine, and Stebby, seeking not so much leadership as security. Fear knotted her stomach. Was this another trap? They could trust no one. Reluctantly, they decided to do what the guards advised.

The five of them quickly gathered their possessions together and came around to the large dormitory where the Belgian women and nuns slept. They each chose a mattress, not daring to ask, "Why the nuns and not us?" Were they really going to shoot the nuns, or had they some other humiliation in store for them? No one dared or wanted to think about it; their own personal terror was as much as they could bear.

They had hardly settled down when the dormitory door suddenly opened. Everyone held her breath, and all movement was suspended. A guard poked his head inside. "Will one of you go and turn the generator off?"

Helen was now conscious of eyes on her. She had the reputation of being a mechanic who knew something about engines. Normally, however, the generator which provided electricity for the entire convent compound was Sister Marie Frances's province. Helen knew nothing about generators of this size. As she hesitated, she saw Amy looking at her. "I'll come with you," she volunteered.

"Thanks," Helen murmured. Followed by the two soldiers, carrying a storm lantern, they walked the length of the cloisters, which were now eerily quiet and deserted. The generator was housed in a small lean-to at the end of the kitchen. They ducked under the low doorway and faced the enormous, throbbing machine. There were cobwebs overhead, oil on the floor, a panel of switches and dials which could be seen dimly on the far wall, but as to which switch or lever turned the machine off, there was no clue.

Helen stumbled over a length of rope in the oily sludge at her feet. She was still scared, because she sensed that unless they managed to switch the generator off fairly quickly, the young guards would suspect that they were being mocked and that the two women were trying to put something over on them. They were both ignorant boys, and, without officers or NCO's to command them, they were liable to turn nasty very easily, especially after having witnessed the violent scene with the nuns.

Amy sensed the danger, and her voice was urgent. "What do we do?"

Helen stared back. "I've no idea. Watch this amp meter. I'll try every switch in turn. See if we can make that needle drop. Tell me what happens."

She moved to the biggest switch she could see and threw it up. Nothing happened. She tried another. Same result. In a kind of desperation she turned and reversed every knob and switch she could see. Still nothing. The monster roared and whined with a vibrant life of its own. Helen could sense Amy's growing disquiet, the distrust of the guards, and felt her own inner hysteria. During all her years in Congo she had always had to handle the engines: grease them, repair them, make them tick. She had a knack for keeping ancient, secondhand vehicles on the road long after they should have been abandoned in the jungle.

Now, not only was she beaten, she was scared of the great oily throbbing monster which seemed to threaten their very lives. She circled it in terror, took a step towards the darkest corner, slipped, and grabbed at a rag hanging on some part of the machine. The rag came away in her hand and the engine throb died away.

Amy's head turned from the amp meter. "You've done it."

Helen felt enormous relief. She lifted her eyes to heaven in thanks. She gulped—she couldn't speak. They backed away from the machine on tiptoe, as if they might wake it up again, or as if it might suddenly blow up like a time bomb.

Outside, on the veranda, the night was full of stars, and was so quiet that even the normally shrill cacophony of the cicadas seemed muted and far away. Helen drew in a deep breath; they had defeated a malevolent generator, and that seemed equivalent to ending a war. They hurried along the veranda and began to sputter with suppressed, near-hysterical laughter. Then she remembered what had happened to the sisters and prayed, "Dear God, please help them out there in the darkness."

Back in the dormitory Helen pulled off her sweater, kicked off her sandals, and rolled them up together as a pillow; they always followed the Mother Superior's advice not to undress. She pulled her blanket over her head to shut out the mosquitos, which invariably whined in her ears as soon as she settled down. The darkness was impenetrable now, the sense of fear and tension as unyielding as a brick wall.

But what was happening to the Mother Superior, Sister Marie Frances, and Sister Dominique? Were they undergoing the same sickening humiliations as before? She tried to switch off her mind as she had the generator. "Oh God,

please protect them," she whispered. She tried to will herself to find a few moments of relief in sleep, but found
herself straining to listen. What was that noise? A car? A
man's footsteps?

Suddenly a baby whimpered, and immediately her throat
constricted with fear. She pressed the angry "Keep it quiet!
Shut it up!" back in her throat. Poor mother and baby.
How much worse off they were than she!

She lay rigid for a few seconds more, then sat up, pulled
on her sweater, and fumbled around for her glasses. She
felt better sitting up, crouched with her arms around her
knees. The breathing all around her grew steadier, more
rhythmic, as the women slept. The mother had quieted her
fretful child. Helen lay down again, and was trying to sleep
when suddenly the door opened and a shaft of light from a
storm lantern fell across her mattress. She grabbed her
glasses. Fear choked her, and she felt her heart pounding.
She could not have screamed or spoken even if she had
tried. The two guards peered in at her. They were solicitous.
Was everything all right? She nodded, and the door closed
behind them. Her relief was so great that she could actually
feel her muscles slacken their tension. How much longer
could she go on existing under this strain? Nothing had
happened. That was what was so terrifying. Nothing had
happened, yet her heart had almost stopped.

Sometime during the night she must have fallen asleep,
for she woke at 6 A.M., hearing the sound of a key turning
in the lock. Her eyes saw the early morning sunshine moving on the pale walls, and she sensed the unfamiliarity of
the scene around her. This hard cot. These movements and
sounds, so different from the noises she was used to—those
made by Elaine, Amy, Stebby, and Jessie. Then she remembered the horror of last night—the terror of that great
throbbing engine. The guards would want her to restart it
this morning, and how was she to do that?

She sat up. This dormitory was very different from their ten-foot-square cell with its two hard beds, desk under the window, wash basin, and the upholstered mattress—softest place of the lot—on the floor for Jessie. Being locked in from 8:30 P.M. until 6:00 A.M. had meant a free-for-all sprint for the bathroom every morning, with each of the seventy women trying to get in first. The Mother Superior had always gently suggested that the others should really let the sisters have precedence, as they had to hear mass at 6:30 A.M. Helen, as resident medical officer, had countered with the view that in this situation all their needs were the same. No hurry this morning, however; instead, an orderly, dispirited procession. Everyone wondered, were they really going to murder the sisters, as they'd murdered the priests and the other civilians? It was obvious that the "weaker sex" meant nothing to the Simbas: They'd destroyed hundreds of women over the past few weeks.

Then a gust of hope. A whisper suddenly went around: There was someone at the door . . . not Simbas . . . friendly voices . . . two of the sisters . . . oh, thank God for that! Helen could have wept as she confronted the broad grin of Sister Marie Frances. She had a cut on her head, a bruised face; as usual, she'd taken as many blows as she could withstand. The two guards made no attempt to stop them from talking, and Sister Marie Frances's grin faded as she described what had happened.

"It was terrible. They beat us and punched us and tore off our veils. That wasn't so bad as the filthy cell into which they pushed us for the night. Human excrement everywhere. The stench made you sick."

She caught Helen's eye and paused; she knew what Helen was going to ask. She nodded sadly.

"Was Sister Dominique—" Helen began quietly.

"She and Sister Clothilde. Both taken and abused again. The poor things, we could do nothing to help them."

Marie Frances and the other "gray" Belgian sister had been released to return to the convent to prepare food for the imprisoned nuns. They had to hurry. Sister Marie Frances gave Helen all her keys, took her along to the generator, and instructed her how to start, stop, and service it; she showed her everything, adding with a wry smile, "just in case." Then she went off to see how her adopted pygmy daughter was getting on, and to feed her dog. Her warmth and vitality were so all-embracing and giving. Helen watched her go out through the front door, carrying the basins of food, with a sense of personal loss.

At two o'clock that afternoon, the front-door bell rang again, and the guards opened it, to reveal another group of sisters gathered outside. They filed in slowly; almost unconsciously, in agonized suspense, Helen realized she was counting them. The Mother Superior, Sister Marie Frances, Sister Sylvaner, the old Spanish nun with a face like a wrinkled orange whose name she couldn't pronounce, Sister Dominique—her face as set as if it had been molded in wax—Sisters Johannes, Clothilde, Gertrude, Wilhelmina. They all shuffled in.

They were *all* back. Oh, God be praised!

They were filthy. Their robes were matted with mud and excrement. The Italian sisters' snowy robes with their pretty little red buttons were covered with dirt and effluent. Their headdresses had been torn off; their eyes stared without seeing, their cropped hair was towsled; there were bruises on some faces, blood on others. They were humiliated, cowed, bereft of dignity. It was heartbreaking to see their shoulders rounded, their heads bowed, and to see the way they stood, so fearful. They had returned from the edge of destruction, and they had been stunned and shocked by the experience.

Helen knew they hated to be seen like this and wanted

to creep away and hide. But standing there, the women who had been spared and those who had been tormented, facing each other like two hostile groups, and suddenly recognizing in the other faces such anxiety, such compassion, such love . . . it was too much for all of them. They swept together into one weeping, brokenhearted congregation— a crowd of terrorized women beaten into abject humiliation, yet no longer strangers. They were no longer Catholic, Protestant, civilian, religious, Spanish, Belgian, Italian, British; instead, they were women all together, clutching each other in a communion of grief, seeking in one another's arms some scrap of comfort and coherence.

It was, as usual, the Mother Superior, tiny, disheveled, bruised, who issued the dominating order which gave purpose and energy to everyone.

"We are dirty!" she snapped. "We must all wash. This very minute we must wash our clothes. Do you hear? Everyone to the laundry to wash their clothes."

There was a chorus of agreement. They must cleanse themselves. One had to get clean. One had to wash. The stains must be removed. Like a chorus of fallen angels, they trooped along the veranda, many still weeping, some singing, all borne along by this compelling purpose.

Helen drew Sister Dominique into a quiet corner. Her hair was short and silky, like a boy's. Dirty and bruised, her cheeks stained with tears, she was still beautiful and vulnerable. Helen, who simply wanted to show that she understood and cared, couldn't think where to start. "I know," she murmured, "I know."

Sister Dominique, who had kept her face composed since she first came in through the door, was completely undone by the sympathy. Her face crumpled, and, covering her eyes with her hands, she began to weep uncontrollably.

Helen let her cry for a few moments, then gently prized

the fingers from her cheeks and drew Dominique's head down to her own shoulder. As she held the young girl tightly in her arms, she found that her own cheeks were wet, and realized that there was purification as well as relief in their tears.

PART TWO

CHAPTER 5

In February, 1953, when young Dr. Helen Roseveare sailed from England heading for Congo, she felt totally elated as the ship, so sleek and splendid in her colors of pale blue and maroon, slid through the Mediterranean and the Suez Canal and then down across a dark blue ocean.

Mombasa fascinated her, with its white colonial buildings shaded by the heavy branches of the mango trees, the slanting sunlight, the heat, flies, noise, black faces and glinting teeth. On the overnight train to Nairobi she simply could not sleep; she had to jump out at every halt so she could try to breathe in the very sound and spirit of Africa.

The steamer which crossed Lake Albert at night was stiflingly hot, but not even mosquitos and the airless darkness under the mosquito net could disillusion her. The moon was reflected in the surface of the lake; the water lapped endlessly past the bows like skeins of black silk. Everything was strange and beautiful. She was up before daylight. The turbulent sunset she had witnessed and this vast, quiet dawn represented nature in its most romantic mood, and the romantic Dr. Helen hugged the experience to herself in an exultation which was almost unbearable.

The great spiny ridge of Central African mountains barred the route to the west, then slowly emerged from the white mist rising from the surface of the lake. High among the peaks rose the mountains of the moon. Because of this enormous watershed, the old civilizations far to the north had been born. From these high and beautiful lakes of legendary importance, rivers flowed north, east, and west: The Nile, the Zambesi, and the Congo were started off on their long journeys to the three oceans.

Beyond, deep in the rain forest, Pygmies, gorillas and other animals, birds, and plants of rarity and beauty existed unaware of the polluted civilization from which she had come. Farther to the north she would see great herds of wild elephants—bulls, cows, and calves—jet black, their huge tusks curved and shining as they stood belly-deep in the shallows of the White Nile, forking trunkfuls of green lilies and water weeds into their mouths, occasionally pausing to squirt jets of water over their skins. Mainly they just ate quietly, ruminatively, totally at peace with the world and their surroundings. And somehow their very placidity and the irrelevance of her own presence on this ground gave her the feeling that this was indeed a wild and primitive part of the world.

The event which brought the young lady doctor to this remote heart of Africa was simple but crucial: her conversion to Christianity. Not that she wasn't a Christian to begin with, as far as her family, friends, and relatives were concerned.

Helen's childhood memories of Cornwall, where her family had lived for generations, were uniformly happy. She had been lucky; she had had so many things in her favor. She passed examinations without trouble, though she would much sooner have kept up as an athlete with her adored older brother, who could out-jump, out-run, and out-fight her. Her father had been one of the most brilliant mathematicians of his day, knighted for his wartime work with the civil service, and it was natural that academic honors came easily to her.

She treasured those memories of long walks in Wales

when she was at Howells, the exclusive girls' public school, and her father would snatch a day or two off to visit her. They would tramp over the mountains as he briefly acknowledged the great sweep of the countryside, the remoteness of war, the soft wind in their faces, and then patiently explained some knotty equation of advanced mathematics.

She always remembered those three wonderful holidays in the thirties when he had piled her, Mother, and the other kids into the family car on top of tents, blankets, and cooking utensils and they had driven off to "do" Europe. All was so simple then for a small girl: You ate, you slept, you laughed, you played; there was no time or room for emptiness. Growing up was a time for satisfying appetites.

Adolescence ended at Newham College, Cambridge. She started off there doing all the things she was good at and liked. She was good at sports. She loved knocking balls about. She got her "blue" two years in succession for both cricket and hockey, though she would admit that it was largely a matter of simply being willing to play cricket which earned her the honors.

She also discovered that a medical education at Cambridge University led to many hazards for the young and ingenuous. She was the only girl student in a study group of six medical undergraduates. Every Wednesday morning they each took turns acting as guinea pig while the others administered an experimental treatment and made notes. On one particular day Helen, nineteen, and bashful in the presence of five aggressive males, arrived in the laboratory to find out that it was her turn.

The self-appointed leader handed her a glass of clear liquid. "Now drink this up like a good girl."

Helen smelled it and didn't like it. "What is it?"

"Gin."

"Oh!"

"What's the matter? Haven't you ever drunk gin before?"

"No."

"Well, it's about time you did. And there's no backing out now. You've read your syllabus, haven't you?" Helen decided it was a bit late to admit she hadn't. "You know the subject: 'The Effect of Alcohol on the Human Constitution.' It's your turn. Go on, drink it down like a good girl."

Helen drank.

"There! Didn't hurt, did it?"

Helen agreed it hadn't hurt.

"Obviously no point trying this sort of experiment on this lot; they're ginned up to the eyebrows already. You're the ideal virgin subject. Now just knock back this next tot and we're ready to take a blood sample and measure the alcohol content."

Hardly could an innocent have fallen into more cunning hands. By the time she had gulped down four large gins, she was barely aware of voices saying, "Better top her up with another double, Godfrey," and "If she has any more she'll float upwards of her own accord."

Some two hours later, with the ritualistic pomp of young knights bearing their dead queen back from a glorious battlefield, five solemn undergraduates bore a horizontal Helen back through the interested bystanders on the streets of Cambridge as she waved arms and legs in all directions like a disoriented spider crab and roared out incoherent verses of "Onward Christian Soldiers."

They deposited her gently at the front door of Newham Ladies College, an establishment noted for the decorum, gentility, and educational qualifications of its lady students. They did not wait for the reactions of the principal but scurried away, breathless with laughter. Helen was sick. The principal, wise to the ways of young medical students, took no action over the episode, maintaining a tactful if frosty neutrality.

Work, music, amateur dramatics, sport, and friends all engaged Helen's attention. But something was missing. The trouble was, she did not know what was missing. The belief grew inside her that surely there must be something more to life than participation in a score of pleasant activities. She simply could not just sit back and say, "I'm all right!" and let the rest of the world go hang. She had to be involved in life.

Reading philosophy was all very well, but *that* was somebody else's philosophy. How did you create your own? She was aware, of course, that the world was in a desperate state. She had grown up during the most disastrous war in history. People were always starving, miserable, terrified, or exploited. She tried joining political parties. Power was the end product of all their rhetoric, argument, and dreams, however, and history seemed to prove they abused power and were corrupted by it as soon as they attained their desires. Each was so certain that *their* philosophy and *their* way of life was the only well-paid and well-fed route to eternity; each certain, without doubt, that they alone had been chosen by God.

God really wasn't much help either. Ostensibly Helen was a Christian. She went to church, she paid lip service to all the good causes, but in the second half of the twentieth century, how could you *really* believe in God? He didn't seem to have much to do with paying the rent, pacifying the boss, soothing an angry wife or boyfriend; what did God have to do with fast cars, overdrafts at the bank, strikes, or package tours? The Christian Church represented "religion," but there was no relation to a personal God. Religion made its ritualistic appearance only at births, christenings, and funerals.

The word "God" seemed somehow to have become too powerful a noun to be accepted simply or naturally. People simpered to children about "the little Lord Jesus." God seemed to have been taken over by those strange people carrying banners at street meetings.

To Helen's astonishment, some of her contemporaries at Cambridge seemed to have found "belief." How, Helen didn't know, since she felt her own emptiness internally and knew no way of filling it. It was not in her nature to join the "in" crowd and mouth empty phrases.

Something about the religious life, however, drew her towards it. Mainly, perhaps, it was because she was ready to try anything once, and because she had looked so hard for *something*, she often found herself joining in at Christian Union prayer meetings and Bible studies. She discovered she loved singing hymns; she adored all those rousing, swinging choruses, the plaintive melodies, the appeals, the confirmations of faith she didn't understand or even expect to understand.

When she eventually came to the hymn which started "More about Jesus would I know . . ." the idea intrigued her, although she was perplexed by the thought. People committed themselves to music, art, gambling, sport, sex, drinking, gardening, sailing . . . a hundred things. Was it possible she could commit herself to God?

She "slogged," to use her own description, through the New Testament, and then found, to her amazement, that she had actually been captured by the great mystery, by the clear compassion, by the simple message. She was still bogged down by the dogma, the theology, the pomp, ritual, and ceremony encrusted on Christianity like the barnacles on the hulk of a great ship.

Christmas came with the news that her youngest sister had the mumps. All three sisters had shared chickenpox and then measles several years earlier, and that had been very unpleasant, because Helen's eyes had been damaged permanently. It would be better if she avoided mumps, wrote her mother, and not come home until January.

Two friends told her of a vacancy at a Christmas house-party at Mount Hermon Bible College, Ealing. She applied and was accepted, although when she arrived she felt at once lonely, bewildered, and unqualified. On the second day there her study group was led through the book of Genesis and shown how to annotate and summarize the message and information to be found there. Helen, with her logical, orderly mind, thought it a fascinating exercise. Next day they were going to follow the same procedure with the Book of Romans. Would they try to read as much as they could before tomorrow morning's study session? She curled up on a sofa in front of the fire and began to read and make notes. "Through its orderly array of facts I gripped the essential basic truth of man's need in his lost state of sin and depravity, and of God's provision to meet that need through the substitutionary death of Christ . . . ," Helen wrote later in her diary.

When she finished she started off for bed. She met two girls just leaving the bathroom. "You're late," she said. "You're early," they replied. She looked at her watch. It was 6:30 A.M., and the girls were reporting for early kitchen duty. Helen had worked all night. To her intense disappointment, she fell asleep in the study session she had prepared for with so much anticipation.

On the last evening she got into a vehement argument with her associates about her conception of Christianity. And as she argued, she realized she did not know or understand enough, and that their theology was miles ahead of hers. She lost her temper and the thread of her argument. They laughed at her and she left, humiliated and close to tears. In her room she threw herself on her bed and wept. Despair and loneliness were all she seemed to have come to in her search for God. Then she raised her reddened eyes to the large printed text of a psalm on the wall. She didn't seem to have taken it in before, although she must have read it a hundred times:

Be still, and know that I am God.

Eight small words which drove into her heart and brain; eight small words which shone like a searchlight through her despair. Suddenly she understood the essentially simple yet contradictory fact that it was *not possible to understand.* Not intellectually. Not as you would work out an equation or a problem in logic. To understand with the intellect was beyond the mind of man. An understanding of belief lay beyond the horizons of brain or computer. Belief was a color unseen in their spectrum.

Be still, and know that I am God. The reasons and the finality were in His hands; at last she understood. There were to be many more emotional fences to surmount, but at last she had achieved an individual relationship with Him.

That evening she went down to the meeting still overcome by her own almost incommunicable awakening. Their leader always asked for testimonies, and usually, once on her feet, Helen could never stop talking. This time she couldn't speak at all. Eventually, feeling foolish, she managed to blurt out that she had met with God. It was difficult to explain that the great light which had blinded Paul on the road to Damascus had shone down for Helen Roseveare from a psalm on the wall of a bedroom in Ealing.

The Africans of the Congo rain forest are a pagan people. Since the era of prehistoric man, no one had disturbed them in the peace of their dark forest glades. Nothing there had ever excited the curiosity or avarice of the outside world.

Gold, silver, and precious stones were not easily available. It was far simpler to poach and transport ivory across the vast plains on the eastern side of the central African watershed. No one searched there for lost civilizations or Cro-Magnon Man. Even when Europeans became obsessed with their nineteenth-century dream of empire and the scramble for portioning out Africa—the carving of the continent into neat geographical joints—no one was very anxious to get hold of the clammy, fever-ridden jungles of equatorial Africa. Obviously, for geographical, anthropological, and medical reasons, the white man could not survive there.

In 1482 the Portuguese navigator Diego Coa discovered the mouth of the Congo. He could hardly avoid it. Thirty miles out at sea, the sludge emitted by one of the world's mightiest rivers stained the immaculate blue of the Atlantic a deep cocoa-brown. Diego built a marble pillar on the southern-most bluff of the river bank and with grisly justification called it Shark's Point. Seven miles away across the river mouth, a long, fat, yellow bank of sand was named Banana Point (for its color rather than its fruit, for no bananas have ever grown there).

During the following three hundred years, a succession of tiny outposts at the mouth of the river traded in slaves and ivory. But generally the great African bight and southern coastline between latitudes ten degrees north and ten degrees south continued to live up to its generic name: the white man's grave.

In 1816, the British Admiralty, unsure whether the Niger and the Congo were one and the same river, despatched Captain J. K. Tuckey, R.N., to resolve this matter with a well-equipped expedition. Captain Tuckey penetrated less than a hundred miles upriver to Isangila, just past the first rapids. There he and sixteen others died very quickly of fever. They were speedily buried, and with equal haste the expedition turned back towards the ocean.

The first frustrating topographical obstacle to any exploration of the hinterland is revealed not far above Matadi. From the smooth and enormous reaches of Stanley Pool two hundred and fifty miles upriver (overlooked these days by the modern city of Kinshasa), seven foaming cataracts fall half a mile in height over a comparatively short distance. There are also some thirty rapids. The seventh and last cataract, the first encountered coming in from the sea, is the most dramatic. The natural terrain compresses three thousand miles of river draining the equatorial basin of Central Africa into a channel eight hundred yards across, most of which is occupied by a large island. The righthand outlet is thirty yards wide, and the roaring torrent emerges from it leaping and foaming.

The three European expeditions which followed the ill-fated Captain Tuckey did not penetrate far enough to witness this spectacle. The combined deterrents of terrain and insect-borne disease, plus the danger of cannibalism, reinforced the theory that there was no way in along this waterway. The determined missionary Livingstone, who died exploring the headwaters of the Congo, and had declared with dour Scottish candor that he had no wish to become "black man's pot," was one of many who was wary of the natives but warier of the jungle itself. Indeed, long after the Americas, Asia, Australia, and the oceans and islands of the world had been colonized or conquered, Congo, sweating under its equatorial sun and drenched by its tropical rain, remained inviolate.

It was not until 1876 that H. M. Stanley, starting from Zanzibar, on the east coast, crossed the great central mountain barrier on foot. He came down from the high grasslands into the unbelievable tangle of jungle, swamp, and river. It was one of the epic journeys in man's long history of exploration. A stone set in the roadside a few miles away from Helen Roseveare's present medical school at Nyankunde records that Stanley set up camp there before beginning the descent into the rain forest to the grave of Captain J. K. Tuckey, some sixteen hundred miles down the twisting river.

The drama of Helen's first entry into Congo in 1953 was heightened by the first demand for her services as a doctor. Jack Scholes, Jim Grainger, and two Africans were waiting at the border to meet her with a two-ton truck and a three-quarter-ton pickup. She helped to load her luggage and the supplies with which she had been entrusted and climbed into the cab.

The heavy tires skidded on the gravel road as they toiled up the escarpment, and it was dark when they reached the mission station at Nyankunde. She stared at the cluster of huts and houses perched four thousand feet up in the high grasslands which slope down towards the vast rain forest.

They rested there for the weekend, and Helen was a little disappointed at the garden-party atmosphere of it all. She played tennis on their court and played her violin at a sort of musical evening which had been arranged.

The concert was interrupted by the news that a doctor was needed in the nearby village. The doctor at Nyankunde was away on leave; could Helen attend the case?

She climbed back into the truck with one of the older missionaries, and with headlights blazing they bumped along a winding track deep into the bush. They stopped near the village, and Helen stepped out. She was immediately aware of the enormity of the star-filled African sky, the fireflies, the sense of loneliness, and the high-pitched monotonous shrieking coming from the cluster of conical huts which she could barely see in the darkness.

The missionary said quietly, "I think we're too late. That's the sound of the death wailing."

There was no light in the village, and only a smoky fire in the hut, which made Helen's eyes smart. On the earth floor lay the thin, emaciated body of the chief, already stiffening in death, surrounded by his six wives, naked and keening their grief. They were already aware of his condition, which Helen confirmed by a cursory examination.

On the way back to Nyankunde, the missionary sensed her bewilderment and asked, "Bit more primitive than you expected?"

"Yes," Helen answered. To her it was a confused, barbaric place. What could she possibly do here? How could she make herself useful?

"You'll get accustomed to it," he said. "Don't worry."

Her arrival at Ibambi was far more reassuring. The truck braked to a halt under a wide banner of red bunting stretched across the road between two palm trees. The words "Welcome to Ibambi" had been picked out in cotton-wool letters upon it. An old man, the pastor, stepped forward to say with much emotion, "We welcome you, our child, into our midst."

Pastor Ndugu, who became a close friend in later years, was gray, gentle, and kind. He had started his Christian career as houseboy to the famous C. T. Studd, who had first reached this part of Africa in 1913 and who, indeed, was responsible for the primary conception of the Worldwide Evangelization Crusade.

Charles Thomas Studd, English gentleman, famous cricketer, captain of Eton and Cambridge University, had been inspired by the American evangelists Sankey and Moody. In 1885 he announced that he was giving away his inheritance, abandoning his mode of living, and obeying the divine instruction "Go thy way, sell that thou hast and give to the poor . . . take up thy cross and follow Me." The British public had received this news with consternation and disbelief.

He spent twenty-five pioneering years in China and India before returning to England, but he did not intend to rest. Over fifty, in poor health, and with almost no money, he set off for equatorial Africa. He reached the village of Nala and heard of Livingstone's reports that cannibalism was widespread in this vicinity. Ten years prior to Studd's arrival, the first white man ever to be seen, accompanied by thirty-five African soldiers, had entered the village. His declared intention: to subdue and control their district. When he was told to go away, he refused. That night his force was surprised, overwhelmed, slaughtered, and, with all the ceremony appropriate to such a rare occasion, eaten.

Studd trekked on through cannibal country, penetrating deep into the Ituri forest to the *kraal* where the great chief Ibambi held omnipotent power. There, in a bamboo hut, Charles Studd pioneered what he at first called the "Heart of Africa Mission." He worked tirelessly until his death in 1931, leaving behind instructions that his body should be buried in the forest, in the green place where he had labored so long and so hard for God.

Helen felt her feet very small to follow in such footsteps. Twenty-eight years old and apple-green on her first arrival in Ibambi, she was uneasily aware that there was much more to becoming a doctor in Africa than holding a Cambridge University medical degree. But as she listened to Pastor Ndugu's welcome, she felt the tears sting her eyes, and the response to her carefully rehearsed sentence in Swahili, "I have great joy to be here among you," was an immediate and spontaneous eruption of hugging, kissing, cheering, and singing. She had never in her life experienced such an overwhelming emotional reaction, having come from a background where feelings were sublimated and channeled into safe, calm behavior. In Ibambi she found that love and affection were a normal part of the human relationship. And later she discovered that not only could she reciprocate their affection but also she could enjoy an intimacy with her patients and parishioners which would have been inconceivable in a British society.

Next day, in the large bare room which Jack Scholes had set aside for her work, the women and children had crowded in to greet their *own* lady doctor who had come from so far away across the mountains. They had smiled at her, touched her, and occasionally indicated a mysterious ache or pain. In those first few weeks, with no drugs and no command of Swahili, if her patients rubbed their heads she gave them aspirin, and if they rubbed their stomachs she gave them Epsom salts. Nevertheless, at the end of that first day, utterly exhausted with trying to cope, she was filled with an enormous exaltation. Christ had said, "Go ye into all the world and preach the gospel to every creature." She could preach, she could heal, and she knew intuitively that God had guided her to this special destiny.

CHAPTER 6

When Helen arrived at Ibambi in 1953, the two people most intimately concerned with her work and future were station leader Jack Scholes and his wife, Jessie, and they watched her progress with solicitous, kindly, and sometimes wry smiles.

"We loved her because we knew her," Jack said. "She lived with us for almost three years from the time she first came out. And what a worker, a real worker. But she couldn't drag everybody after her at her speed. You can't keep pace. You're walking stride for stride and suddenly she's a hundred yards ahead. And just when you're catching up, she's off two hundred yards in another direction."

Jack was a contemplative Lancashire man built like a farmer of medium height, his hair now beginning to turn white. A man whose eyes were shrewd and watchful, who thought before he spoke; a man of silences. He helped young Helen set up her dispensary at Ibambi, and before the year was out he was listening to her plans to reform not only the enormous country of Congo, but, as far as he could make out, the entire African continent, from Cape to Cairo. Few people except for Livingstone, Cecil Rhodes, and Zulu chief Cetowayo could ever have approached Africa with such all-consuming zeal.

When Helen discovered God, the idea of becoming a medical missionary naturally followed in her mind. Her affinity with WEC, still known as the Heart of Africa Mission when she first arrived in Congo, also fitted into her pattern of Christian endeavor. Nine A.M.-to-five-P.M. missionaries were not part of the Worldwide Evangelization Crusade's thinking. You either had a vocation or you had nothing. They said: "If you've got a vision, go and do it, but we're not interested in mere visionaries. You can expect hard, endless work. You'll go into the field with practically no salary, and we'll expect you to live alongside the nationals of that country."

Americans, Australians, British, Swedes, Swiss, all worked side by side in projects all over the world. They recruited their members not only from the professional and university levels but from working- and middle-class people as well. They asked for devout belief. They asked for volunteers who were prepared to devote their lives to hard work in remote outposts without praise, attention, or reward. Their allowances were meager, and they paid their own fares if they had any money.

There were missions already established in the Congo, the administration told Helen, and there was a Christian church, and schools of many varieties, but in the province they suggested for her, WEC ran no medical services. She would work under enormous disadvantages, but the need for a doctor was desperate. That was enough for Helen. Congo sounded wild, challenging, far away, and there was a need which should fill her own emptiness. Her room at Ibambi contained a tea chest, a camp bed, and a camp chair. As soon as she had settled in, she had a talk with Jack Scholes. He pointed out, with dour north-country candor, that if, as a young lady doctor, she thought her university education, medical degree, or the excellence of her church work conferred any sort of preference or favor upon her, or was going to make her a good missionary, then she'd "better have another think coming."

Humbly, Helen agreed. She realized that you had to make a fundamental assessment about your *use* as a missionary, your *right* to be a missionary. You had to rationalize your impertinence at living in another people's country and trying to alter their habits by shattering their beliefs in the old gods of sun, wind, and rain, and the black spirits they feared.

Jack came from the older school of missionaries. He'd been accepted for training at the missionary colony in 1921. The next year, he left by tramp steamer from Liverpool for Alexandria. He traveled through Africa by riverboat, lake steamer, and a steam train, which plugged slowly over never-ending steel rails. Across deserts, plains, and jungles he went, secure inheritor of that Livingstone legacy of belief that Christianity and commerce must push in side by side, that they can exist together.

Two final days in a vintage car over a bumpy road took him and his two companions to the northeastern corner of Congo, where the great tropical rain forest began. There were no more roads—you walked. Long lines of African porters carried your boxes and bales on their heads; you smelled animals at night, listened to the chatter of monkeys by day. This was country of heat, flies, dark rivers, suspicion, tribalism, and witchcraft.

The Belgian District Officer gave them every help. He recruited the seventy porters necessary to ferry the three white men and their luggage to their destination. Every fifteen miles or so, a rest house had been established. It was a three-day journey to Faradje, another six days to Dungu. Then six more to Nala, and the first of the Heart of Africa Missions. Jack had stayed there; the other two pressed on to Ibambi. Time had ceased to be important. It stretched from sunup to moonrise. It stretched through the cool night and the long hot day. It had a slowness, a cadence, and a rhythm which were full and satisfying.

Jessie left Blackpool on the twenty-fourth of November, 1924, journeying by sea to Kinshasa (since then renamed Leopoldville, and then Kinshasa again), which lay above the great rapids two hundred miles from the mouth of the Congo. It was then a small European outpost with a high mortality rate. She waited for three weeks for the upriver boat to take her to Stanleyville, and arrived in Ibambi on March 7. The journey had taken her three months and thirteen days. She had been engaged to Jack back home, and they were married the following January.

There was something very rare and splendid about those early days of evangelical work in this almost untouched and certainly unknown corner of Africa. Even when Helen first arrived, in 1953, it was still primitive. Diseases of every variety were borne by animal, insect, water, and food. Biblical diseases such as leprosy were prevalent; tropical diseases such as elephantiasis, yaws, hookworms, ulcers, malaria, yellow fever, and black-water fever were common-place. There were crocodiles in the rivers, snakes and leopards in the forest. Elephants could trample your crops, and locusts could devour what was left of them. Driver ants could arrive at your gates—as they did once at Helen's—in a wide, dark, endlessly flowing river. With their bite, they would kill every living thing which did not move out of their path: chickens in their coops, goats in their pens.

In the tropical rain forest there was a species of red fly, the chrysops, which stung like a horsefly, and every morning Helen would see several in her classroom. Its bite implanted larvae in one's tissues, which developed into tiny hairlike white worms, called filaria. These infested your body for most of your life. They crawled about inside you, often surfacing just under the skin, so that you could observe their slow progress across your hand or arm. When they crawled across an eyeball or the lobe of an ear, it was quite painful. Getting rid of these parasites was a difficult job, and the cure, Helen found, was worse than the worms.

Her patients from the rain forest were always fascinating. Her first Pygmy patient had been pure delight: a ten-year-old boy, a perfectly proportioned miniature of a child, with smooth, shining skin, and darting, inquisitive eyes. He had broken his thigh, and in her mud-and-thatch hospital at Ibambi she'd reset it under local anesthetic. With the help of a carpenter, she built a highly effective, if surrealistic-looking, trapeze of blocks and pulleys which kept the leg stretched and the bone correctly in place.

To the primitive eye, however, it must have looked terrifying, for when she returned from lunch she found her Pygmy patient gone. "But what happened?" she demanded in exasperation of the apologetic ward orderly. It appeared that the boy's father, not much bigger than his own son, had suddenly arrived in the ward, examined Helen's superb traction apparatus with terrified eyes, and decided to remove his son from the hospital.

"But was he frightened by the apparatus, or did he think we had already cured the boy?" demanded Helen.

"I'm not quite certain, Doctor, but I just couldn't stop him." The father had unhitched Helen's contraption, gathered his son into his arms, and carried him back into the forest, never to be seen again.

By the end of her first week at Ibambi, not fewer than one hundred and fifty patients a day were pouring in, with terrible ulcers, running eyes, septic wounds, earaches, abscesses—the bewildering range of afflictions never ceased to astound her.

As a doctor to a parish covering several thousand square miles of territory, Helen's cases were often of great medical interest, their treatment highly unlikely to be found in any textbook. On one early occasion a group of Africans carried in a man slung on a blanket between two poles.

"What's the matter with him?" Helen asked. The oldest African explained. "There was a quarrel," he said. "A spear was thrown. It went in through his back and came out through the front of his stomach. It stuck out at least two feet."

"So what did you do?"

We pulled it out the other side. What else could we have done?" It was a good question. Helen didn't know.

"We have brought it with us to show you." As if it might be of some medical interest also, one of the pole-bearers stepped forward, holding out the spear. It was vicious-looking weapon, nearly six feet long with a thin, pointed blade. She touched the point gingerly. It was very sharp.

There was no possibility of Helen operating on the man. The thought of trying to trace, repair, and antisepticize the track of a spear wound through the middle of a man's body gave her the shudders. She dressed and bandaged the entrance and exit wounds and put the victim to bed. Less than a week later, he got up and walked home. The people of the rain forest were a hardy race.

As she was returning from Wamba one day, a party of villagers had waved her down. They needed a doctor immediately. Helen had protested in her painstaking Swahili, "I've been shopping in Wamba. I've no medicines, no drugs, no instruments, not even a thermometer."

The spokesman had brushed aside the excuses. "You are the doctor. Our village elder is dying."

"I'm sorry," said Helen and spread her hands. "But I have no instruments, no drugs." Helen made one last effort. "Listen, I'll come back as soon as I get my equipment from my dispensary."

"He will die before that. You must come. Please come."

There was no alternative, so she'd trudged for more than an hour deep into the dripping forest along overgrown trails, half dreading what she could find: the last stages of T.B., perhaps, an inoperable cancer, a strangulated hernia? What could she do then? By the time they reached a clearing among thatched huts and she saw the silent crowd gathered around the fire, it was almost dark. An old man twisted and turned in delirium before the fire. She touched his forehead. It was fever-hot. Nervously she looked around at the orange firelight flickering over dark, absorbed faces. They were all strangers, and it was a long way back to the road and the car. Supposing the old man died while she was trying to help? What would they do? She pushed the thought abruptly out of her mind and examined the feverish, emaciated body. To her relief, the source of his illness, an enormous inguinal abscess, was patently obvious. Immediate medical aid was necessary, even though it had to be of the instant-first-aid variety. Helen had no instruments at all; that was the crux of her dilemma, since the abscess had to be lanced.

Then she saw the small group of Pygmies, who, in their strange intuitive manner, had somehow scented drama and drifted into the clearing to watch. Tiny, lithe figures, naked except for loincloths, skins shining, utterly still, they clutched their bows and bundles of arrows, their eyes wide and fascinated.

Helen nodded at the pot bubbling on the fire and said: "I'll need that boiling water." She walked across to the Pygmies. Even at her height of five foot three, she towered above them, and they drew back nervously. She smiled reassuringly, reached forward, and indicated that she wanted to borrow an iron-tipped arrow belonging to the nearest man.

He handed it over, and she walked back to the fire with it. Lifting her skirt, she tore off several strips of petticoat and dropped them into the boiling water. She thrust the iron arrowhead into the flame. It began to glow red hot, and she heard the speculative murmurs of her audience increase. They hushed as she approached the old man. She motioned to two of his friends to hold him steady; then, deliberately, she stabbed the arrowhead deep into the festering swelling. A torrent of pus emerged. The hiss from the crowd sounded like a bicycle tire bursting. She used the boiled strips of underskirt to clean the wound. She drained and plugged the hole, and with more strips of petticoat bound up the abscess, leaving instructions as to how it should be treated until she returned.

Rarely can a doctor have enjoyed such a swift, total, and remarkable victory. With a few moans and groans, the patient changed from a delirious, dying old man into a weak but quite coherent human being. By the time she had returned the arrow to its owner and rinsed her hands, his temperature had plummeted. Before she left, he was talking softly but clearly to his audience.

The walk back to the car was slow and tiresome. But she was conscious of an intense feeling of relief and triumph. The British Medical Association might not have adopted her treatment for the textbooks, but she hoped they would have understood its necessity. Thank God it had been effective. Over the years in Congo she did all she could for her patients, but realized, so often, that when their lives hung in the balance, God had to decide the final issue, not she.

The young African boy had stood uncertainly before her, his eyes wary, his face buttoned up to hide his nervousness. His clothes were clean but worn, and generally he gave

Helen the impression of a school truant suddenly surprised by the headmaster. Six months at Ibambi, however, had blunted Helen's capacity for surprise.

"God has sent me to see you," he said. It was at least an original and promising start.

"I'm glad."

"My name is John Mangadima. I am a Christian."

He intrigued Helen with his determination that the interview proceed logically and at his own pace. "How old are you?" she asked.

"Sixteen."

"I see. And what can I do for you?"

"You are a doctor?"

"Yes."

"Will you teach me to be a doctor?"

"Is that what you came for?" she asked. She was taken aback.

"Yes."

She wondered how she could explain in her rapidly improving Swahili how long and complex a task it was to become a doctor. First of all, there was the necessity for vocation or calling. And then, the years of study. Even becoming a trained male nurse took quite a long time.

He was, however, one step ahead of her.

"I have already worked for one year at the Belgian Red Cross Hospital at Pawa," he announced abruptly.

"Oh, have you!" said Helen surprised. The hospital lay fourteen miles to the north of Ibambi, and as part of her government medical education to fit her for work in Congo Helen had spent a month there shortly after her arrival. Mainly she had worked under Dr. Kadoner, a fine doctor of the old school who had spent twenty-five years in the Belgian colonial medical service. Helen admired him greatly. He taught her surgery in twelve hectic days, performing a daily average of two hysterectomies, eight herniorrhaphies, and several other minor operations between 7 A.M. and 2 P.M. She became acquainted with the tropical diseases endemic to their area, studying the diagnosis, treatment, and laboratory tests connected with them. She had also met Dr. Swertz.

Dr. Swertz was younger than Helen, short, square, and dark, his gaze direct and hostile. He was a capable leprologue and laboratory pathologist, under whom she was expected to spend two weeks of instruction. Dr. Swertz plainly did not like women, and in particular women doctors. He never uttered one single word to Helen during her stay, preferring a monosyllabic grunt, and so the period was nonproductive.

Helen looked at young John Mangadima with new interest. "Why did you leave?" she inquired.

He said simply, "I reprimanded one of the Belgian doctors."

Helen carefully replaced a roll of cotton wool in the drawer, and screwed the top back on her fountain pen.

"I see," she said thoughtfully. "*You* reprimanded one of the Belgian doctors."

"Yes."

Helen had no doubt at all which doctor he had reprimanded. Dr. Swertz always considered a swift kick in the backside or a clout across the head to be routine and necessary disciplinary procedure with any African staff, patients, or students who happened to get in his way.

"What had the doctor done?"

"He kicked a leprosy patient."

"What did he do after you reprimanded him?"

"He struck me across the face."

"What did you do?"

"I turned the other cheek."

"Very Christian," said Helen. "What did he do then?"

"He struck me across the face again." Helen nodded understandingly. "I thought he might," she said.

"Then he kicked me out of the hospital."

"So you came here?"

"Yes."

Helen knew there was no point in trying to take the matter to the authorities; kicking Africans was currently acceptable in Congo. Some of the doctors were good and conscientious men, and she understood their practical difficulties. There was never time for the kindly advice, the good-natured suggestion. A slap across the face often merely indicated that the African concerned had transgressed and must do better next time. Certainly, she knew that Dr. Kadoner always had ten times too much to do. All the physicians were vastly overworked and incredibly understaffed; demand always outstripped the bounds of human time, strength, and patience. She'd cycled past a queue of Africans a hundred yards long the first morning she arrived at Pawa hospital; she cycled past a queue of the same length on her last morning. And while she could never approve of or subscribe to physical abuse of Africans, she understood how it could happen.

While she was under training at Pawa, an old man from Ibambi, a good church worker and a respected elder, arrived for an operation escorted by his two teenage granddaughters, both pretty girls. He was not operated upon, but sulfonamide pills were prescribed for him every four hours. When the local male nurses arrived at 6 P.M. for night duty, they took one look at the pretty granddaughters and gave the old man an ultimatum: No pills unless the granddaughters spent the night with them. Indignantly the old man refused, and sent the girls away. Because they all came from Ibambi, Helen was informed of this occurrence, and she confronted Dr. Kadoner with her disapproval. He shrugged noncommittally, his face expressionless, his interest minimal. It was obvious that he considered the retention of his trained male nurses more important than the virginity of two local girls. "After all, this is Africa," he remarked, and took no action. The fact that the old man died the following morning increased Helen's feeling of bitter injustice. She realized how desperately trained nurses were needed in Congo and how little she knew about that profession.

She knew already, from her visits to other isolated Protestant mission stations scattered about the province, that a clinic, a dispensary, and one trained African could be a God-send. All of these thoughts flashed through her mind as she talked with the young African boy standing before her. Now here was John Mangadima, who might provide the beginning of the answer to that need.

"Where do you come from?" Helen asked.

"The rain forest. I was born in a village deep in the forest. We were very poor."

Helen had already seen many such places: huts and mud and straw thatch, where you worked in the cleared land from sunup until darkness, you ate just enough food, the chief and the witch doctor ruled your life. You never earned enough money to buy even a single cow, so the purchase of a wife was always beyond your reach. You were born, existed, and died in the rain forest, as oblivious to life and the outside world as a worker ant in a rotted tree stump.

"Parents?" asked Helen.

"My mother and father are lepers. They had to leave the village and go to a leprosy camp."

"I see," said Helen. "Now, to be working as a student nurse in Pawa means you must have had some education?"

"Yes," said John Mangadima. "But not enough." By Western standards, his education was rudimentary: about equal to that of a British eleven-year-old. But he had done a year as a student nurse. Surely that made a difference? He looked at her appealingly.

"I will work very hard, do all you instruct me to do."

The large brown eyes in the earnest face were filled with perplexity and anxiety. The voice quavered. He had failed through his sense of Christian justice at Pawa. This might be his last chance.

Helen made one of her quick, intuitive decisions. "All right, John. If you're willing to work, I'm willing to teach you. It's a bargain."

She knew at that moment that John Mangadima's appeal was the catalyst to her own goal. His spirit and determination matched her own exactly. "Teach me," he had pleaded, and by heavens she was going to teach him! She was going to teach the Africans to start their own medical services so that no one in the world would have the right to hit them in the face or tell them they did not understand.

The arrival of John Mangadima in Helen's life had far-reaching consequences. It completely altered her vision of what she was going to do in Africa. From an early age she had suspected that the world inhabited and organized by men was one which, in her opinion, could do with a great deal of alteration. Far better for all concerned, she decided, if she forgot about marriage and a family and used her female intelligence and talents to chart a life of her own.

What else was there to do other than become a doctor? As a university graduate, she seemed to have a choice between doctoring and schoolteaching. Telling your friends that you were going to be a doctor sounded the superior of the two; most people raised an eyebrow with interest and looked impressed. Besides, an emergency measure had been passed at the end of the war that enabled medical students to compress a nine-term university course into two years.

So Helen became a doctor, but it was young John Mangadima who influenced her to change direction. From the very first at Ibambi she was determined to remove all language barriers between herself and her patients, and was already studying Swahili with a fanaticism worthy of a Marxist disciple. Now, with John to coach her, she quickly became fluent; within months she lived and dreamed in the language. (Later she passed an unusual proficiency test to her own satisfaction. After coming out of a severe bout of fever, she was told she had raved in Swahili for two days.)

Ibambi provided Helen with her first experience of being doctor-in-charge. At the beginning, in the empty room where she did her work—the crowd of patients waited out on the veranda—she used assembly-line techniques: all the coughs in this line, the headaches in that, the ulcers here, the unknowns over against the wall. Then she'd check the coughs to see if there was any pneumonia, treat those who showed any symptoms, and ladle cough mixture into the others.

She kept her case histories on pieces of paper torn from an old exercise book, and for those first few months she had no help from either Europeans or Africans. It was apparent, however, that if she was going to make any impact upon the medical scene she had to have a hospital, with wards and nurses, not only patients. With John Mangadima's arrival, the need to teach and train became paramount.

Building the hospital was probably the simplest part of her program. There were many skilled and willing workers among the African Christians at Ibambi, and within a few months they had built two large mud buildings with thatched roofs and shuttered windows, whitewashed the walls, and filled each unit with wooden beds. She now found herself in possession of a twenty-four-bed ward for women and eight-bed ward for men, and various small rooms for maternity, minor surgery, and special cases. They were filled almost overnight.

With difficulty Helen recruited seven other boys to train with John Mangadima. The idea of training female nurses at that time was completely impracticable; very few girls had any education at all. Half of the boys were educated to the standard of English eleven-year-olds, the others to that of eight-year-olds. On the credit side, however, they had a specialized knowledge and awareness unknown to the Western child. They knew about agriculture and forest craft, about birth and life and death. On the debit side, they had no notion of science, not even a primary conception; neither they nor their parents had ever thought in a scientific or logical manner in their lives, and after her first few lessons Helen wondered if she would ever be able to overcome this daunting disability.

On the very first occasion, she had stood up in front of her class, looked down at the eight shining, expectant faces, and held up a thermometer. "Now," she had asked, "what is this?"

The faces remained clear and untroubled. Only John Mangadima knew.

"This thermometer," she went on, "has a Fahrenheit scale, so we have to turn it into a centigrade scale."

Seven blank faces stared at her. To conceal her slight confusion, she turned to the blackboard, drew a picture of the thermometer, and began to mark off the readings at the side: 98.2, 98.4, 98.6.

One of the boys inquired very politely: "Excuse me, madam, what are those little dots between the figures for?"

Helen put down her chalk and sighed. "You don't know what a decimal point is?"

"No, madam."

"Do you know your twice-times table? Twice one are two, twice two are four—"

"No, madam."

Helen put the thermometer back on the table and started with a short course in mathematics. Then they spent hours, days, weeks on the thermometer.

"Inside this glass tube is a metal which expands," she said. Then she paused. "John," she asked, "what's the word for 'metal' in Swahili?"

"There is no such word as 'metal' in Swahili," he answered politely.

She found a small metal ring and a metal ball. She demonstrated that the metal ball would not go through the ring. They tried pushing, but it would not go through. She boiled the metal ring and showed that now the ball went through quite easily. Metal expanded when it got hot. "Here, hold it and see." She passed it to the first boy, who exclaimed in pain and dropped the ball. "Now do you understand? That's 'metal,' and that's 'hot,' and when it's *hot* it expands, and we can get this *cold* metal ball through it. 'Expands' means it gets bigger. Now, that drop of metal in the thermometer, which we call 'mercury,' gets hot when you put the thermometer under the arm of someone who's got a fever. It has nowhere else to go upward, except *up* the ladder. It walks up the ladder."

The whole thing was rough, yet she was going to teach them, come what may. The class quickly shrank from eight to five boys, yet Helen loved it. In teaching them, to her joy and great excitement, she broke through into new regions, new worlds, new experiences she had not dreamed existed inside her own heart and brain. For the first time in her life she understood why she had sat as far away as possible from the surgeon in the operating theater, kept her eyes closed as long as possible when he did "the nasty bits." She hated being a doctor; she knew that, having committed herself, she had no alternative, and she steeled herself to the thought that for the rest of her life she would have to go on being a doctor—but she was not going to like it.

Medicine involved her emotionally. Watching people suffer through sickness or injury worried and upset her. She would become so committed that she could not sleep. When a patient died in the hospital, she grieved as though he had been a close relative. She realized this was a terrible weakness; she knew she was supposed to be detached, clinical, aloof, but she also knew she would never be able to train her heart to adopt this attitude.

Teaching, however, was different. She discovered teaching as a young girl discovers her first love. She was no longer hesitant, nervous, and afraid, as she was in medicine; she soared over the obstacles like a topflight steeplechaser. All right, if the boys could not think in a logical Western way, they certainly thought in a logical African way, so she would find out how to use their logic and harness that to her teaching methods. She had come to Africa with no "vision" of teaching, yet her own father had been a teacher, so perhaps it was in her blood.

Teaching obsessed her. She began to feel that there was nothing she could not teach; she became convinced that *anybody* could learn *anything* if the teacher could teach. Suddenly her life and outlook achieved a direction, an impetus, and a fulfillment she had never expected.

In those early months of schooling, she had one stroke of great good fortune. She had started with only a Red Cross first-aid and home-nursing guide as textbook. Then one of WEC's outstanding senior missionaries, Arthur Scott, heard of her plans when he returned from a leave. He had been trained in Belgium; his experience in training African health workers had entailed years of sweat, toil, and patient observation. Now, with love and good wishes, he passed all his notes over to Helen. A gold mine! She knew she would never be able to thank him enough.

She based her teaching on his notes, and through the years she added to them and modified them. She found that her own methods of teaching, of necessity, were primitive, but had good effect.

She would march through a ward trailing students in her wake and stop by a bedside.

"This patient," she would announce, "has pneumonia. How do I know she has pneumonia?"

Five pairs of eyes were mystified. No voice answered.

She draped her stethoscope around John Mangadima's neck and told him to listen hard. She placed the end of the stethoscope against the patient's chest.

"You hear that noise? You can hear its rhythm, its depth?"

"Yes, madam."

"Right, now put it against your own chest."

John Mangadima did as he was told.

"There is a difference?"

"Yes, madam."

"Now put it against Yokana's chest. See if the noise is different or the same as your own."

John's eyes opened respectfully as he listened. "It is the same as mine."

"Right, now listen to the chests of these next three patients and tell me if you think any of them has pneumonia."

John did as instructed and made his selection. "This one has pneumonia."

"Correct," Helen confirmed triumphantly, and she was thrilled with the results.

"Listen," she said to them another time. "You are going to learn about the ten basic diseases in this part of Africa. You are going to learn how to recognize them and learn what to do about them and how to treat them. Now, let's start with malaria. In Congo there are always thousands of people with malaria in various forms."

She showed them how you pricked the finger of a patient and took a drop of blood on a microscope slide, how you smeared it around and let it dry, how you used the little bottles of stain, and how you slid the tiny pane of glass under a microscope. There, through the magnifying lens, you saw the evidence you were looking for; the type of malaria the patient had, which confirmed or disproved your diagnosis. She taught them how to stain slides and to do ten basic laboratory procedures; how to bandage, take a temperature, give an enema and an injection, how to recognize bacillary dysentery, intestinal worms, tuberculosis, and pneumonia, how to treat wounds old and new, tropical ulcers, yaws and syphilis.

Her immediate aim was simple. To become accepted as a trained male nurse in Belgian colonial Congo, a man had to have a diploma issued by the government which gave him the title of Aid Nurse. The examinations were held once a year at the Red Cross Hospital at Pawa. She wanted all of her students to get this diploma.

In October, eighteen months after she started the school, the day arrived for the great test for which she had prepared her pupils. Shortly after sunup she piled five tense and nervous youths into the back of her Chevrolet truck and set off for the town. She had secured freshly pressed khaki shorts and shirts for all of them, and they looked very presentable. There was practically no talking on the drive through the lush tropical forest, for Helen was far too busy praying for divine support to make polite conversation.

She parked at the back of the hospital and led her charges inside. The doorman was about to see them out again. Examinations? What examinations? This was a hospital, not a schoolhouse. After half an hour's discussion, Helen finally got out of him that yes, the examinations were going to be held in the laboratory at the back of the hospital. A government doctor was driving specially from Wamba to administer it. Would they please assemble there?

Waiting in the anteroom next to the laboratory were twelve other students, trained by the Red Cross hospital. They looked at Helen's class with contempt. Didn't the boys from Ibambi speak any French? No? How ridiculously gauche and primitive. So Helen's five spoke only Swahili? Indeed! How quaint! It meant they were obviously jungle boys. The arrogant twelve did not inquire what she—a white female—was doing with such youths; *that* defied imagination. They thought themselves very grand; they laughed, they chatted gaily in French, and Helen could almost hear the confidence seeping out of her pupils like air from a slow puncture. She wished she could have struck up a rather militant hymn to aid morale, but, as they were in a Catholic hospital, she decided against it.

Helen was allowed into the examination room with the pupils to help with necessary translations, and once the questions started, her pride began to grow. The examination was entirely oral, and she saw at once that the hospital-trained students were merely capable of making glib, rehearsed answers to set questions. They were utterly lost when anything other than a textbook question was asked. On the other hand, John and Yokana and the others listened when it was their turn; they considered each question; their answers revealed that they knew what they were talking about and were thinking before they spoke.

When the examinations ended, Helen sat in the anteroom, digging her nails, like small knives, into her palms. The examining doctor cleared his throat: "First, with ninety-five percent, is Yokana from Ibambi . . ."

No mother has ever felt more pride than Helen at that moment. She took off her glasses and polished them industriously to remove the dampness which had settled on them.

The doctor's voice droned on. John Mangadima was third, with eighty-five percent. Two of the others had passed with high marks. The fifth was put back until next year. Four out of her five had succeeded magnificently: The first male student nurses had been trained at Ibambi. The drive back to Ibambi was as glorious as any in Helen's whole life. They cheered, they sang, they chattered incessantly. When they got back to Ibambi, to Helen's intense disappointment and disillusionment, no one else was the slightest bit impressed. Didn't they understand that all those months of work by the boys who had come out of nowhere yearning to accomplish something had succeeded? For the boys, it was like a journey to the moon! Helen wanted a celebration; she wanted a church service, a diploma-award day; it was all so important, the first nurses trained in Congo by their mission. Yet no one was interested.

She felt certain that Jessie and Jack would have celebrated with her if they had been free to express an opinion. But Jack was mission leader, Jessie was his wife; they had to be impartial. Those in charge had obviously never approved of Helen's project, and Jack was not in a position to protest.

Next day he came to see her. "Helen," he began, "Helen, as you know, the mission's field committee are in session at this moment in Ibambi."

"Yes," said Helen, still upset from yesterday's reception. At this point she would have been happy if the whole mission field committee fell into the lake.

"They've asked me to tell you their decision."

"Yes?" said Helen.

"They'd like you to move your entire medical center to Nebobongo."

Helen's breath seemed to stop for about five minutes. So this was her reward! To get shunted off into the forest!

"Nebo?" was all she managed to get out.

"It's only seven miles down the road. And there's a hospital—or a sort of hospital—there already."

"There's nothing there now except an old leprosy camp!" Her voice was an outraged squeak.

"It's the committee's decision, Helen."

"But I've already started here. Ibambi's ideal. We've built our first hospital. You know the first-ever students passed their exams yesterday."

"The committee feels it would be better for everyone."

Missionaries were just like other people; while many disagreed with her—she had expected that—they disagreed with everybody else, too. A short time earlier a similar committee had been held at Ibambi, and Helen had received one of the biggest shocks of her missionary career.

When Helen, with only nine months' experience behind her, had stood up in a meeting to talk about her vision of training Congolese, to her astonishment there were all sorts of objections. Training, particularly medical training, should, they said, be the work of the government, not of a Christian mission.

"But Christianity must be teaching . . ." she began, then faltered and sat down, bewildered and confused. Nevertheless, encouraged by Jack and Jessie, she had gone ahead with her plans, and now that she was really making headway, they sprang this on her. This idea of moving to Nebobongo was ridiculous!

"Can I make my views felt to the committee?" she demanded hotly.

"Helen, you'll only start a big row."

"Yes, I expect I shall."

Jack pursed his lips. "All right," he agreed doubtfully. "Come this evening."

She seethed all afternoon. One by one she marshaled her arguments. Point by point she rehearsed them. She bathed, changed her dress, combed her hair, and marched across to the committee room, waiting for the trumpet call which would sound the charge.

Jessie was waiting for her in the outer room. Helen could hear the voices within.

"Helen," said Jessie. "Shall we pray together?"

"Pray?" exclaimed Helen. Pray, when her mind, soul, and heart were poised for instant raging controversy? She was ready to strike argument aside with the fury of her rhetoric, the justice of her cause, the passion of her belief. Pray?

"No," she said.

Jessie eyed her solemnly. "Then I'll pray for both of us."

She knelt and prayed that Helen would find grace, humility, and understanding. She then delivered a little homily on pride and its fall, on the virtues of Christianity and brotherly love. Helen sat stony-faced.

Jessie got up and went on talking. There were two, three, or even half a dozen sides to this question. Surely Helen must realize that? The purpose of Ibambi and all the other mission stations was to teach the word of God to the Africans. Many missionaries thought that training and various forms of education were outside their sphere altogether; many believed that starting a hospital and training school would change the character of Ibambi; hundreds, possibly thousands of people would be pouring in who weren't even Christians.

Helen felt, however, that this idea crystalized practically her entire conception of religion and life: Through healing you introduced a vast new audience to Christianity.

How would they feed all these people? Jessie asked. New departments would have to be set up. The Heart of Africa Mission would take second place to the Heart of Africa Hospital.

Helen sat and listened. No missionary in all Africa possessed more kindness and love for her fellow man and woman than Jessie Scholes. Helen did not doubt for one second her motives or her sincerity. Therefore, if Jessie could make this strong appeal to her, perhaps she should examine her own motives.

She knew that if she went to Nebobongo she would be faced with an immense challenge. The place was an overgrown wilderness enclosing a tiny maternity center, an orphanage, and a leprosy camp—all that was left of a huge government scheme of ten years before. Helen would have to assume station leadership and all the responsibilities that such leadership entailed: care of drains, hygiene, rations, roofing repairs, orderlies' wages, a hundred and one calls on her time and attention. And she knew she really wanted to train nurses, to set up a successful hospital and medical school sheltered under the umbrella of Jack's experienced leadership.

The door opened and a senior missionary from the north smiled at her. "Hello, Helen," he said. "Sorry to have kept you waiting. Please do come in."

She felt Jessie's X-ray eyes on her back as she walked through the door. She listened politely to the committee's point of view. They were certain she would have great scope at Nebobongo; it was a big problem, but under her leadership they were confident that it would be successful. They realized she might be disappointed after having made such a fine start at Ibambi; however, all things considered . . .

"Yes," she agreed meekly, trying not to smile at the

dumbfounded expression on Jack's face. "Yes, I'd like to give it a try. Thank you for the confidence you have in me."

A week later, with John Mangadima and her students and several other Africans and their families, she loaded all her possessions into a truck and headed for Nebobongo. Her apprenticeship served, she was on her own.

CHAPTER 7

On October 31, 1955, the day after her arrival at Nebobongo, Helen started work. With two African helpers, she
walked backwards and forwards across her new terrain,
measuring, plotting, sketching and discarding, her mind
absorbed in problems of drainage, sewage, and building.
The feeding, clothing, and other logistics had to wait until
after dark. But her days were very long for the next few
years, starting at 5:30 A.M. with hospital-ward rounds, and
finishing—after dealing with paperwork and administrative
details—at about 10:30 every night.

Her first task was to decide what could be rescued from
the jungle, what abandoned and what rebuilt. She drew up
her list of priorities: a new workmen's village in a healthy
spot to the west of the hospital site, adoption for many of
the orphans, and a practical, experienced teacher for those
who remained. She also listed a new hospital and all that its
construction entailed: clearing land, digging water holes,
starting new food gardens, providing toilets, building a kiln
to fire the thousands of new bricks . . . the tasks were
endless.

Still, she had to admit she had a few things in her favor:
a small brick maternity unit run with loving attention by
Florence Stebbing, an orphanage for thirty-eight happy
juniors, and a few houses in reasonably habitable condition.

But the water ditches were muddy, overgrown, full of
mosquitos and perfect breeding grounds for disease; the

leprosy colony had all but disappeared in encroaching jungle. What remained of the African Protestant community eyed the "new-broom Helen" with deep suspicion, and she realized that one of her first jobs must be to gain their respect and trust.

Medical work, of course, never stopped. The patients were merely transferred to the new site. Attending to their needs was not always easy; sometimes it was totally impossible. Certainly, God *had* to have come to her aid that night of the first Caesarian, and Stebby had been there to witness her panic. Dear Stebby! Clichés like "salt of the earth," "faithful unto death," "solid as a rock" jumped into Helen's mind whenever she thought about her. She was short and homely, but there was a durability, a sense of security, a matter-of-factness about her which reassured hundreds of patients before operations. When Stebby entered a ward, common sense and sanity prevailed. She was older than Helen, and, fortunately, she was a trained nurse and midwife.

Stebby had woken her with the urgent news, "Pregnant Pygmy mother just brought in. Far gone and probably dying. Think she needs a Caesarian—better hurry."

Helen uncurled. The light of the hurricane lamp which Stebby had set down at the side of the bed hurt her eyes. She fumbled for her glasses to peer up at her colleague. "Hurry up!" urged Stebby and was gone. Helen knew she could never live up to the inflated reputation which Stebby built up around her. Yes, she was a doctor and had been to Cambridge, but regardless, the idea of performing her first solo Caesarian filled her with terror. Oh yes, she'd read all the textbooks about Caesarians—she should be able to proceed from A to B and on to Z without difficulty. But the difference between theory and practice was enormous. In the calm, antiseptic security of a London hospital she'd listened to the lectures, but had never actually attended or assisted at a Caesarian birth. And this was not a well-equipped London hospital; this was wildest Congo in the middle of a dark night.

Helen sighed and slid her bare feet onto the concrete floor. As she slipped on her dress and walked along the corridor into their living room and out onto the small veranda, a cloud of insects were already dive-bombing the hurricane lamp. Outside the air was hot and humid, the moon large and white behind the trees, the cicadas as shrill and constant as a radio signal. The gravel was sharp and crunched under her feet, the lamp making swinging circles of light as she walked the seventy yards to the brick shed with a corrugated iron roof which served as the maternity block. She quickly closed the door behind her and went into the labor ward. Mosquitos and night-flying insects battered at the wire-screened windows; the pressure lamp hissed loudly. Grotesque shadows fell across the whitewashed walls. And there on the table, mute, shocked, naked, and vulnerable, lay the small, nut-brown Pygmy woman, swollen with child.

Helen examined her carefully: temperature, pulse rate, heartbeat. She shook her head.

"We've got to try," said Stebby stiffly.

Helen nodded. She looked at Stebby without speaking. Both knew that the little Pygmy woman hovered at the edge of death.

Stebby said, "We might save the child with a Caesarian."

Helen agreed. Then she added, "I've never done a Caesarian before."

It was Stebby's turn to nod. "Now's your chance, then."

Stebby was already wearing her mask and gown. Helen went into the outer room to scrub up and change.

A few minutes later she began to operate. Half an hour later, hopelessly confused in a sea of blood and amniotic fluid, she delivered a malformed dead baby. She looked at what might have been a human being, certain now that she should never have tackled the operation. Regardless of the fact that she had had no alternative, the sense of failure was bitter. Drenched in sweat that formed a pool about her bare feet, she stared in anguish at Stebby.

"It's hopeless. I'm lost. She's going to die. I've no idea what to do."

Stebby's voice was commanding. "Don't be silly! You've got to do something. We can't let her die on the table."

"It's no good. I can't find any landmarks. I can't even find the uterus."

"Listen, I'll put my hand up from below. Feel for my fingers and sew around them."

"But I . . ."

Stebby's eyes above the white bandage of her mask caught and held Helen's. Her voice was clear and imperative. "You work. I'll pray," she said loudly.

The precise instruction spurred Helen on. Afterwards she admitted that in the history of unorthodox surgical procedures, unsterile conditions, and peculiar techniques, the next hour broke all records. With no suction apparatus, no proper retractors, with nothing but faith and determination, they continued. Helen sewed the ruptured womb back onto the cervical stump. The little Pygmy woman survived the surgery. Ten days later, however, she died from a puerperal infection. A few years afterwards, with the introduction of multiple antibiotics, they would have saved her. But not even a veteran Helen—with the hundreds of the Caesarian operations she would eventually perform behind her—could have altered that final outcome.

She was saddened and wiser from her experience. She understood more fully one of the fundamental truths of her profession: Often those you attend and hope to cure will die, and their death diminishes you. No matter how expert Helen became, the death of one of her patients would always cause her sadness and self-reproach.

It took her a year to get things going at Nebobongo and every day provided a new experience from which to profit. Her ideas about an airy dispensary with a roof supported by brick pillars, cool, simple, and utilitarian, had to be revised somewhat when the first hurricane blew the roof in the direction of the Indian Ocean. There were smaller, personal irritations: letters from other missionaries saying they had need of her services also—after all, she was not in Congo only to look after Nebobongo's affairs, was she? They were under the impression that her function was to act as the *mission* doctor.

Blithely, she had already decided she could exist almost without food, sleep, or holidays—a belief she retained for most of her years in Congo. Food had never interested her; during her twelve years at Nebo, she managed without any difficulty on native food, including plantains, casava, bananas, and coffee. She never saw fresh meat; she used a tin of corned beef once a fortnight, and a tin of Kraft cheese had to last for three days. She would eat if she felt hungry, but more often than not, she was too busy to remember she was hungry. The result, and she admitted this herself, was that occasionally she grew impatient and irritable. On one occasion her behavior earned her an admonishment from John Mangadima, whose candor grew rather than diminished through the years.

She had finished her weekly eye clinic and was ready for ward rounds when an orderly came in to tell her that an old lady was waiting on the veranda, wanting her eyes tested. Helen was exasperated. The eye clinic was finished.

She would have to come back next week. An hour afterwards John Mangadima burst in upon her accusingly.

"You would not see that lady."

Helen was defensive. "She can come back next week."

"Didn't you know she was blind? Even to get here at all was a tremendous trial for her?"

"No, I didn't know!" Helen answered, but she realized immediately that this was no excuse. Because of her irritation and impatience, she had rejected someone badly in need of her services, and John was right to admonish her.

"She waited at the roadside all morning, asking if someone would please take her to the Christian lady who heals people." He went on, "She waited there for many hours; she couldn't find the way by herself. She is a soul for whom Christ died, and you have harshly turned her away. Would He have done so?"

Helen stared at him, her eyes full of contrition, not knowing how to reply. That the boy born in the rain forest of leprous parents should lecture the Cambridge graduate on her duties to mankind was unusual, perhaps, but it was also significant that she could accept his admonishment and profit from it. Never again did Helen fail to see someone who needed her help, no matter what the hour or how tired or distressed she might be. The memory of John's rebuke remained with her always.

Twelve months after her arrival, Nebobongo was flourishing. In the maternity department they delivered some forty babies a month; twelve pupil midwives were in training, three qualified girls were in charge, with Helen and Stebby keeping a careful shop-steward's eye on the scene. There were two hospital wards and often fifty patients filling them. On an average, one hundred and fifty people, from miles around came in each morning for outpatient treatment.

Helen also trained twenty male student nurses in a two-year course; there were thirty children in the primary school; there were acres of land growing peanuts, rice, manioc, plantains, pawpaws, and pineapples. All this meant that administrative work was a never-ending headache: government forms in duplicate and triplicate, accounts, inquiries, correspondence—all needing attention.

She knew there was criticism about some of the activities she undertook. Many of her colleagues reiterated that missionary activity should begin and end with the Gospel. It was true that WEC did not wish to put any of its funds into either educational or medical projects. Helen ran all her medical activities from the funds she received from her friends in Britain.

Her outlook was simple: The need was there, therefore she would fulfill it. Had she left it to the government to provide medical and educational facilities in the enormous province of the northeast, then thousands of children would have grown up without schooling of any sort, and thousands would have died because of a lack of medical attention. "Help them so that they will be able to help themselves" was her credo, and it still is.

She was obsessed with Nebobongo. As leader of a huge "family" of workmen, teachers, students, and nurses, she was confident that they had made something out of nothing, and she believed that the pride she felt was not sinful pride, but the pride of achievement. Surely God would see no harm in that?

She accepted the criticism that she was dictatorial, but maintained that there was no alternative. Her attitude was simply "I would be very pleased to have more trained medical help."

This became a distinct possibility during the missionary conference at Ibambi in 1957. John Harris, a young British surgeon working in the north with his wife, wanted to move, and was selected to join Helen at Nebo as her superior. Helen, in true Christian spirit, told the conference, "Certainly. Dr. Harris is a better surgeon than I am. I can learn an enormous amount from him. Of course he must take over leadership of Nebobongo; he's a man and naturally must be in charge. We shall be able to expand and I shall really be able to get moving on my pet scheme to set up a whole series of out-station clinics."

She smiled happily, said all the right things, and at the time thought she meant all the nice things she said. She certainly had no conscious awareness that somewhere deep down a short fuse leading to an explosive charge of deep anger and frustration had just been lit.

Four months later, Dr. Harris and his wife arrived at Nebo, and Helen welcomed them cordially, insisting they live with her and share her home. From the first, they clashed over keeping the books. Helen knew that meticulous bookkeeping was not one of her strongest points; she was aware that her method of fourteen account books carefully cross-indexed to match fourteen carefully labeled porridge-oat tins was unusual, but *she* always knew where she was. Dr. Harris did not seem to like her system at all.

She gave in to him happily here, pleased that he wanted to get on with that mundane side of the work, since she had more important projects. She had worked out a plan whereby she would spend one week at Nebo training her students and doing her routine jobs, and, with the blessing of the WEC committee, she would use every other week for the establishment of forty-eight village clinics spread in a wide figure-eight around Nebobongo. She wanted each clinic staffed by a trained male nurse—what else was the point of all the training she was doing? A supply of drugs would be necessary, enough to treat the diseases endemic to that area. Each clinic was to consist of a single-roomed house with a big veranda (the village headman to be cajoled into providing this), and in the room there would be a bed, a table and chair, utensils, and a cupboard. One unpaid church worker—the village evangelist—would look after the clinic if no male nurse was available. Basic drugs: quinine solution for malaria, Epsom salts for constipation, a kaolin mixture for diarrhea, eye drops, boracic powder for ulcers, a more powerful mixture for deep tropical ulcers, potassium permanganate crystals for snakebite, aspirins, cough mixture, antiseptic solution for disinfecting wounds, and a special H. Roseveare formula for treating both hookworm and roundworm. Helen herself, on her rounds, would be able to identify the beginnings of tuberculosis, leprosy, malnutrition, and other diseases, and remove those affected to the Nebo hospital before they became too ill.

So began what were really the most exciting and thrilling years of all she spent in Congo. She visited each of her forty-eight clinics once a month: twenty-four in the first week, and twenty-four the following trip. Twenty-four villages a week meant six a day, so she started at five thirty in the morning and finished in the dark at the last village, where she spent the night.

She made the journeys in her old International three-quarter-ton pickup truck, kept running only by faith, hope, and continuous attention. In the back she carried a set of surgical instruments for minor emergency operations, a microscope and a pharmacy balance, stock medicines of four to eight times their required strength (to be diluted into the mixtures), creams and powders necessary to restock each clinic when she called.

Beneath a large sun helmet, wearing a large printed cotton dress which ballooned around her slender figure, openwork leather sandals over bare feet, spectacles set on her nose, Dr. Helen Roseveare of Nebobongo always looked more like a slightly nervous butterfly collector than the heir to Dr. Schweitzer of Lambarene.

Invariably she and her assistants were greeted by a reception committee at each village. The talking drum would sound, the crowd would gather, and work would begin. Worm medicine had to be administered to primary-school children whether they had worms or not, expectant mothers had to be examined, those who needed surgery had to be told which day to arrive at the hospital in Nebobongo. Endless queues formed: the eye treatment queue, the T.B. queue, the leprosy queue.

And, of course, the handshake queue. People would come in from every hut for miles around, and very often even shy Pygmies would emerge from their tiny, cone-shaped leaf shelters deep in the forest to produce a sick baby or exhibit an arrow wound. She shook hands with everyone. There were rarely fewer than five hundred and more often a thousand people to greet her. This was a ritual in rain-forest Congo. Perhaps only a hundred needed medical attention, but everyone needed to shake the hand of this strange female who seemed to be able to do more for a sick baby than all the witch doctors in the province. Helen felt that those wearisome, sleepless months were the most rewarding ones she ever experienced in her life; she was doing her job!

The condition of the roads from one village to the next was beyond belief: The roads were merely tracks of beaten earth of varying density which wandered through jungle. When it was very thick, she could drive for fifty miles or so without a sign of human habitation. The giant trees branching across the roads dripped water constantly, before storms, during storms, and after storms. All the bridges across the endless streams consisted of two planks in line laid over tree trunks, which hopefully were centralized under the wheels. Often it depended entirely on the choice of the local bridge-builder—who might favor a wide wheel base rather than a narrow one—as to whether you drove across or drove in.

Everywhere she went, the Africans wanted to give her and her medical team a meal, and the team was always anxious to have a meal. It was discourteous to refuse, they said. "Discourteous, nonsense!" Helen retorted. "We're not eating five meals a day, we're eating *one!* And that will be after the last patient has been treated. Our job is medical aid," she insisted. "We're fulfilling a need which has never been met before. If we can't do it here, we'll bring them back with us." When she found a seriously ill person who needed immediate treatment, she would send a runner to Nebo and arrange for transport to take the patient back to the hospital.

The wet season was worst of all: lakes of mud, rain pouring down day after day, roads virtually impassable. Keeping the truck running was a daily chore, and she lost count of the hours she spent lying underneath it or probing beneath the bonnet. Broken springs, filthy plugs, dirty carburetor, exhaust pipe dropping off, punctures—these were the commonplaces of her motoring life. She paid for the entire operation—forty-eight clinics, drugs, petrol—out of her donations. Sometimes she would receive as much as thirty pounds a month, although even in the best year the total never came to more than two hundred pounds. But she managed on that sum.

Certainly she had her share of arguments, and would admit that practically all were caused by her own impatience and weariness. She wanted to get things done five times quicker than anyone else; she was always glancing at her watch, while they did not even know what a watch was. But whether she got to her clinics on time or not, she always got there.

She never forgot the embarrassing scene at the village of
Deti, which stood on the top of a steep, muddy hill. She
reached it towards the end of a long day at the end of a
long week, and the road up to the village seemed to be
covered with liquid glue. She tried to climb it again and
again, she churned from one side to the other, she tried
every gear, but the wheels simply would not grip in the
mud. Eventually, frustrated and weary, she slid down to a
lower level and sent a passerby up to the village to tell
them that she would hold the clinic at some accessible spot
near the bottom of the hill.

Within minutes the village evangelist, Peter, had
descended, followed by a crowd of villagers. Helen got
out. She was cold, wet, tired, and irritated. Peter only made
things worse.

"But what's the matter? Why don't you drive up to the
village?"

Helen said bitterly, "Can't you understand that for the
last half hour I've been trying to do just that?"

"But they're all waiting for you. Why can't you get to the
top?"

Helen controlled her desire to scream. "Because the road's
too slippery and you didn't send anyone down to give me a
push."

"Well, we didn't know."

"You should have known. It's pouring with rain. Haven't
you any sense at all? You knew when to expect me."

"Doctor, we simply didn't know you'd arrived yet. Everyone is willing to help."

Irritation and frustration overwhelmed her. "Well, it's too
late now. They can come down here. I'm not going to try
again."

The argument continued, loudly and forcefully. Helen
regretted it afterwards, for the spectacle of the local evangelist and the lady missionary standing in the rain harangu-

ing each other was disillusioning to the village people. Only the arrival of Pastor Akawa from the village ended the quarrel.

"Dr. Helen," he called loudly, "shut up!" It was the first time Helen had been told to shut up during her stay in Congo. But the pastor was an older man and a capable minister. To her surprise, she shut up instantly.

"Now you go straight to the top of the hill on your own feet," he said sternly. "We will meet you there."

Helen was defeated. "All right."

She turned on her heel and started off up the hill. She knew she was wrong to quarrel with Peter; it was not his fault, it was hers, and she felt solitary and alone trudging up that muddy slope. Suddenly she became conscious that someone was walking alongside her, and she realized it was one of her friends from the village. An arm was slipped around her waist in support, and then she sensed rather than saw that a dozen village women had formed themselves into an escort group to take her up the hill. *They* understood how she felt; their hands and arms and sympathetic murmurs told her that. Let those unfriendly men push that ancient truck up the hill—that was all they were good for. Hot coffee awaited her in one of the huts, and she could sit by the fire to dry herself.

When the pastor and Peter arrived, they found Helen recovered, shaking hands with the six hundred or so people who had gathered to see her. After watching them direct the villagers to push and maneuver the truck into the square, Helen shook hands with them too, said she was sorry, and started work.

At least that quarrel lasted only half an hour. The one with Dr. Harris lasted a week. Daniel, her chauffeur, had been told by Dr. Harris to collect a patient and bring him to Nebo. If the patient's house was near Adzangwe—where

Daniel lived—he told him, then he could visit his parents, but if it wasn't near, then he could not. Daniel collected the patient, visited his parents, and returned. Dr. Harris examined the kilometer gauge and declared it wasn't *near* at all; it was miles away. Daniel had had no right to go and was undoubtedly untrustworthy. He was therefore dismissed.

When she heard this news, Helen was furious. "No!" she blazed. "He's *my* chauffeur, and I haven't dismissed him!"

"What he did was dishonest," Dr. Harris replied mildly.

"No, it wasn't," Helen insisted, knowing she would get the worst of the argument because, as usual, she was growing furious and, as always, Dr. Harris was keeping his temper. "It's such a piffling little thing. Daniel used the word *karibu*. All right, it means 'near.' But how near is near? You can say the earth's near the moon, can't you?"

This row was the explosion point reached after weeks of simmering conflict between two people of utterly incompatible personalities. Helen, at heart, was a pioneer; she liked to start from scratch and build up. Dr. Harris was thoughtful where Helen was impulsive; he was slow, whereas Helen acted immediately; his attitude towards the Africans was completely different from hers. His deepest interest was leprosy, and Helen disagreed with him about the urgency of treating that disease as compared to others. She knew that back in England if you stood on a platform and talked about the needs of leprosy patients, the contributions would roll in. But if you drew attention to syphilis, tuberculosis, yaws, hookworm, malaria, and the other unpleasant but less dramatic diseases from which a far greater proportion of the Congolese population suffered, then the money barely trickled in.

So Dr. Harris and Helen constantly rubbed each other the wrong way. For a week after their quarrel, no word passed between them, and Helen bottled up her fury. She thought he misjudged the Africans, was unkind to them, and didn't trust them. She'd always lived on a system of trust; nothing in her house was ever locked. *He'd* put padlocks on everything; *he* hadn't even got used to the place before he'd changed everything! And this stupid business about the chauffeur . . . it was the last straw.

When Mr. Coleman, a missionary from the south, arrived at Nebo for medical treatment, he immediately greeted Helen in his friendly Christian manner, "How are you, and how's Dr. Harris?"

"I don't know," snapped Helen in an utterly exasperated, un-Christian manner, only just preventing herself from adding, "And I don't care!"

Mr. Coleman realized quite easily that the relationship between the two doctors was at freezing point. Each ignored the other's existence.

"Now, you can't go on like this," protested Mr. Coleman. "It just doesn't make sense. I'm driving you both to Ibambi and you're going to have this out with Jack Scholes." He marched them out to his car and they drove in silence to Scholes's office. Jack nodded wisely while Helen made it plain what an awful person she thought Dr. Harris was, and Dr. Harris said how much he admired Helen and how thoroughly capable she was. At the end of an hour Jack said, "This is perfectly ridiculous. You're both out here for missionary purposes and all you're doing is destroying the essence of our cause. What you're trying to preach doesn't make sense any longer. If you can't make peace with each other, how can you instill peace in anybody else's heart? Now we shall all pray about this matter."

Jack Scholes, Jessie Scholes, Mr. Coleman, and Dr. Harris all prayed. Helen did not. She knew she could not say to God all the things she'd been thinking: that Dr. Harris was a beastly man, and that, even though she accepted the fact that he was a good doctor and a fine surgeon, she disliked him intensely.

Basically, however, she knew the reason for her hostility. She knew she hated Dr. Harris's takeover. She accepted the fact that she had brought it on herself, but that only made it worse. In her terms, he'd just taken over Nebobongo—*her* place, which she'd built up out of nothing, out of her dreams, out of her heart, out of the money she'd raised. This was the place where she'd dug the water holes, cleared the ditches, fired the bricks. She had acknowledged the facts that you could not have two people in charge, that he was a man, and that in Africa a man was the superior being, so she had handed over the keys. Then she found she couldn't take it. Perhaps she had been her own boss too long. But now she had lost everything. She had always taken morning prayers; he took them now. She had always taken Bible class; Dr. Harris took it now. Dr. Harris organized the nurses, and Helen had always done that. Everything that had been hers was now his. Of course she knew she was being uncharacteristically selfish, but she could do nothing about it.

Jack Scholes, however, knew Helen rather well by this time. He had learned from years of experience among Africans that you had to take your time. You let things quiet down; you were patient. He took his time now, and Helen simmered down. Eventually she prayed. Eventually she shook hands; eventually she climbed into the car and they all drove back to Nebobongo. On the surface things were all right again.

Helen realized, of course, that she was not doing her own cause any good with this sort of behavior. She knew that while the African members of the Church wholeheartedly applauded her idea of clinics, many of the white members felt that she was wasting her time. She was not going so much against their wishes as against their expectations. They felt the work was so hard and exhausting that she would probably work herself to death—which, quite possibly, she might have done. They did not understand or appreciate why she risked her own personal safety while performing her job. Indeed, some of her journeys around Congo during those years were so adventurous that only a person as committed as Helen would have undertaken them.

One midnight, on the road near Boyulu, she was scared literally speechless. She had turned off the main road onto a narrow, winding forest track, heading for the isolated mission station at Opienge. Enormous trees, dripping and dark, lined the endless miles of switchback road, which was crossed by at least forty plank bridges. Baboons and monkeys swung between the trees. She was in wild, uninhabited, animal country.

Susan, one of her assistants, sat in the cab with her. Matthew, a student nurse, two Africans, their wives, and their families slept peacefully under the canvas in the back. Great black bolsters of clouds loomed over the mountains as darkness closed in. When Helen switched on the lights, nothing happened. She stopped the truck, and after fiddling under the dashboard and bonnet for twenty minutes, she still could not raise the slightest gleam. A storm was imminent, and moonrise was not due for hours; therefore, even though the chances of another vehicle approaching were minimal, the safest thing to do was to stay put. They obviously needed some form of signal indicating that their truck was blocking the so-called road, since Congolese lorry drivers invariably blundered along with no more than a cursory

glance through the windscreens. They might run straight
into the truck if they were not forewarned.

There were two hurricane lanterns in the cabin. Helen lit
them both and placed the first about fifty yards away in
front of the truck. She had just returned for the second
when Susan's shrill, horrified squeal of "Danger!" made
her shoot through the door and slam it behind her. The
whole window area was suddenly blacked out by an enormous presence of fur or skin which moved. She was petri-
fied. Silent and stiff, Helen watched a great, hairy black
arm rise in the air and a huge hand plop gently down on
the cabin roof. Finally, a giant, beetle-browed, yellow-eyed
face stooped to stare in through the window at her. She
could neither move, breathe, nor think. For perhaps ten
seconds her face behind the glass window was no more than
twelve inches away from the monster's. Her mind was frozen. She suspected her hair was standing on end.

The thing then slowly shambled around the front of the
car. It walked on all fours, but the front arms seemed like
mighty pillars fastened to giant shoulders which supported
an enormous dangling head. When it reached Susan's side
of the car, it stood up to a height of what appeared to be
about eight feet. Later Helen realized it must have been a
gorilla that so frightened them and that probably he had
simply been full of amiable curiosity. After all, gorillas live
on green shoots of trees, far from inhabited villages, and he
had undoubtedly never encountered anything on all his
mountain peregrinations so ludicrous as these two humans,
one white, one black, enclosed in a sort of see-through nut.
He examined them with avuncular curiosity, decided they
were worth only his passing attention, and shambled off
into the darker shadows.

Helen could remember only that they sat there in petri-
fied silence. A few spots of rain pattered on the roof before

the deluge began, the loud drumming on the cabin roof blotting out the few words they exchanged. It was cold and the roof leaked. They became wetter and wetter. Naturally, Helen did not place the rear hurricane lamp in position; the entire lorry force of southwest Africa could smash into their truck for all Helen cared—she was not getting out to risk meeting that animal again.

The hours passed slowly. They dozed; they were wet and miserable. At about 2 A.M. a bright round moon rose over the trees, and Helen saw that they were perched on the top of a slight rise. The rain had run into other tire tracks leading ahead which formed two silvery guidelines marking the road they had to follow.

"No point in staying here any longer," she said to Susan. "If we go slowly, I can see the trail. Anything's better than waiting here."

The engine started fairly easily, surprisingly enough, and they moved off. Although she was tired and cramped, it was not really very hard to follow the tire marks. They crossed three swollen streams on plank bridges stretched over tree trunks, crawled down a rather steep hill, swung around a bend, and this time a wider, deeper stream faced them. The tire tracks ran to the edge of the river precisely in line with the planks. But the river had swollen so that it just covered them; the water swirled across like a smooth silken platform. This was not atypical in the forest; you simply crawled across the bridge with your tires half submerged. Helen ground down into bottom gear, pointed the bonnet in the right direction, and accelerated. There was one snag in her calculations—the bridge. It had been washed away. She drove slowly forward, straight into the river! The bonnet disappeared under the swirling water. Helen and Susan were flung against the windscreen; the sleeping passengers in the back slid forward; the children began to wail. For-

tunately, the truck stuck in its upended position, the cab
half full of water, the back perched on the bank. Swinging
open the door, Helen tried the river depth; hanging onto
the door handle, she touched bottom at six feet. She crawled
up the bank, muddy and soaked. Matthew and two African
families had now scrambled out of the back, and they joined
her.

"The battery," she pleaded. "We must get the battery
out. All our acid will drain away."

She was not quite certain of her facts, but it sounded
practical, since without a battery the truck couldn't move.

It was now about three o'clock in the morning. The
moon was passing in and out between great masses of dark
clouds. Some of the time they could see, and then suddenly
there was blackness. Helen found the tool kit and took out
a wrench, and she and the three men dropped into the water
and pulled themselves out against the force of the river.
Helen took a deep breath, ducked under, and fumbled for
the bonnet catch. At the third attempt she managed to prize
it open. The engine was completely under water, but she
managed to unscrew the two battery leads. The four of
them heaved the heavy case onto the bank.

"That's enough," Helen gasped. "Nothing more we can do
until dawn comes. Let's light the primus and see if we can
brew some coffee. You women must go and collect wood so
that we can start several fires to scare off any animals."
Already in the cold night air the smell of elephant was
acrid, and the sound of elephant quite close.

They brewed Nescafé and sipped it gratefully, cupping
their hands around the hot enamel mugs and crouching
near the fire. Helen knew that the mission station at Opienge
lay some twenty-five miles ahead. It was better, therefore,
if they could try and find the missing planks and get the
truck across the river rather than attempt a return jour-

ney. As soon as the first grayness appeared in the sky, she announced her plan.

"First," she told the two Africans, "we'll see if there's anybody around to help us. One of you can swim across the river and go forward for a couple of miles, the other can walk back a bit. It's possible we could have passed a hamlet in the darkness. Meanwhile, the rest of us will try and find the planks to rebuild the bridge."

The rain had stopped, and in the two hours which had elapsed since their plunge into the water the level of the river had dropped considerably. They struggled downstream to find the planks, submerged up to their waists and sometimes their necks. Sometimes they had to swim. All Congo's rivers are infested with crocodiles, but they were too busy working to reflect on this.

They had collected about half a dozen planks from the reeds at the river's edge when one of the Africans appeared from the road behind them. He brought good news: A gang of half a dozen road workers whose job it was to keep bridges intact and the road open were nearby. The man had found their camp and had woken them. As they approached, Helen was delighted to see they carried axes, saws, and adzes. Using slender tree trunks from the forest, they levered up the front of the truck and dragged it back onto the road. The whole gang joined Helen's expedition, salvaging planks from downriver, but it quickly became clear that they were not going to recover enough; the torrent had undoubtedly taken many of them miles downstream. Helen pondered, and finally she said, "We'll replace the planks as far as the middle of the bridge and then push the truck out that distance. Then we'll take the planks from behind the truck and re-lay them in front of it across to the other side. At least if we get the truck over I can strip down the engine and see if we can get her started." The plan worked well and they got the truck across. The workers told Helen that there was a village not far away, and she sent off the women and children to buy food, borrow or buy a saucepan, and make them all a meal.

She and Matthew went to work on the truck, stripping down the carburetor, petrol pump, everything that looked as if it might be waterlogged. The battery, fortunately, seemed to have survived in reasonable condition. The only thing which worried her were two small steel balls which were part of the steering mechanism. They had disappeared in the river. Several dives into the muddy water failed to locate them, so Helen decided she would simply have to manufacture a replacement.

From a bed of stones on the river bank she selected two pebbles in the shape of the two missing steel balls. When the two African women had finished preparing the meal, she sat them down with orders to grind out the stones until they were roughly hollow in the center. Grinding one stone against the other, as if they were preparing cornmeal, they started work. Work on the truck continued until dark; then fires were lit again, and they all slept in the truck.

Early next morning Helen discovered that one pin was missing. She contrived to twist a hairpin into the right shape, and after she'd fiddled with the choke, the engine fired and they were ready to start. They had spent two nights on the road, but this was not unusual in those pioneering days of Congo motoring. They arrived at Opienge that day, where Winnie Davies, the mission nurse, welcomed them warmly.

Helen spent three days at Opienge, seeing all Winnie's patients, admiring the maternity wards, and accompanying her friend on several trips to outlying villages to visit the sick. The two missionaries there serviced her car and tried to remedy some of her improvisations, but they could do nothing about her stone ball-bearing on the traction rod. They hoped she would make it back to Nebo without further incident. But Helen's adventures were not yet over.

The following day, the journey to Bomili was appalling. Ninety kilometers of rough, switchback forest road separated her from the mission station. The first sixty kilometers were through deep mud, and she crossed two wide rivers conscious that if her muddy tires slipped on the wet planks there was nothing to prevent the truck from plunging into the river. On the other side, the exhaust fell off. She picked it up, tied it to the roof, and continued, although the truck sounded rather like a Sherman tank.

She reached a rudimentary ferry made of huge logs bound together on top of dugout canoes and drove the lorry aboard. The boatmen cast off and they were swept down current until the oarsman managed to pole them to the other bank. Twenty-five miles farther on, as they began to climb into the mountains, the steering gear held together by ground-down stones and Helen's hairpin disintegrated. The wheel spun uselessly in her hands. The truck lurched across the road and dropped down three feet into a mountain stream.

"There is," said Helen, trying to be cheerful, "a white man's house about eight miles from here on top of the mountain. I don't know him, but I think he's Belgian and he runs the gold mine here. I'm sure he'll help us."

She, Susan, and Matthew climbed from the car and waded out of the stream. Before setting off, Helen tied the laces of her sandals together and draped them around her neck. Shoes were precious; it was difficult to obtain replacements, and she decided she would sooner wear out her feet than her shoes. It was now almost dark. At the beginning the climb was quite easy, in spite of the fact that the rain kept pelting down. They had experienced so much trouble on this journey, however, that nothing could exceed what they had already endured.

They were now in real elephant country. They knew that wild elephants are apt to charge immediately at any moving target. The muddy road was almost obliterated by pad marks, and they could hear a herd moving through the forest not far away. But, strangely enough, although there were tracks everywhere and they could constantly hear the huge beasts moving in the forest, they did not glimpse a single elephant.

It took them three hours to reach the top of the mountain. At ten o'clock they stood outside the white man's house, to find it locked and deserted.

"Well," Helen said with her last weary attempt at cheerfulness, "the church and our evangelist are only another half mile on. He won't be able to pull us out of the ditch, but he may know someone who can help."

Her feet were hurting, so she decided to put on her shoes, only to find that her feet were so swollen and painful that she could not get the shoes on. By the time they arrived at the evangelist's house, she could scarcely hobble. The evangelist and his wife made them welcome. They built up the fire, for it was cold on top of the mountain, and produced a bowl of salted hot water in which Helen could soak her feet. The brine stung but her feet felt better for it. The evangelist's wife did her best to be helpful; she carefully cleaned and bandaged Helen's feet; then Helen watched in silent horror as she cut off the tops of her shoes. It was only because of her vain determination to save the shoes in the first place that her feet were now in this condition. However, the remedy was successful: Feet plus bandages fitted in comparative comfort. Ironically, the Belgian had left his house that morning and gone off to his other residence, which was only about two miles from the place where their truck had plunged into the stream.

"Fate," Helen observed philosophically. "So the sooner we get back to ask his help, the sooner we get the truck out of the stream."

The evangelist was worried. "But please wait for the morning light," he urged. "The sun will be up very soon."

Helen shook her head. "No, if he's at the other house we'd better catch him before he leaves for somewhere else."

The evangelist volunteered to show them the way. After a meal, a rest, and several cups of hot coffee, Helen felt ready to start. Nevertheless, by the time they reached the foot of the mountain, both she and Susan felt worn out: they had walked roughly sixteen miles that night.

The evangelist led them through the sprawl of the gold-mining compound to the Belgian's house and left them to go ahead of him at about 2 A.M. He told them he would catch up. When they reached the veranda Helen sat on the steps, too tired to go any farther. She was quite prepared to curl up and sleep. The idea of waking a stranger and giving all the necessary explanations was too much to contemplate. She told Matthew and Susan to wake the houseboy and ask him to find them some place to sleep.

Matthew and Susan did as she suggested, and five minutes later the Belgian's houseboy opened the front door. "The master will see you," he announced, and the lights came on.

A large man in a dressing gown came to the door and regarded Helen in unfriendly fashion. "Who is it?" he demanded.

"I'm sorry to bother you," said Helen. "I'm a missionary from Bomili. My car's broken down; the steering has gone, and it's run off the road into a stream about two miles from here."

"A missionary from Bomili?" repeated the man with the same sort of intonation he would have used for "an escaped convict?" He then added, "I must tell you I have been suffering with malaria. I have been very sick."

"I'm very sorry to wake you," said Helen. "Please go back to bed. I shall be quite all right here."

She found the man's attitude very strange. In Congo there is a camaraderie among whites; help is given freely and quickly, even more quickly when a white woman is concerned. Yet this man seemed quite indifferent to the idea of her spending the night on his veranda.

The evangelist who had escorted them had been lagging behind, but as he came up to the veranda, the Belgian brightened immediately. "Hello. What are you doing here at this hour of the night?" he asked.

The evangelist sounded surprised. "I'm with my missionary."

"*Your* missionary?"

"Yes, the lady sitting there. She's our doctor. She's from Nebobongo."

The Belgian turned to stare at Helen. "You said you were from Bomili," he stated accusingly.

"I left there today. I'm doing a tour of missions and clinics."

"My dear young lady," said the Belgian, quite overcome, "please come inside. I'll get my headman out with the truck and chains at once."

Helen could not understand why his attitude had changed so suddenly. They drove down the track with a crowd of workmen recently roused from their beds. With the Belgian's heavy equipment, it was a fairly simple matter to haul her vehicle out of the stream. The headman towed her back through the mud to the Belgian's residence.

When she walked into the bungalow, she saw that he had left instructions for her to be given the royal treatment.

Hot soup, milk, sandwiches, clean linen on her bed . . . oh, and such a lovely bed! She fell into it. Next morning she woke at nine, to find an enormous breakfast waiting and the Belgian kindly and avuncular, begging her to stay for at least another day and night. He felt she must be exhausted and in need of a rest.

Helen thanked him and said she must press on, for she was due back at Nebobongo. He then smiled and apologized again for thinking she was from Bomili, and she discovered why he had been so boorish the night before. His gold mine employed local labor, which divided spiritually into three different Christian groups. The community guided by Helen's evangelist was apparently his favorite: They never demanded time off for prayer meetings or Bible classes; they were conscientious, hard-working, and impeccably honest. None of them objected to working overtime, as did the workers whose evangelist's headquarters was in Bomili; if the Belgian needed a difficult job done, it was always the workers from Helen's evangelist's flock to whom he turned. When Helen had told him that she was a missionary from Bomili, he had reacted accordingly; his theory was that she must be in some way responsible for the attitude of those workers.

Three days later Helen arrived back at Nebo, having discovered en route that she had acquired a terrible nervousness about crossing plank bridges. She insisted on having her passengers walk over while she navigated the crossing alone in the lorry.

At Nebo, Dr. Harris met her outside the house. "Oh, back again," he said cheerfully.

"Yes," said Helen.

"Jolly good. Did you have a good trip?" he inquired politely.

"Not bad. Everything all right here?"

"Quite all right, thank you."

With such banality do the English, on certain occasions, describe incredible adventures, great misfortunes, and the fall of empires.

All of Helen's exploits, however, were not totally successful. She had grave doubts about herself, if the truth be known. At the end of her first five years in Congo, Helen had reached the conclusion that she was a complete failure: She had succeeded as neither a doctor, a missionary, nor a woman; she had antagonized many of her contemporaries; and she had messed up her social and professional relationship with Dr. Harris.

In an agony of indecision, she wrote constantly to Norman Grubb, a senior missionary at WEC headquarters in Fort Washington, Pennsylvania, U.S.A., recounting her spiritual doubts and agonies. She had always enjoyed a warm father-daughter relationship with him; he tried to reassure and guide her. In reply to one of her more difficult bouts of soul-searching when she felt certain she was of little use either to God or missionary endeavor, he wrote her, "I have a deep conviction that you are a precious instrument of the Lord." Helen replied sadly, "Oh, how far from the truth this is. If you only knew all the meanness and littleness and pettiness of my heart you'd be shocked. The pride—it makes me sick to look at myself—the rotten pride in achievement. No wonder He had to take the leadership away and give it to Dr. Harris . . ."

From the first moment of her arrival in Africa, she had been troubled by these doubts. From the very beginning, despite the adventure, the triumphs, the achievements, there was this emptiness, this lack of lasting spiritual peace. She worked almost around the clock, ignoring the divisions of daylight and darkness. But there was still no peace. Other missionaries, like Jessie and Jack Scholes, Stebby, Elaine, and Amy, seemed to have arrived at a haven and a fulfill- ment in their Christianity. Why wasn't she fulfilled in the same way?

Sometimes she wondered if a marriage, a husband and child, might perhaps be the answer to that sort of fulfill- ment. But she knew this was a hypothetical solution, so meanwhile all she could do was go on working with a fierce and dedicated concentration. In every letter she wrote to her mother and to her friends, she declared her loyalty to, belief in, and love of the Lord, but in her own heart she could not grasp what seemed to exist just beyond her reach.

Each evening she looked out at the beauty of the night, the bright dust-bowl of the moon, the silvery scrapings of the stars, through the eyes of a small and insignificant woman who believed desperately in God but could find no spiritual security. And because God, in her terms, must *be* that security, this, above all, disturbed her. She did not doubt God; she doubted herself. Somehow, she decided, her own communications system must be at fault; somewhere a switch was not turned on, or a fuse had blown. She looked for miracles, she discerned miracles; some people felt that *she* worked miracles herself, but it was still not enough, and she did not know what would ever fulfill her. She realized that her belief in God would have to suffice until death provided the final answer.

Early in 1958, after she had been in Congo five years, she considered whether she should leave Africa and WEC altogether. She had reached the conclusion that the whites were not needed any more as pastors, preachers, and good shepherds; the Africans could take care of that aspect of Christianity by themselves. She wrote: "To hear Pastor Ndugu preach does my heart good . . . they [The Afri- cans] have a spiritual grip and deep discernment that just humbled me to the dust. It's not what I can, or have done, for *them,* but what they are doing daily for *me!* There's a fierce, fighting spirit of independence inside me that just won't bow the knee to any old Tom, Dick or Harry—but with the Africans I discovered that it isn't there—rather the reverse, a deep, hungry dependence, a longing to lean on them, to confide in them, to receive their advice, to be received by them into their families in a oneness that knows no racial barrier—I almost hate my white skin at times, and this makes me separate when I long to be united."

Helen's disillusionment increased when she heard that some of her missionary colleagues had said about her, "She knows everything, therefore she is impossible to work with." She was also in very bad health. For all of these reasons, therefore, she did not object when her name was placed on the leave rota two years before it fell due. Most WEC missionaries went on leave after seven years; Helen was leaving after only five years in the field.

Before going to England, she completed one last task, which she had been meaning to finish for several years: the typing and stenciling of the pages of a medical textbook in Swahili for use in training male nurses. In the middle of 1958, feeling that it was unlikely she would ever return to Congo, she started the long journey home.

She arrived in London, outwardly smiling but inwardly perplexed about her future as a woman, a missionary, and a doctor. She spent a month in Cornwall with her mother, and then went into the Tropical Hospital to be treated for chronic amebic dysentery. Her health improved, and she set out traveling all over the British Isles on a series of deputation meetings.

Ostensibly one of the reasons she had been granted early furlough was the fact that her training was incomplete:

She needed more surgical training if she were to fulfil a useful medical role in Africa. In February she applied, and was accepted, for the position of houseman and Casualty Officer at the Mildmay Mission Hospital in Shoreditch, East London, and she enjoyed the job enormously. The work, the regular hours, and a salary check at the end of each month meant that for the first time in her life she could buy clothes for herself and gifts for her mother. And one other thing interested her: She worked closely with a good-looking senior houseman. Her duties constantly led her into his company, and he watched over her progress with a keen interest. She found that she was thinking about marriage seriously for the first time in her life.

Helen decided, with typical impulsiveness, that the young houseman was just the man for her. Mentally she began to prepare for the marriage, daydreamed about the welcome they would receive when they returned to Nebo, the house they would live in, and the work they would accomplish together. She was rather disheartened when she discovered that he had no desire at all to go to Congo on missionary service. He was a good Christian, but not as Christian as all that.

Helen decided she must alter her approach. She needed more time. Collecting a husband took longer than she had thought. She bought herself new clothes, had her hair permed, applied to WEC for a year's leave of absence, and set out to lay her loving traps. She even considered the possibility that perhaps her new career as a young bride might rule out missionary work altogether.

She had, however, made one major error: She had not taken the man's feelings into consideration. Slowly, to her dismay, she discovered he did not return her affection. Obviously he liked her, clearly he enjoyed her company, but he had no inkling of that web of romantic intrigue being woven around him. He was a handsome, healthy, and hearty young doctor who patted her cheerfully on the head and said, "Well, old girl, I suppose you'll be off to the Congo soon?"

When Helen told him she'd decided to ask for a year's extension of leave to get more medical and surgical experience, he replied casually, "Oh, jolly good show, old girl. Well, let's get back to work."

After some months Helen realized that he thought she was "a very nice girl," but that was all. She had to accept the truth that he had not given her the slightest encouragement and that the "love affair" had existed solely in her own heart.

Nevertheless, she was bitterly hurt. She was aware that not only had she humiliated herself, she had failed God. While she should have been thinking about a lifetime spent helping others, she had instead been concentrating selfishly on self-gratification and personal achievement. She saw clearly what a fool she had made of herself, and realized that she had to forget, survive, and start again.

She applied for and was accepted as House Surgeon at Newport Hospital, Monmouthshire. She arrived at Newport determined to work as she had never worked before and, fortunately, she discovered the medical routine at this hospital was so taxing that it encouraged the speedy healing of her broken heart.

She assisted in the obstetrical department, and although she had performed more than twenty Caesarians since that first traumatic night at Nebo, now she accomplished her first solo Caesarian in Britain. For three weeks she took over as Acting Registrar while the Medical Superintendent was away on leave and learned something of the difficulties of running a large hospital. Also, she had time to reflect upon her years in Congo, and to realize how acutely she missed Nebo and Ibambi. With the new knowledge and confidence she had acquired at Mildmay and Newport, surely she could now return without making the same mistakes, and find that peace of spirit and body she so urgently needed.

She wrote to Mission Headquarters. Would they please have her back? John and Elsie Harris at Nebo would be seriously in need of leave by this time. Would they allow her to take over at Nebo again? If so, could she leave at the latest by May of next year—1960?

Headquarters agreed to her request, and as a result of their decision Helen suddenly found herself humming as she walked along the corridors of Newport Hospital. She had won the most precious of opportunities, so rarely achieved —a second chance. This time she was determined she would not fail.

Dr. Helen Roseveare, newly-arrived at Ibambi Station, four maternity nurses and John Mangadima.

A crowd of Congolese villagers watch "our doctor" comforting an old man dying of cancer.

Helen Roseveare's long journeys to isolated villages involved many incidents like this: rescuing a car from a flooded road.

Simba "cubs." Large numbers of these children were trained for service with the rebels.

As doctor, surgeon, schoolmistress and missionary, Helen found time to play games with the children at the leprosy settlement of Nebobongo.

Simba recruits being trained during the northern rebellion against the central Congolese government.

Helen Roseveare revisiting the convent at Wamba where she was for weeks a captive of the Simbas.

In a remote village Helen instructs a group of women in hygiene and maternity welfare.

Helen helps bathe her houseboy Benjamin's two small sons.

White mercenaries serving Tshombe rescue terrified African nuns in 1964.

Tearful Belgian nuns rescued by Congo mercenaries in 1964.

Mercenaries rescuing an injured
child.

The moment of deliverance: Dr. Roseveare with Lieutenant Joe
Wepener of 54 Commando. Helen left immediately on a plane
with this Polaroid print. Wepener was killed shortly afterward.

Jack Scholes, Helen and Jessie Scholes at Ibambi with a young man who once saved Jessie's life.

Helen, Richard Dix, Dr. Carl Becker and Richard's wife, Dr. Ruth Dix, at Nyankunde. Helen and Carl planned this medical center, connected by a flying doctor service with remote jungle villages, and Richard designed it.

Helen and John Mangadima.

Helen with two of her pupils.

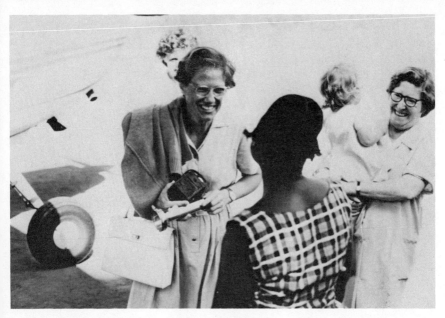

Helen welcomed on a visit to Nyankunde by Florence Stebbing,
nurse-midwife.

Nyankunde: Helen built her medical school here in the grasslands
above the rain forest to complement the hospital pioneered by
Dr. Becker and other American doctors.

Dr. Helen Roseveare and the author, Alan Burgess, in Africa.

PART THREE

# CHAPTER 8

In the middle of 1960 Helen set off for her second tour, knowing that getting back into Congo might itself prove to be the most difficult part of her journey. A cablegram from WEC reached her at sea suggesting that, with the approach of independence and the hurried departure of the Belgian colonial administration, it might be better to wait in Nairobi and see how events turned out.

Helen turned a deaf ear to this advice, but there was more trouble awaiting her and her traveling companions, Elaine de Rusett and Bill McChesney, at Mombasa. Traveling to Congo? Were they mad? They would not be allowed to disembark until they had deposited return fares with the immigration authorities. The officials felt it their duty to lecture the missionaries severely. Did they not know that all hell was about to break loose in equatorial Congo? Were they unaware that hundreds of white refugees were already pouring out of Congo into Kenya?

"Congo is my home," Helen replied mildly. "There is still two weeks to go before independence is declared, and I intend to be at my hospital in Nebobongo before that date." She remembered the history of this country during the past century, the trials it had undergone and the changes it had seen, and she was proud to consider herself a part of it again.

It could be asserted that the modern history of Congo began when Stanley made his historic east-to-west traverse of the central African continent in 1877. The man most intrigued by Stanley's determination to exploit this territory turned out to be King Leopold II of Belgium. Even in an era when princely domination of Europe still rested on the principle of divine right, it was something of a surprise that Leopold felt he could annex Congo as his own private domain. Britain, France, Germany, and Portugal gave his act a nod of acquiescence. Leopold administered the territory for the next twenty-one years, oblivious to the many critical voices alleging that the conditions of the African workers in the rubber plantations of upper Congo were identical with those of slavery. Forced labor, floggings, brutality, and mutilation were among the normal conditions of employment. In 1904, when Leopoldville was forced to appoint a commission of inquiry, it confirmed these "great abuses," and it became evident that the Belgian State itself would have to take over responsibility. It did so in 1908, "assuming its heavy task with a determination that as a colonial possession the Congo territory should be honestly governed, and in real agreement with the humanitarian principles which Leopold II has never ceased to profess."

In 1955, when it became evident that the Congolese wanted to govern themselves, a Belgian Professor M. van Blisen proposed that in thirty years' time Congo be granted independence. The proposition raised the temperature in Brussels to such a degree that the shout of horror which greeted this radical heresy could almost be heard in Leopoldville itself. While Britain and France were shedding their African colonies with resolute speed, understanding that either the Europeans went gracefully or they would be forced out with a revolutionary kick in the rump, the Belgian authorities seemed hardly aware that such a thing as Congolese nationalism existed.

It was Patrice Lumumba, a left-wing politician returning from a pan-African congress in 1958, who demanded immediate independence. He was ignored. In 1959, when the colonial government tried to ban a public meeting in Leopoldville, fifty people were killed in the ensuing riots, and African mobs surged through the European neighborhoods, firing, looting, and destroying property to the value of millions of dollars. The point was made. King Baudouin of Belgium reacted quickly, promising independence without delay.

But the new state of affairs would obviously make many situations difficult for Europeans entering Congo. To Helen's great relief, Frank Cripps was waiting at the border with the mission truck, and they crossed without difficulty. She was welcomed joyously at Nebo, and John and Elsie Harris, very tired after seven years of intensive effort, were pleased to hand over the station to her.

But the unsettling mood of approaching independence was everywhere. In that first week Helen was requested to attend a meeting of station elders and male nurses where she was told, "At the Red Cross Hospital at Pawa, Dr. Kadoner has already handed over his authority to the senior African medical worker and Dr. Kadoner has become the new executive director. Should not something of the same sort happen here?"

Helen sat quiet, a little tense, not quite knowing how the situation could be resolved. John Mangadima was in no doubt at all how it should be settled. He got slowly to his feet. "I am the senior African medical worker, but let me add at once that I am not a doctor. I don't mind being in charge of the nurses and the general administrative work, but we can't do without *our* doctor and I certainly can't be over her."

So that was that. On June 30, when Independence Day arrived, the headman of the nearest village and senior men from the district all arrived at her front door wearing native dress and carrying presents of fruit and little bouquets of flowers. The headman made a short speech. They would like it very much if the "strangers in their midst" would agree to join them and stay with them in this new independence. Helen was very moved. It seemed that independence was going to usher in a new spirit of cooperation among everybody.

A week later she sensed that the mood had altered as she watched cars trundling back and forth from Ibambi. Every African knew that something important was happening, but it was nearly dark before they came for Helen.

"Everyone's collecting at Ibambi. You've got to come too."

"But what's the matter?"

"There's trouble all over Congo. Just outside Leopoldville the missionaries have been knocked about. Several of the white ladies have suffered." This was the first time Helen had heard the word "suffered" used in this manner. "The feeling is that all white women should get out while there's still a chance."

"Oh!" Helen exclaimed. "Is that so?" And she thought but did not say, "If you think you're getting me out when I only got back in by the skin of my teeth, you're quite mistaken."

Twenty missionaries were crowded into the room at Ibambi when she arrived, and Helen sensed this was going to be one of those occasions fraught with anxiety, suspicion, indecision, and occasional outbursts of anger.

A tall missionary with a long sad face began: "The reports that drunken Congolese troops are raping, murdering, and looting in Leopoldville are undoubtedly true."

"This isn't Leopoldville," said Helen quickly, but she was ignored. A short, sunburned missionary from the south took over when the first man had finished.

"The trouble is obviously going to spread all over Congo. All American missions have ordered their personnel to evacuate across the Ugandan border as quickly as possible. I think we should do the same."

Helen already knew exactly what she was going to do. Although she was one of the younger ones there, she was a second-termer, if only by a matter of days. And she was firm in her conviction. God had called her out and had not told her to go home; it was as simple as that. And whoever else was going to be needed, a doctor would certainly be a necessity. She also felt very strongly that at this time of crisis the mission they had started in Congo badly needed her support and presence.

When her turn came to speak she made her position clear, and she knew at once that there was great hostility towards her position; the men felt that she was making it harder for them.

One of the married men said huffily, "It's all very well for you, but you're not responsible for a wife and children."

"I accept that," admitted Helen.

"And how shall we be able to protect you women missionaries when it becomes necessary?"

"You won't have to."

"It's all very well you saying that, but in the long run you'll be our responsibility."

That made Helen furious. She hadn't been anyone's responsibility since she left college. This was pure male chauvinism. "Not at all. We're out here on God's calling, not yours. You're not responsible for us—God is. Surely this is a case for a free choice."

The argument grew more heated, and Helen noticed that

the three senior women missionaries—Margery Cheverton, Agnes Chansler, and Daisy Kingdon, women in their forties, fifties, and sixties respectively—were sitting together on one side of the room. They had already made it clear they were not leaving.

Helen rose and went across to sit next to them. "This looks more like my side," she said. She realized later what a formidable quartet they must have seemed, and how really unfair it had been on the men with wives and children to consider.

Those who decided to go packed their cars and streamed out at four in the morning. They arrived at Paulis, where a plane was supposed to be coming to fetch them. They waited all day, but no plane arrived. That night they set off in convoy for the Ugandan border and crossed without incident.

Helen returned to Nebo alone and went to bed, but she could not sleep. Suddenly everything was different—she was full of strange fear. It was quite an uncanny feeling. By 2 A.M. she was exhausted listening to every tiny noise: the sound of a nightbird, a rat scurrying across her bamboo ceiling. Then she heard a tapping on the front door, and she approached on bare feet, almost expecting to open the door to her own murderers. She was overjoyed to discover that her two wonderful friends from different ends of the village, Mama Taadi and Mama Damaris, were waiting outside. They rushed in and hugged her. Each, making her own decision, had decided that Helen should not be allowed to sleep alone in that house. Tiptoeing through the darkness, they had met at her front door. The next day Agnes Chansler and Margery Cheverton, the two women from the meeting at Ibambi, arrived from their mission station at Egbita, about eighty miles away. They had made a similar decision: The medical work and Helen's safety were of

prime importance; for the time being they would abandon
their own mission and come to work with her. What needed
to be done? Agnes was very good with children, so she
could take over that department, couldn't she? And Margery would act in a general capacity. There would be a
great deal of work to do. Within a two-hundred-mile
radius, only Helen and Dr. Swertz, the leprologist and
pathologist, remained of the seventeen doctors who had
been working in the area a few weeks ago. Helen was
deeply moved that these women had come to help her out.
It was good to have friends.

During those next four years of independence, life in
Helen's part of Congo changed beyond recognition. A few
weeks after her return she wrote home: "Today is Sunday
evening and it has been such a quiet and lovely day with the
mass of yellow acacia blossoms brilliant against a clear blue
sky; doves cooing, hens clucking, birds humming—all the
sounds of peace and beauty—I listened to the kiddies, some
thirty-five of them singing hymns in the children's ward
opposite. Congo still writhes in the convulsive grip and
tempestuous storm of political unrest and intrigue. How
one's heart longs to see an end to it all, and peace restored
to this poor republic. Economically, even without this political upheaval, the country is in the depths of the most
abysmal need—there are just *no* technicians, no doctors,
no senior school teachers—*none*—and UNO says that even
with the most rigorous program of intensive training, it will
take five years to produce enough for Leopoldville alone.
Drug shortage is growing acute. Already I have had to start
to refuse treatment to adults and conserve supplies for
acutely ill children. Also food is becoming a problem—no
more rice or salt or flour available locally, nor matches, and
milk will be running out again soon. . . ."

Independence had indeed got off to a bad start. In Leopoldville, a thousand miles away, it was marked by rioting, mutiny among the Belgian-officered Force Publique, and the near collapse of the hurriedly assembled and unprepared African government. Katanga (the wealthy, copper-rich eastern province without whose financial support no central government could hope to function) seceded almost immediately, under the leadership of Moise Tshombe.

Because of the spread of violence, Belgium rushed in thousands of troops to protect her nationals. Patrice Lumumba, appointed first Prime Minister, appealed to the United Nations for assistance, and later to the U.S.S.R. This second action added another political problem, of course. Secretary General Dag Hammarskjold decided that United Nations military intervention was necessary; however, it was spectacularly unsuccessful. Troops from many countries were flown in, the secession of Katanga was prevented by force, and the UN operation turned out to be costly and incompetently handled. It was evident that no one could feel either affection or loyalty towards an international army. Certainly, the episode discredited the idea of further physical intervention by the United Nations in the arena of world affairs.

Helen was unaffected by these international proceedings. Her reactions to the more commonplace perils of Congo remained practical: She swatted the flies which stung her; she biffed (to use her own terminology) the things which threatened her; she slaughtered the things which attacked her. She was too busy with God, her medical work, and her pupils to be concerned with anything else.

On one occasion she had to defend herself in her bath. The house at Nebobongo was built of red bricks they had fired in their own kiln. The roof was asbestos, painted red.

The rooms were square and utilitarian, the windows shuttered to keep out the glare.

The bathroom was a gloomy place half filled by the bath —a huge concrete rectangle which over years had become discolored to a dark gray. It took ages to fill with water, and Helen in those busy days had no time to waste on such extravagance. Every evening she placed a large zinc bathtub in the middle, filled it with hot water, and sat in it. There, for a divine minute or two, she would slosh soap and hot water all over herself and emerge fragrant and refreshed, ready to eat whatever food was available and get on with writing up her notes, marking the papers, and arranging the curriculum and medical program for next day.

On this occasion, alone in the house, perched happily in her tub, she was suddenly surprised to feel the zinc tub begin to rock beneath her. She leaped out of the bath as if the water had suddenly become scalding hot. Simultaneously, from under the zinc tub emerged the angry head of a black mamba snake, whose bite almost inevitably ensured a quick death. It had slithered up the waste pipe and found the cool, damp recess under Helen's zinc bowl a perfect place to coil in siesta. It must have been mildly curious when the hot water pouring into the bath raised the temperature—and absolutely enraged when Helen sat on it.

Her reactions were as rapid as the mamba's. She fled naked into the living room and grabbed the machete which always stood there ready for any crisis. Scurrying back to the bathroom, she found the six feet of black snake hissing and coiling along the length of the bath, about to writhe over onto the floor. Helen went into action.

Next morning, when the houseboy came in, he goggled in admiration. "You certainly chopped up that mamba good, missus! There was mamba blood on the ceiling! Yes, right up on the ceiling."

Snake bites of all varieties were commonplace at Helen's hospital. Encountering every sort of snake from boa constrictor to adder was a normal hazard in the rain forest, and it was always possible to step on one in your darkened bedroom or, as Helen had, discover one elsewhere in the house. On one occasion, she lay delirious in the middle of a particularly bad bout of malaria. The male nurse attending her observed that Helen's eyes were rolling around in a most peculiar manner. He called his colleague to observe the phenomenon. They discovered that her eyes were following the gyrations of a large mamba circling the supports of the mosquito net overhead as he attempted to find some aperture in the net which would allow him to join her in bed.

But physical difficulties were not the only ones Helen dealt with in Congo. There were other irritations as well. Permits were needed for practically every mode of transport, and every aspect of living. You would be stopped in your car for no obvious traffic offense; you never felt quite safe. The fact that so many Europeans had left gave one a feeling of insecurity. Under the independence government one was never really sure what was going to happen, and during the next four years everything began to fall apart.

When Helen had first arrived in Congo, in the early fifties, the separation between black and white was finite. One did not so much accept as tolerate the Government's attitude that the Africans were incapable of doing almost anything. Therefore, they were given no political or social authority. The missionaries, however, tried to give the Africans both authority and direction. They could, of course, do nothing about the law, and there simply was no justice for any

African in Helen's district. Bribery and corruption eroded all aspects of law; there was no point in a black man trying to take a white man to court, since the decision was always that the white man was right, the black man wrong.

In the area of religion, also, there was injustice. The Government's official faith was Catholic; therefore, Catholic influence, patronage, and authority permeated all aspects of public affairs. The hospitals were run by Catholics, and the nursing staff were Catholic sisters. When the Simbas' rebellion started, they identified anything Catholic with a despotic government and reacted with horrifying brutality.

From the very first moment Helen arrived in Congo, violence was a natural occurrence of daily life. She would never forget her first experience with the authoritarian manner of meting out punishment. She had left Nebo to walk into the village to buy plantains for the patients. In the shade of the trees at the edge of the road, traders were selling limes, breadfruit, manioc, papayas, fat yellow bananas, stalks of plantains. She wandered from one fruit pile to the next, enjoying her encounters and bargaining in her elementary Swahili.

The man she chose to do business with seemed no different from the others. A fat, cheerful, ingratiating character, his vegetables were apparently the same prices as everybody else's. In the crowd, she failed to notice the arrival of a Belgian official and his two uniformed African constables, who stood behind her, listening to their conversation. The vegetable seller, however, recognized them immediately. His eyes became furtive, and he was frightened.

Helen heard the abrupt order behind her and felt the two African constables shoulder past her to grab the man. She could scarcely believe it when the two constables flung the man on his face on the grass and beat him with long, pliant sticks. The noise of the sticks swishing through the air, cutting through the man's thin clothes, was sickening. He screamed as they continued flailing him. There seemed no end to the punishment: ten, twenty, thirty strokes. Helen turned wildly on the Belgian official, protesting in a mixture of English, French, and Swahili. "Stop it, stop it," she shouted, "what are you doing? Stop it, do you hear?"

The official's voice was peremptory and contemptuous. "He was overcharging for third-rate produce. He knew he was cheating; he knows what the penalty for cheating is." She couldn't bear the fact that the man was being flogged because of her. "But he wasn't overcharging me; we were just discussing prices."

The official waved an impatient hand, dismissing her. A crowd had gathered now, watching in silence while the vicious flogging continued. Then the Belgian issued a sharp order and the blows stopped. "That will be a lesson to everybody here," he declared in a loud voice. Helen turned away; the thought of trying to buy anything was now quite repugnant to her.

African chiefs trained in the Belgian administration used flogging as a general antidote to all forms of petty crime, and after independence the brutality of Congolese in power towards their fellow countrymen was much worse than anything she ever witnessed under the Belgians. All through those early years of independence, she treated men brought into her hospital who had been flogged almost to the point of death. Nursing them back to health and sanity was a harrowing task.

Shortly after independence she was asked by the new civil authorities to act as visiting doctor to the Wamba hospital. Although this was inconvenient and meant giving up two days a week, she agreed. Then she discovered that she was also expected to do medical inspections at the prison.

Her first day there horrified her. Certainly, the smells sickened her. In one part of the prison she was shown a series of cells roughly nine feet by twelve, each holding not fewer than twelve men, with no sanitary arrangements, no water, and half the inmates suffering from dysentery or malaria. She did what she could, administering tablets and medicines, knowing that these were of no real use to sick men in such conditions. Then she demanded to see the prison commandant.

"It's absolutely disgusting," she stormed. "You have cases of malaria and dysentery, you have lepers, you have all sorts of diseases, yet the prisoners are incarcerated like animals. You have no hospital facilities at all. How can I treat them when there are no beds for me to put them into?"

The prison commandant's face was hostile.

"This is a prison," he said bluntly.

"I know they're in prison, but they haven't been condemned to death. Should they die because they're serving their sentences?"

"They're criminals. This is a prison."

There was no way around this stony-hearted logic. Helen did what she could for a year, hating every visit she made. She was soon made aware that her visits coincided with particularly brutal beatings for many of the men; the prisoners were beaten *because* she was there, simply to illustrate to them that she had no authority—the prison officials had authority. There was no way she could actually help or alleviate the conditions at the prison while the officials merely paid lip service to having a medical inspection; they made a fool of her and enjoyed it. A year later an official medical officer was appointed to Wamba, and she relinquished her detested position.

Acting as visiting doctor and surgeon to Wamba hospital

was much pleasanter. She quickly established friendly relationships with the Catholic nursing sisters (whom she met again as prisoners in the convent) and with the African staff. There was little hospital discipline, unfortunately, and very little professional conscience about caring for patients or administering drugs.

The weekly journey was irksome, and it meant leaving Nebo at 5:30 A.M. to be ready to start ward rounds at 8 A.M. She was never home before 10:30 P.M. on the day she returned.

It was on one of these journeys that the truck, laden with her weekly quota of passengers, was flagged to a halt at a village about eight miles from Wamba. A group of Christians she knew very well gathered around.

"Dr. Helen, you must not go into Wamba today, it is too dangerous."

"What do you mean? There's an operative list as long as my arm awaiting me. I can't postpone operations. Some of the people might die."

"It is too dangerous, Dr. Helen. Wamba is in chaos. All the white people are either under house arrest or in prison. You might be killed if you're seen on the streets."

"Nonsense," retorted Helen flatly. "I'm needed at the hospital and I'm going in. Anyway, what's all the trouble about?"

There was a despondent air about her friends. One announced, "The news has come through that Patrice Lumumba has been murdered." The passengers in the back of Helen's truck suddenly disembarked. Not a chicken, pig, squealing baby, or pregnant mother remained, and she and John Mangadima were left staring at each other.

"John," she said, "I must get into the hospital. You can stay here and I'll pick you up this evening when I finish. I think I'd better . . ."

She trailed off as she saw the cold look on his face.

"Don't you know me even yet? If you're going into Wamba, then I'm going with you." He held up his hand as she started to speak. "And there's no argument about it. Shall we get in and start off?"

Helen blinked behind her glasses. She'd been thoughtless with him again.

"All right," she said. "Sorry." Three miles from Wamba, soldiers stopped them with leveled rifles at a roadblock, and Helen realized *they* knew all about Lumumba's murder and what it signified. All Helen knew about Lumumba was that he was another politician operating in Leopoldville.

"Out of the car! Where are your papers? Where d'you think you're going?"

The first exchanges were in Swahili, but John, serene and calm, knew that the soldiers were local Wabudus. He replied very sharply in their own dialect.

"You are not to talk to this lady in such a rough fashion. Do you understand me? This is *our* doctor. She is one of us. She is of our blood. If you wish to interrogate us, take us at once to your senior officers, and be quick about it."

Helen knew enough Kibudu to understand most of what he said, and had difficulty in preventing herself from grinning as the abashed soldiers drove with them into Wamba to the local administrative offices. Their discomfiture increased as a small crowd gathered and Helen recognized several of her patients in it. They loudly demanded to know why "our doctor" had been arrested.

The exchanges were noisy, and the administrator came out of his office to see what was going on. The corporal in charge of the squad explained his predicament. "We stopped this lady, sir, knowing that all the whites in Wamba are either under house arrest or in prison. This man with her, sir, says she is a doctor on her way to hospital in Wamba."

The administrator looked at the crowd and said politely,

"Perhaps you could step into my office, madam, and we can see what this is all about."

Half an hour later, equipped with credentials making it clear that she was indeed a doctor and authorized to move wherever she wanted, she left his office, bound for the hospital. When she returned to Nebo the same evening, the guards at the roadblock saluted her.

Three weeks later "our doctor" was not half so self-assured driving through Wamba, this time without John Mangadima. The police jeep which pulled alongside hooted at her angrily and drove her into the side of the road. The policeman swore at her. Didn't she know she had made a right turn without signaling with her traffic indicator? She was under arrest.

"This is absolute nonsense," Helen began, but stopped abruptly as she stared at the policeman's ugly revolver, which was pointed at her head. She was driven to the police station and taken to an officer. For a few seconds he continued working at his desk. Then he glared at her.

"What's all this about?"

Helen had no intention of allowing the arresting officer to get his version of the story in first, so she began to speak. The desk officer stood up, leaned forward, and struck her hard across the face.

"You'll speak when you're spoken to," he yelled. Helen's hand went to her cheek; she was more shocked than hurt.

"And stand to attention in front of me."

Helen stood at attention for two hours, and any attempt to defend herself was met with abuse and threats. The "our doctor" scrap of paper was pushed aside contemptuously— she doubted if they could read, anyway—and they harangued her on her obligations to the new regime. Did she think just because she was white she could drive through Wamba ignoring all the traffic regulations? Did she think she could behave like a white colonialist? Those days were over, and the sooner she understood that the better!

When she drove back to Nebo, this time there were no guards to salute her.

Even Nebobongo, usually a haven of rest compared with the other areas she frequented on her rounds, inherited its share of problems. One almost cost her her life.

She had returned from her weekly visit to Wamba bringing back bales of cloth to make uniforms for the infant school and student nurses. It was after ten at night, and she was exhausted. A student nurse and a workman helped to unload the goods into her lounge. Then she carried her lamp into the kitchen to pick up the plate of food the houseboy had left for her supper. As she sat at the table she felt the cold nose of her Alsatian puppy pushing into her lap in anticipation of a bite or two. He just wanted to remind her that he too was interested in what lay on her plate.

She took one mouthful, sighed, and gave up; she was far too tired to eat. Sensing this, the puppy gave her a second nudge and she sighed again, putting the plate on the floor. The food was eaten, the plate cleaned and polished by a long, appreciative red tongue, in about twenty seconds.

She did not remember getting into bed, but she remembered the hideousness of the next three days: the vomiting, dizziness, and burning in her mouth and stomach. Benjamin, her houseboy, had found the puppy stretched out stiff and dead on the floor when he arrived next morning, and had found Helen in an unconscious delirium.

The house had been stripped bare: All the cloth she had bought, household goods, curtains at the windows, foodstuffs, all her clothing, her watch, and the glasses she kept by her bed, even the blankets, sheets, and pillow on her bed, were gone. The violators had calmly eaten a meal at her table and left only the dirty crocks. They had poisoned her food with native berries of a particularly deadly variety, and two mouthfuls would probably have killed Helen as effectively as it killed the Alsatian puppy. The local police arrived and made a beautiful plaster cast of one footprint they discovered, but this was as far as they went towards solving the crime. Even Helen had to admire this fine example of their craft, and no doubt the footprint is still being exhibited today in some police college in Province Orientale. Naturally, it had nothing whatsoever to do with catching the criminals.

Susan was out at Pastor Ndugu's village running the clinic with her friend Eleanor when a young African walked in wearing a sweater which Susan recognized immediately as one belonging to Helen. Eleanor was injecting patients in the next room when Susan surprised her by whispering, "There's a youth next door with a sweater I want. I'm writing out a prescription for him to be injected."

Unsuspectingly, the youth, in preparation for his shot, handed over his sweater and went in to see Eleanor. When he returned, to find his sweater missing, he began to complain.

"It's over at Pastor Ndugu's house," explained Susan blandly. "If you want it, you'd better go across and fetch it."

When he arrived, Susan cross-examined him with the tenacity of a prosecution counsel at a murder trial, as indeed it might have been but for Helen's good fortune.

"Where," she demanded, "did you get this sweater?" The youth was taken aback. "I bought it at a shop."

"Which shop?"

"A shop in Wamba."

"What was the name of the shop?"

"I've forgotten."

"But you know where it is?"

"Oh, yes."

"Then we can take you there and you can show us."

"Oh, I've just remembered. I'm confusing this sweater with another. My brother bought this from a shop in Stanleyville. There are a lot of shops in Stanleyville."

"You are a liar," Susan told him. "If you don't tell us where you got this sweater, we're taking you to the chief and he'll know how to get the truth out of you."

The youth was weak and easily browbeaten. He admitted he'd bought the sweater from a man in the village next to his. Yes, the man had all sorts of things to sell: bales of cloth, household goods, knives and forks. They were very cheap, and when you bought them he asked you not to tell anybody else.

Susan and some of Nebobongo's senior African staff presented the evidence to the police. Nothing was done about it. Congolese judicial procedures still operated in the same blindly prejudicial manner as they had when the Belgians were in charge, only now the black man was always right. To many Africans, the freedom word *uhuru* obviously implied a right to rob, plunder, and dispossess the whites. On one occasion the local chief wrote to Helen saying that if ever a thief broke into her house, on no account was she to challenge him, because the thief would undoubtedly be armed, and it was likely that he would kill her before she could attempt to kill him. This disconcerting admonition removed all peace of mind she still possessed. She lay in bed with a machete on one side and a spear on the other, thinking how dreadful it would be if anyone came in to kill her, and how even more dreadful if she should strike back and inadvertently kill *him*.

She was in this state of mind one night when she woke conscious of a soft sawing noise at her shutters. Someone was trying to get in. Tense with fear, she put on her glasses, grabbed her machete, and crept forward with a flashlight in the other hand. Standing silent at the shutters, she realized that indeed someone was trying to force them open. Summoning all her courage, she switched on the light and bellowed, "Go away!"

She heard a noise outside that sounded as if the surprised burglar had fallen backwards in fright, and then she heard someone scrambling up and running away. Two inches away from her nose, the point of a long, sharp machete projected towards her. She had at least gained one extra weapon.

These experiences began to proliferate. Another occurred when John Cunningham, a missionary from the north, arrived with his pregnant wife for the birth of their baby. The evening his wife started in labor Helen told them, "It will take quite a few hours, so while Elaine gets everything ready I suggest we all rest as much as possible to be ready for the real work when it begins."

Helen put her feet up on the couch in the living room, Mrs. Cunningham retired to bed, and Elaine started sterilizing instruments and boiling water. The rest period was interrupted by a loud scream from Mrs. Cunningham. Everyone rushed to the bedroom. "There was a black man in the room," she declared in a panic. "I'd just dozed off, woke up suddenly, and there he was at the foot of the bed!"

There was no one in sight. "Now calm down, calm down," Helen soothed. "It was probably only a bad dream due to your condition. You go back to sleep and we'll search the house and make certain that no one's here."

A house search revealed that indeed no one was there, and everyone breathed a sigh of relief.

Two hours later the baby began its journey into the world. In the middle of the process Helen needed something from the bathroom, and Elaine volunteered to fetch it. As she passed Mrs. Cunningham's now vacant bedroom, she glanced inside, to see an African scrambling out through the window carrying a briefcase in his hand. (Later they decided he'd probably hidden under the bed the whole time.) Elaine dashed back.

"An African! In the bedroom! Just jumped through the window carrying a briefcase!"

John yelled, "He's got the briefcase. He's got my briefcase!"

Helen, trying to cope with the arrival of a baby, shouted, "What was in it?"

"Everything we own in the world. Passports, documents, all the church money."

Helen dropped everything and dashed for the back door. Mounted outside was her own personal talking drum, placed there by friends who had taught her how to use it for an emergency like this. Helen grabbed the rubber drumsticks and began to bang away on the talking drum, which imitates the sound of human vowels. In her early days in Congo, Helen had learned to send a couple of messages— "Come to prayers," "Surgical team needed"—half as a joke. One side of the drum played a light tone, the opposite had a heavier resonance. You kept a regular beat going with your right hand and stroked rhythmically with your left. Now into the midnight air went Helen's exhortation, "We need help . . . we need help . . . we need help . . ."

From the first drumbeat, the compound and indeed the whole village was alerted to the fact that "our doctor" was in peril. The village men decided she was certainly under attack from a band of outlaws. They leaped from their beds, mainly naked, grabbed spears and clubs, and ran down the road towards the hospital, ready for battle. John Mangadima and his group of student nurses, nearer at hand, interpreted the message differently. The birth had gone wrong, they thought: A full Caesarian must be mounted at once, and the entire surgical team was needed. Pausing only to leap into white surgical gowns and caps, they raced for the house. Both groups arrived outside the house in a confused crowd at precisely the same moment: naked villagers brandishing spears, surgical team waving stethoscopes.

Helen directed the emergency with a few quick words, and they spread out to search the compound. The thief and money were never seen again, though most of the documents were recovered the next morning since they had been thrown down by the roadside. But Helen's villagers were now very concerned about her. The attempt at poisoning and the burglaries indicated to them that she was in real danger, so until the Simbas finally arrested all of them, they never again let her out of their sight. Practically every mouthful of food put before her was tasted by her cook. Her male students slept at the house and maintained guard in pairs and in shifts. "Our doctor" was an essential and precious part of the pattern of their lives.

CHAPTER 9

Doctor Swertz's expression was, as usual, impassive, serious, and seemingly hostile. "Dr. Roseveare," he said bluntly, "I think you should leave Congo at once."

Helen, who had been into this already with Jack Scholes and the others, had her answer ready.

"Thank you very much, Dr. Swertz, but I didn't leave in 1960 and I don't intend to leave now."

Dr. Swertz's expression did not change. "This is 1964. It is much more dangerous. I think you should go."

Helen would admit that Dr. Swertz's contacts at Pawa among the Africans were probably more solid than her own. He probably knew more than she did about this new rebellion, but he didn't seem to understand that she was driven to stay for reasons of faith, and was not as concerned about her personal survival. It really was most astonishing, she thought, how the passing of the years changed one's opinion about people. Dr. Swertz had figured briefly in that first training period at the Red Cross hospital at Pawa, and had ignored Helen completely. Certainly, his brusque reaction to John Mangadima had been responsible for John's coming to work with her. But apparently, over the years, he had decided, if not to like Helen, then at least to accept her. And, of course, he had one good reason to feel grateful towards her. Four years earlier, she had helped him through a difficult time. Helen had never understood him, but she admired him for his dedication: She knew that as a doctor he gave his life and skill wholly to Congo for a pittance of a salary. At independence in 1960, all Belgian civil servants had been ordered home, but before leaving, he had come to visit her at Nebobongo.

As usual, he came abruptly to the point. "You know I have married a Congolese wife? You also know that she has contracted tuberculosis?"

"Yes." Helen had heard this disturbing news. She knew how much he cared for his wife. In his own taciturn way, he treated her with tenderness, love, and respect, and was never unfaithful to her. This side of his character was so diametrically opposite to everything Helen knew about him that she could scarcely believe it. He generally thought nothing of Africans, and was often physically violent with them.

"I am ordered back to Belgium, but I intend to return as soon as I can. The newly independent regime wants me to go on working at Pawa for them."

Helen was immensely pleased. She was delighted to discover that Dr. Swertz was actually a man of humanitarian ideals, in spite of the kicks and slaps he often administered. She was even more delighted to hear that the Congolese also recognized these qualities in him and wanted him back.

For once in his life, he now seemed at a loss for words. "Would you . . ." he began hesitatingly.

"Yes?" encouraged Helen.

"Would you look after my wife until I return? She is very sick, and she will not get better."

"Of course. I'll do everything I can."

He returned only to help nurse an incurably sick woman. His wife eventually died at Nebobongo in 1963.

In that August of 1964, when the missionaries at Ibambi and Nebobongo heard that Stanleyville was in the hands of rebels who called themselves Simbas, Helen was extremely confused. She had no clear idea what sort of rebels they were or what they wanted. She received half a dozen versions of the news in English on her radio set: The Russian and Peking spokesmen predictably asserted that this was a popular uprising of the downtrodden Congolese people against Leopoldville's imperialist-dominated puppet government—a line followed by Brazzaville's Communist regime on the northern side of the Congo.

The BBC was cautious, the American stations excited, but the rebellion was sufficiently disturbing to halt Helen's impending thousand-mile journey across the border to Kampala, in Uganda, to procure supplies of badly needed drugs. She reasoned that if rebels were roaming about the countryside, it was likely they would either steal the truck on the outward journey, or steal both truck and supplies on the way back; and there was the added likelihood that she might not be able to get back.

During those first four years of independence, Patrice Lumumba had been assassinated and Dag Hammarskjold had died in a mysterious air crash near Congo. During that time, the Central Government, bolstered by the UN, had been dominated by President Kasavubu, and appeared just as unstable as the governments of some Latin American republics.

In September, 1963, Kasavubu abruptly dissolved the parliament, and a variety of left-wing politicians fled across Congo to Brazzaville to set up revolutionary committees. Their avowed purpose was to overthrow the government.

By June, 1964, as the last of the disillusioned UN troops left the country, half a dozen politicians were successfully fomenting rebellion in many parts of Congo. Stanleyville fell to General Olenge and his Simbas with scarcely a shot fired. The General was aided by his chief of witchcraft,

Mama Orena. She was an ancient crone, four and a half feet tall, who wore a leopard-skin wrap and waved her magic amulets as she pranced through Bunia, Paulis, and Wamba, which offered only token resistance before surrendering. The use of drugs, fetishes, magic incantations, witchcraft, and cannibalism in modern warfare was so successful that it terrified whole battalions of the National Congolese Army: In Stanleyville seven thousand soldiers deserted to Olenge's ranks. Communist guns, ammunition, provisions, and advisers were ferried in from Brazzaville and across the borders from southern Sudan and Uganda, and within weeks four-fifths of Congo were in Simba hands. The coup appeared to be complete.

Its hold, however, was tenuous. By a political sleight of hand as mysterious as one of Mama Orena's magic formulas, Moise Tshombe, who had been discredited after the failure of the Katanganese secession, was now recalled to become Prime Minister of Congo, with Kasavubu as his President. His first move was to recruit a force of three hundred white mercenaries under a British ex-officer, Major Mike Hoare, and another force of six hundred, mainly French-speaking, under Major "Black Jack" Schramme. There is no doubt whatsoever that this comparatively small force of mercenaries preserved Congo from the rebels. They stiffened the morale of the National Congolese Army to such an extent that they were able to recapture all the major towns during 1964 and 1965, even though the much more formidable task of flushing the rebels out of the rain forests still remained.

Tshombe did not survive much of this action. In 1965 General Mobutu, a sergeant in the Belgian Army at the time of independence, instigated a military coup. Tshombe was deposed, and he fled to Europe and the comfort of his Swiss bank account. Eventually he was lured to his death in

North Africa under "mysterious circumstances." Deaths under mysterious circumstances were commonplace during Congo's years of violence.

Although Helen had remained oblivious to much of what was going on, she knew Dr. Swertz had not. His arrival at her front door in August, 1964, was therefore not totally surprising. Still, she had made her decision.

"Are you leaving?" she inquired.

"No, but I'm a man."

"And I'm a doctor."

Helen was slightly puzzled why he should be so concerned about her, but then she never had, and never would, understand this enigmatic Belgian physician.

"I've got my car outside," he urged. "I'd like to drive you to Paulis so that you can catch a plane to safety."

"I'm not leaving, Dr. Swertz. Thank you very much for your offer to drive me to the airport. But what are you going to do?"

Suddenly he smiled, and Helen realized that it was the first and only time in her life she had seen this happen.

"Go back to Pawa and kick my patients about."

It was also the very first time she had ever heard him make a joke. She presumed that the story of John Mangadima's departure from his hospital and John's reasons for joining Helen must have reached him sooner or later.

"Gently, I hope," said Helen.

He stared at her. "Yes, gently."

"What about the danger for you?"

He shrugged. "I'll be all right. They'll need doctors in the future; they'll need them very badly."

He said good-bye and left—this abrupt, enigmatic, yet peculiarly gentle and professional Dr. Swertz, who had made his bed and was, for better or worse, going to lie on it. She never saw him again. Certainly, she could not have foreseen the bitter finale life held for him. While Helen was held in the convent at Wamba, he traveled from Pawa to Ibambi to see a patient. Seeing a white man in the street, a twelve-year-old "cub" opened fire with his machine gun, killing him instantly.

When the Simbas first overran the missionaries' district, they were quite reassuring and insisted that, now that they were in power, everything would be bigger, better, and brighter. Their intentions were good, their sense of logic childlike. They had no notion of economics, for example. Their ruling that all prices in the shops would be cut by three-quarters resulted in all goods disappearing overnight. Soon no one had any money and no one was paid any wages. Helen was told to make a list of all the drugs she needed, and this would be sent to Stanleyville. The drugs, she was assured, would arrive within a few hours. Helen already knew that Stanleyville was as short of drugs as she was, and that the Simbas' reasoning depended on the belief that if they *said* it would happen, it *must* happen. After all, they had been given magic powers by the witch doctors.

The omnipotence of their authority was appalling. Legal courts, tribunals, and juries were things of the past. If the Simbas thought you were guilty, you were executed. And from every town and village in their vicinity came the bestial stories of hundreds of innocent people tortured and killed.

Helen's first involvement with the Simbas was frightening. A truck full of soldiers had roared into the compound at Nebobongo. A sergeant grabbed her arm and gabbled away in a peculiar French, of which she understood about half. Even as he spoke, his men were lugging a wounded civilian out of the truck.

"He's been shot in action. Bullets in the chest. His life is in danger. You must attend to him at once."

Helen had a vision of smashed ribs, pumping arteries, and massive internal injuries, and feared she would be completely unequipped to deal with them from an emotional, surgical, or any other viewpoint. The man would almost certainly be dying from his wounds; there was little she would be able to do except pray.

There was no alternative but to examine him. In the operating room she was at once relieved and puzzled to find that his wound had already been bandaged quite professionally.

"Yes, yes," the sergeant concurred impatiently, "the nurses at Wamba did it. But they are not *real* doctors. That is why we have brought him to you."

Helen undid the bandages and saw at once that the wound was not serious: A single bullet had struck the man high up in the chest, ricocheted along his clavicle, and emerged at the point of his shoulder. She cleansed and rebandaged it and reassured them all. But when they had gone she sat down and contemplated the future with dread: She knew she would never be able to cope with bullet or shrapnel wounds in the stomach or chest; the very thought of such injuries unnerved her. What would the Simbas do to her if she could not treat their wounded?

Soon, the house inspections started. Claiming that they were in effect "liberating" the equipment, the Simbas went wild looting radio sets, tape recorders, typewriters, and anything else they fancied. On October 23, a gang of young hooligans armed with spears and knives invaded Nebobongo. They rushed into Helen's house demanding the keys to her car and the chauffeur to drive it. "I'm the chauffeur," declared Helen, and then, stalling for time, she asked, "Who is in command?"

The truth was unbelievably ridiculous. The leader was twelve years old, a swaggering little boy whose feet wouldn't even reach the clutch pedal of her car—yet he intended to drive it away. Vainly Helen protested that the vehicle had no lights, needed its plugs cleaned every ten miles or so, and its tires were likely to blow apart at any minute. In spite of this, the car was commandeered.

To save her house from destruction by a boy who could not drive forwards, let alone in reverse, Helen backed the car out of the garage and gave him a short course of instruction. It was quite hopeless; every time he tried to accelerate, he stalled the engine, and it was obvious that unless she drove, they were never going to move in any direction.

Without lights she drove the car to the palm-oil factory beyond Ibambi, and the local mechanic accepted responsibility and took them to Wamba. Again, Helen could only be thankful that nothing serious had happened. She was still safe and well.

But the real terror which culminated in the missionaries' arrest commenced during those first weeks of November, 1964. They knew from radio reports that fighting between Simbas, the National Congolese Army, and white mercenaries was taking place at various points within a hundred-mile radius, but they had no way of confirming these broadcasts and no means of communication with anybody.

On November 1st, after Helen's rape and their move to Ibambi, a gang of Simbas arrived to arrest Bill McChesney. In the course of the confused argument they wanted to know why, as doctor, Helen was not at Nebobongo. She tried to avoid the issue by making formal application for permission to stay at Ibambi. This did not please them at all.

"But your hospital is at Nebobongo. It is your duty to be at your hospital."

"At this moment I request permission to stay here."

"Why don't you want to go back?"

Helen's face was swollen and bruised; the traumatic effects of the night of her rape only two days previous still haunted her. "Because I'm frightened."

"Frightened. What is there to be frightened about?" Exasperatedly Helen exclaimed, "Two nights ago I was hurt. I was struck in the face."

This was beyond belief, they told her. Who had struck her? A Simba officer, she replied. Was she not aware that a Simba would never molest a white woman? They were blessed by magic powers and cleansed of desires to commit such acts. A statement would have to be made about this whole affair and forwarded to the proper authorities. Paper and pens were produced, questions and answers duly noted, the whole unfortunate story revealed. At the end of it she had to sign a document. Because of it Lieutenant George was arrested and spent a short period in prison. And Helen earned the continuing enmity of the Simbas.

So the series of dangerous incidents continued, until the Stanleyville massacre brought everything to a head. A Belgian parachute drop on the town precipitated the murder of white civilians. On November 24, two days later, Brian hurried in with alarming news. Contingents of angry Simbas fleeing from Stanleyville and other battlefronts were driving through Ibambi in stolen cars and trucks, looting and wrecking property. It was rumored that the Greek traders were being beaten up and murdered.

The senior African mission workers thought it would be an excellent idea for the missionaries to hide deep in the forest until the danger had passed. Mama Anakesi, one of the most respected Ibambi midwives, was chosen to lead them to such a hiding place. She led them along muddy paths, across streams, and into the deep silent forests. "You settle down here," she said, "I will come back tonight when the Simbas have left."

Helen looked around, her eyes appraising the beauty of the forest. Enormous, smooth black tree trunks soared up to support a thick canopy of branches and leaves. Sunshine filtered down in a golden haze. Little pools reflected light and were occasionally fragmented by the plop of a rain-drop from high overhead. Insects hummed and buzzed.

Brian broke into her thoughts. "We'd better not stay in one group. Much better if we split into pairs and find hiding places about a hundred yards apart, make ourselves comfortable, and read our books. I'll bring sandwiches and coffee around at lunchtime."

The forest floor was wet and slushy, but Amy and Helen found a small island of dry ground among the gnarled roots of an enormous mahogany tree and sat down. No more than an hour had passed when suddenly they heard the planes overhead.

"It could be the mercenaries," exclaimed Amy excitedly. "Supposing they did manage to capture Ibambi!"

The thought was enormously intoxicating, but only served to increase their tension, and it wasn't until Brian brought around the coffee and sandwiches at midday that they calmed down again.

"No sign of Mama Anakesi yet," he reported. Helen looked uneasily at Amy. "I hope we're not supposed to stay here all night," she said. The idea of staying there after dark was intimidating to all of them. For perhaps half an hour after Brian had gone they sat in silence. There had been no sound, not even a whisper, a twig snapping, a rustling in the undergrowth. Suddenly the fierce war chant "Simba! . . . Simba! . . . Simba! . . ." virtually enveloped them. About twenty men armed with crowbars, spears, and clubs herded the missionaries back through the forest, jostling them out onto the red gravel road which linked the mission station with Ibambi village.

The missionaries would be taught a lesson this time. "All shoes off! All hats off!" As Amy began to wipe her muddy feet on the grass, one of the Simbas yelled, "Do people wipe their feet when they're going to be executed?"

Barefooted and bareheaded, they were prodded in the direction of the village.

"Run!" their tormentors shouted. "Run." Pointed sticks and iron bars were shoved into their backs. "Run, run!"

Each victim was pushed by at least two men. The stones and gravel cut into Helen's feet; the sun on her head and neck was blisteringly hot. Two hundred yards and it was unbearable; three hundred and she knew she could go no farther. Her chest constricted, she could not get her breath, she staggered, and suddenly the red gravel road came up to meet her face. But there was no respite. The Simbas yelled and kicked her to her feet again. Gasping, Helen looked around for Jessie. She too had fallen to the ground. One of her tormentors hit her, getting her up on her knees, then jerking her upright. Helen had no time to see more. She was prodded and pushed onwards. Their feet bloody, their bodies sweating, and staggering from exhaustion, the seven of them were chased and jeered through Ibambi village and up the hill to the factory which the Simbas were using as headquarters and jail.

The five women were herded into one room, the two men taken elsewhere. There was a bed in the center. The Simbas crowded in after them, ready for the fun to start. The leader shouted the orders. "Sit on the bed. Now stand up. Now sit on the floor again. Now stand up. Sit on the bed."

It was childish and petty, but there was something positively evil about this manifestation of viciousness and anger. You did what you were told. Death or brutal punishment was a threat as close as the fists waving in their faces. Their captors were drinking spirits and beer now; half of them already had the glassy look in their eyes which indicated that they were under the influence of native drugs.

"Wait till tonight," they threatened. "We'll show you what women are for."

Two men lurched into the room and began to fight, striking and screaming at each other and cannoning into the women. Then suddenly they stopped, roaring with laughter; this had been only a mock fight to disturb and upset their captives.

At this moment one of the men recognized Helen. "That's the woman who accused Lieutenant George of raping her," he shouted. Now they had a specific point of hatred on which to concentrate. Helen was separated from the others and pushed outside.

"Give her the same sort of justice that Lieutenant George got," they cried.

They set up a mock tribunal, which delighted them no end. It was as if choosing a judge and jury and calling upon a variety of hostile witnesses helped them fulfill some democratic process of exemplary virtue. Helen was thrust into the center of the ring.

"You accused Lieutenant George of raping you?" Helen knew that unless she answered their questions, she would certainly be beaten up.

"I did not accuse him of anything."

"You accused him of raping you."

"When I was forced to by your examiners."

"There was no reason for you to open your mouth. Why did you open your mouth to accuse an African?"

Helen did not reply.

"Did he beat you? Tell us that."

"Did he hurt you? Tell us that."

Helen thought of the smashed teeth, the cuts and bruises.

"No."

"He used you as a woman, that was all?"

"Yes."

"Aren't you a woman?"

"Yes."

"Well, what are women for? You were used as a woman, weren't you?"

"Yes."

"Yet you have accused our comrade of a dreadful crime, when anyone knows that such things are no more than the natural order of events. Tonight we'll show all of you what the natural order of events can be."

She was pushed back into the other room with her friends. The immediate future seemed to hold little peace for any of them now.

A little later they heard a truck tear into the factory compound, the noise of a dozen drunken soldiers. They reeled into the room to communicate the latest rumor. There were great battles going on at Paulis and Wamba, they said; the National Congolese Army was attacking with planes and guns. There were air raids and slaughter everywhere. Suddenly, someone remembered the five women again. Weren't they responsible for all this trouble? Yes, another run would do them good, wouldn't it?

They were jostled out of the room and into the sunshine again. Shoes off! A lot of exercise was necessary for white women. The soldiers jeered and applauded the spectacle. But only three guards could bother to run behind and prod them along now; the beer drinking and the heat of the afternoon had diminished their interest. After two hundred yards, only one guard was still with them.

Jessie Scholes collapsed once they were around the corner and out of sight of the soldiers.

"We'll have to carry her," said Helen. "Can you get on my back, Mrs. Scholes?"

"I'm all right," said Jessie faintly. "I'll get up." But she could not get up, even with help. Elaine and Helen made a chair with their hands and carried Jessie, but before they had gone twenty paces Helen knew it was hopeless. The pain caused by the sharp gravel cutting into their feet was excruciating; the extra weight made it intolerable. Helen caught a glimpse of Elaine's face and knew they had to stop. The remaining guard came up behind them.

"All right," he shouted. "Put her down. Put her down."

For an instant Helen thought he was going to strike them, but, oddly enough, he turned and stooped, offering his back. "Go on, help her up. I'll carry her."

In silent amazement, Helen and Elaine watched him jogtrot off down the road carrying Jessie. Half convinced that he planned some fresh outrage, they hurried after him. But he gave Jessie a piggyback ride to within a hundred yards of the factory gates before lowering her to the ground.

"Now go on, all of you," he ordered. "Run, so it looks as if I'm chasing you." Jessie later told Helen and Elaine that she had recognized the man as an ex-mission worker from Ibambi. Of course he would have tried to help them when he could. The other men, however, were not so kind. There was no respite for the women as they stumbled into the factory compound. The soldiers were drunk and ready for another opportunity to humiliate them.

"Get into line. Quick march!"

They were pushed across the compound and lined up in

front of the temporary Simba headquarters. A large crowd of jeering Africans quickly gathered.

The Simbas began to taunt them. Were they tired? Didn't the poor missionary women look tired? Were they thirsty? Would they each like a glass of beer? Bring beer from the store and give it to the ladies. The crowd applauded. This idea offered new excitement. Everyone knew that the Christians adamantly refused to drink beer or any other alcohol; several African Christians had been badly beaten up, a few killed, for sticking unwaveringly to their principles.

"I'll not drink it," Jessie Scholes exclaimed loudly. "I'll not touch a single drop. I'd sooner die."

Helen knew her colleague well, and felt quite certain that she would not drink it, and it was likely that she might be killed for this. Fortunately, in her agitation Jessie had forgotten her Swahili and had shouted her refusal in English.

The first glass of beer was thrust into Helen's hand. She had occasionally wondered what she would do in such a situation. She hadn't tasted alcohol since her unfortunate experience at medical school. She knew that the consumption of strong drink of any sort was frowned on in her missionary circle. Generally she thoroughly approved of the principle, but she was not at all sure whether she approved strongly enough to sacrifice her life for such a cause. She knew there was no scriptural necessity for such a stand and that God could see the exigencies of their present situation. Would He wish any of His hard-working and hard-pressed followers to die in an anti-drink campaign? Helen felt she now had a clear choice of being thrown to the crowd to be raped, mutilated, and probably killed—the soldiers' threats made this quite clear—or drinking the glass of beer. She was conscious that Jessie Scholes was eyeing the glass as she might a black mamba poised to strike.

Helen raised her glass high in the air. "I am drinking this liquid in the name of the Lord Jesus," she said loudly and swallowed it to the accompaniment of loud cheers and laughter. To her slight surprise, it made her feel better almost immediately. And she had certainly deflated the beer-drinking joke: If all the women were going to behave as Helen had, there would be no fun in this missionary-baiting. The Simbas downed the rest of the beer themselves, and then herded all the women back inside. Not long afterwards Jack Scholes and Brian were thrust back in to join them. They had also had an unpleasant time, but for the moment they were being left alone. The soldiers were bored with them, and in any case another truckload of Simbas had just arrived with more stories to tell.

Helen was therefore a little surprised when a sergeant, one of the younger Simbas and a local leader, approached her. He wanted a word with her outside. It was quite dark as she followed him out on to the veranda. Obviously, the fact that she had been raped and now drank beer gave her a certain glamor in his eyes. It was all very simple, he explained. All she had to do was agree to make love to him, act as his wife, and the other missionary women would not be molested. He came closer and put his arm around her. He tried to kiss her, and she turned her face away.

There was no doubt, however, that *he* believed her silence meant acquiescence; she realized this by his change of manner. He adopted the same possessive attitude towards her that Lieutenant George had shown after that terror-filled night at Nebobongo. He took her back inside, gave her a chair, and offered her a glass of water. The other missionaries, he announced to everyone in the room, would be taken across to a nearby European household. They were not to be harmed; no one was to touch them.

When they had gone she felt very isolated and vulnerable.

The arrivals and departures of the Simbas continued, and a noisy lieutenant who had just come inside seemed to be the man in authority. He began to harangue the others at the top of his voice, and Helen understood the gist of his message quite clearly. It brought a chilled feeling to her stomach.

"All Simba units are falling back," he shouted. "There must be no mercy shown to any of the whites in this area—none of them must survive. Civilians, missionaries, Catholic and Protestant, are to be executed at once."

He paused and there was silence. The Simbas drew back with dramatic slowness to reveal Helen sitting on her chair. They had a victim already in their midst.

Their movement brought her to the lieutenant's attention. He went across and stared at her. Helen was now almost too exhausted to care what they did to her, but she was stunned when the lieutenant bent down respectfully and touched her shoulder.

"You are the lady doctor?" he said in surprise.

"Yes."

"Well, don't you remember me, Doctor?"

Helen glanced up. The lamps in the store were dim and smoky. She couldn't see him very well.

"You saved my life," he told her.

"Did I?" Her eyes widened in bewilderment.

He turned back to the others, his arms stretched wide. "This woman is good. She saved my life. No one will touch or harm her. D'you hear me?"

And then she remembered. He was the wounded civilian the soldiers had brought in for attention during those first days of the rebellion; she had been terrified that he might be suffering from massive internal injuries, but he had only caught a bullet in his chest. He had authority among the Simbas because he was one of the magic ones: A bullet had struck him and should have killed him; instead, he had survived. He had demonstrated that the witch doctors' powers were potent and real—bullets could not kill those who followed their doctrine. Small wonder he had risen to his present military rank.

"Where are your friends?" he demanded with overwhelming solicitude. "They must not be harmed either. And you must be with them. What are you doing here by yourself?" Helen was quite content to be taken across to the European house to rejoin the others, and did not waste time explaining.

As the hours passed the situation became completely confused. The Simbas argued, but there was no one authority to issue orders; the missionaries became an embarrassment to the warriors. During the night, they were marched in various directions and then marched back again. Eventually some temporary authority decided that the best way of solving the problem was to send them all home. At 6:30 A.M. they were loaded into a truck and driven back to Ibambi. Two days later they were rearrested and taken to the convent in Wamba.

PART FOUR

# CHAPTER 10

All through that long hot December of 1964 in the convent, a spring of tension inside each woman slowly tightened towards breaking point. The nights were agony: A footstep in the corridor, the sound of a voice outside in the darkness, was enough to grip the mind in terror.

There was growing evidence that the Simba revolt had failed—that, slowly and inexorably, the insurgents were being ejected from town and village—but it seemed also inevitable that they would continue to fight as a guerrilla organization in the forest for years to come. And this news did not reassure Helen or any of the others at all. The preservation of their lives as front-line hostages depended entirely upon the National Congolese Army and the mercenaries keeping their distances; the closer the fighting crept to Wamba, the greater was the threat to their safety. Each day brought some new crisis.

One Saturday, Helen, Amy, and Elaine were clearing tables in the dining room when they heard a commotion outside. They crouched behind the refrigerator for more than two hours, listening to Simbas storming up and down the corridors and racing across to the dormitories of the black nuns. Occasionally they heard the Mother Superior's voice raised in protest as she tried to bring some sense into the total and horrifying confusion. When the noise subsided, they crept out of their hiding place. Apparently the colonel had come for Sister Dominique; he wished to declare his love and continuing determination that she become one of his wives. She had pleaded illness and he had left, disgruntled, without her.

Early next morning the guards rushed in, herded them all back to their rooms, and locked them in. They were let out in the early afternoon. Apparently another convoy of fleeing Simba troops had passed through Wamba, looting and shooting, and had driven to the convent, looking for trouble. Eventually the guards had persuaded them to leave, and they had departed after stealing bread from the kitchen and some underwear which was hanging on the clothesline.

That afternoon the commandant from Wamba arrived, accompanied by his second-in-command and a twelve-year-old "cub," one of those protected by local magic. Helen had met the cub before. He boasted he had fought in the war at Beni and killed a white man. He asserted that bullets fired by the National Army had passed harmlessly over his head. He was therefore one of the elite, and the other Simbas, many much older than he, treated him with the greatest respect. Helen also discovered that he had managed to reach sixth grade in a primary school and had passed his scholarship examination to secondary school, but that now he had reached his present eminence these "childish ambitions" no longer interested him.

The purpose of the commandant's visit was to assure the Mother Superior that he was wholly on her side, and when the delivering troops arrived, should it be in his power, he would certainly hand over the women unharmed.

"I seem to be the only one in authority left," he admitted sadly. He had obviously decided that in the very near future the moment to stand up and be counted would arrive, and he had no wish to be counted on the wrong side. "Everyone else has run away. However, I must warn you that hundreds of Simba soldiers are passing through Wamba, and the next few weeks will be very dangerous. The safest place is definitely the convent, and my guards will do their best to keep you safe."

The women were worried. The fact that their safety should now depend upon the very guards who had used them so brutally was hardly conducive to a feeling of confidence. The Mother Superior gathered them all together.

"We must all sleep in the dormitory," she ordered. "We are plainly safer if we stay as one group. Your windows," she said to Helen and the other missionaries, "are much lower, and open onto the outside. If shooting started, you would be vulnerable."

Helen and Jessie obtained permission from the guards to move their bedding, and they settled down in one corner of the big dormitory. They wedged a large wooden cupboard against the most vulnerable point, the French window, and settled down to sleep. But all of them were uneasy. The commandant had not made a special journey to warn them without good reason, and anticipation of attack was almost as unnerving as the real thing.

The siege was not long in coming. As they lay there, still on edge and unable to sleep, suddenly they heard the war cries outside. "Simba! Simba! Simba!" Then a great battering and banging at the French window.

The Spanish nuns, who were nearest, leaped for the shifting cupboard and braced their backs against it, all of them holding and pushing back, panic-strickened and desperate. A second hammering started on the shuttered windows, so that the whole room echoed to an enormous drum roll of sound. The children yelled; Sister Maria Frances's big Alsatian began to bark. Helen, Jessie, and the others were paralyzed with fear, so much so at first that they could not even run to the Spanish sisters to aid their delay-

ing action at the door. There were ten minutes of pande-
monium, which ceased as abruptly as it started. They heard
the voices of their own guards as the jeering, laughing
Simba invaders went away. There was little sleep for any of
them after that. Helen sat with her back against the wall,
her arms curled around her knees, and dozed fitfully and
uneasily.

She was still tired next morning when a summons arrived
for her to proceed into Wamba town. An armed guard and
driver with van appeared at the front door, bringing orders
from the commandant. She was needed to give medical
attention to the Greeks, several of whom were sick. The
message was vague, the dangers obvious, and Helen was
reluctant. She distrusted all directives coming from Simba
authority, and how was she to know this one was actually
from the commandant? Danger was always magnified when
one was alone, and this might be a trap.

It was then that Sister Ignacio, an Italian nursing sister
who had served for five years at Wamba hospital and whom
Helen knew quite well from her work there, offered to help.

"We will go together, Dr. Roseveare," she said.

Sister Ignacio was a thin, pious woman; her long Italian
face, patrician nose, and hooded eyes could have been
inherited from generations of Borgias, and Helen was
aware that her sense of humor was as curiously contorted
as that of an Inquisitorial Jesuit. But she trusted God, did
her duty with scolding severity, and at a moment of trial
like this she was as reassuring as a dozen paratroopers.

They were met in Wamba by Mr. Preostos, one of the
leaders of the Greek community. He came from Cyprus,
and usually his seamed brown features broke into a white-
toothed smile at the sight of them. But his face seemed to
have changed since the women had last seen him: It was
gray with strain. The Greeks in Wamba had managed to

hold their own basically because they maintained a tacit support of the uprisings. They sweetened their hypocrisy with bribes, gifts of food, clothes, and commodities. They were obviously acting out of self-interest. The Simbas were now the sole authority in the area, and to oppose them meant imprisonment or death. So how else could they behave? This was the only way they could protect their stores, livelihoods, and families.

However, their good fortune was now apparently over. An army commander arriving in Wamba had informed them that the Greeks in Paulis had taken up arms against the Simbas and were fighting with the National Congolese Army. Revenge against all Greeks now had immediate priority.

"They came for us yesterday," explained Preostos to Helen in a low voice. "They arrested all the men, tied us up, beat us, marched us off to prison, threatening they were going to kill us . . ."

He paused, the memory of the outrage returning. "It was worse for the women and children. They stripped them of their clothes and beat them when they resisted. All night they terrorized them by telling them that the men had been murdered."

He looked at Helen with dark, somber eyes. "We are kept under guard in three houses, and we have little hope." He led her across to the first. Thirty women and children were packed inside, and Helen was devastated by the children: They sat absolutely still, cowed and silent; even their eyes did not move.

Preostos took her around. "This woman," he said, indicating a young girl lying on a bed, "is seven months pregnant. They knocked her down and kicked her again and again. We think the baby is dead. She cannot move her left side . . ."

The dark, despairing eyes of the girl looked up at Helen as she bent to examine her. She placed her stethoscope against the woman's body and listened to the heartbeats. The baby's heart was beating normally. Further examination revealed that the girl was bruised but not seriously hurt. Shock had helped to contribute to her breakdown. It was the same with all of them. They were in a state of intense emotional shock, and their morale was at its lowest ebb. The magic lubrication of their existence—money—had always secured their salvation before; everything and everyone had had a price. Now, suddenly, financial considerations were meaningless, and they had nothing of spiritual value, no inner strength, to fall back upon; they were bankrupt and defenseless. Helen felt that somehow she had to restore their value as human beings, and with an instinct and inspiration which was half medical and half missionary, Helen began to talk.

She spoke in English. "Now, there's a guard here who will be suspicious of what I'm saying. He'll understand Swahili and I'll ask medical questions in that language, but I want to tell you something else as well . . . something I don't want the guard to understand . . . and I'll tell you that part in English, which he doesn't speak. Some of you are from Cyprus, so you can translate what I say into your own language. Don't translate the Swahili—translate the English."

To the woman she said in Swahili, "Now tell me what happened to you? Where does it hurt?"

Then, as if translating these words, and without taking her eyes off the patient, she began in English.

"I know you are desperate. I know you are all lost. But don't despair. Don't lose hope. We are Christians. God will protect us. Believe me, God is on our side."

She told them of the situation at the convent, of the plight of the nuns and the Protestant missionaries. She told them of the strength of her faith and how, because of that faith, she—and they—could stand the strain of the terrible times they were undergoing. God *did* know what was going on, God had *not* deserted them, God *did* love. They must put their faith in God.

During this speech she also told them in Swahili that the girl was not badly injured, that the baby was unharmed, that they would all be secure if only they had enough faith and strength to pick themselves up off the ground.

"Many of you must belong to a church," she said. "But it's not the church that matters, it's you. A belief in God is a personal and individual thing. An individual can touch God. I have this faith and it supports me in times like this when I most desperately need it. It can support you now. *Now* you need it."

It was quite strange, almost electric, how the atmosphere in the room changed. She gripped her audience, inspired and charged them with her oratory.

Towards the end she said, "I'm going to pray for you. And I want you to pray with me . . ." She bowed her head. "Father, will You pass to these in need the love You've given me for You? Will You reach out to them with that same love that kept us sane and whole through all the wickedness and evil? Give us Your peace in our hearts. Keep us sane and fill us with hope. Make these here believe this, Lord."

They gripped her hand when she stood up. Their faces were relaxed; there were tears in many eyes. The children were moving and smiling. In a place which had been without hope, now there was hope.

Helen sensed that through her actions she had accomplished God's work, and it filled her with an intense feeling of spiritual joy. So rarely in our modern world do we face the fundamental issues of life and death; so seldom do we find the means necessary to quiet our feelings of despair.

Once again Helen had witnessed the consolation her faith brought to people so deeply in need. It had lightened their hearts and given them strength and hope to journey through another day and another night.

When they left, to be escorted back to the van and driven to the convent, Helen was so full of elation that she could not prevent herself from telling the Simba guard, in Swahili, what she had done.

"I was preaching the Gospel to those people," she said bluntly. "Did you know that? Did you know that woman might have lost her baby? Her suffering is mental as well as physical, and it's my responsibility as a doctor to help her find a mental balance in a situation like this. Explaining the Christian faith helped them greatly. Do you understand that?"

The Simba driver and the guard with the rifle stared at her with serious eyes. They did not say anything. The one with the rifle scratched himself. But Helen, full of her work for the Lord, was not stopping now.

"Do you understand how Christianity can help you also? Support you and give you strength at terrible moments like this? Do you know what joy it gives you to have somebody bigger, all-powerful, all-loving—God, in fact—to call on in agonizing moments of stress? Do you understand that if you had this faith, this belief in Christ, it would give you a sanity and a joy to fill every day?"

Even in Swahili Helen was not quite sure if they understood it all. But they understood enough, and Sister Ignacio nodded approvingly. The guards, whether they liked it or not, were cooped up in a small lorry with a militant Helen, and had no alternative but to listen to the sermon. When they left Sister Ignacio and herself outside the convent door,

Helen had a feeling they were not really sorry to say good-bye. Fighting a war against good, saintly women is always a trial even for the most determined fighting men.

Their feeling of triumph ended abruptly, however. At eight o'clock that night the doorbell rang, and Helen sensed trouble. As usual, eyes met and hands were tightened into nervous fists, the sickness churning in their stomachs.

A sister came down the corridor to fetch Helen. Her eyes were grave. "The Mother Superior wonders if she could have a word with the doctor?"

Helen followed her back along the veranda. At the entrance to the large dormitory she could hear voices crying and sobbing in confusion. She looked through the door and decided that the five distraught, dirty European women inside must be Belgian civilians, newcomers probably brought up from the hotel in Wamba. They had five children with them. The Mother Superior saw her and came out to confirm Helen's guess.

"Five wives of Belgian planters. They've been kept down in the hotel for three weeks. Every night the soldiers have used them—threatened them that their husbands would be murdered unless they accepted a succession of men."

"But I thought—" Helen began.

"Yes, the husbands are all dead," said the Mother Superior, finishing the sentence for her.

"Then they must know?"

"Like the others, they refuse to believe it. They have suffered all this time believing they were helping to keep their husbands alive. They have been brutalized beyond belief. Every night, hour after hour, with the children there. But they will not believe their husbands are dead."

"How can we help?" whispered Helen. It was impossible to know where to start.

"We can comfort them."

Helen watched her as she turned back to them.

"You're all going to have a nice hot bath. Then you'll feel better. Yes, the children too. Then clean clothes and a hot meal. You can share a room between two of you. There's no need to worry." She put her arm around a young woman in her early thirties. "You're all right now. You're safe here with us." Helen suddenly realized one sad little figure was looking in her direction. She turned to focus on the solemn blue eyes and pigtails. The little girl was about nine years old, she guessed.

"Hallo," Helen said, "What's your name?"

"Godeliefe."

"That's a pretty name. Are you glad to be here?"

"Yes, but it was better at home. My daddy had a plantation."

"Yes, but this is nice. It's quiet, and there's lots to eat. And other children to play with."

Godeliefe was hardly listening. "I expect my daddy will come and fetch us soon."

Helen, stung to the heart, put her arms around her. She lied, as any good Christian would have. "Yes, darling. I expect he will."

They waited for Christmas with an almost desperate expectancy, as if the arrival of the holy festival might in some way alleviate the tension and solve some part of their dilemma, for almost every day brought some sort of crisis. Soon, there was a new development. Halfway through the month, Amy approached Helen, fairly bursting with her news.

"Have you heard? The National Congolese Army and the mercenaries have captured Paulis. It's only a hundred miles away. They could be here tomorrow . . . the Greeks picked it up on the radio. The Mother Superior knows! Helen, d'you think . . . ?"

"*Wapi*," retorted Helen, using her favorite Swahili expression, which signified collectively "Stuff and nonsense" and "I'll believe it when I see it."

"It's true," Amy insisted. "It really is true."

And it was. They had captured Paulis, but neither the National Congolese Army nor the mercenaries arrived the next day, or by the end of the week. Nevertheless, no matter how firmly they tried to close their minds to this dream of freedom, no matter how hard they tried to forget that they were front-line hostages under threat of immediate execution, it was impossible not to hope, impossible not to be filled with the most desperate longings.

The days leading to Christmas inevitably made it worse. Childhood memories of church bells echoing across the snow, the lights on Christmas trees, red-breasted robins, log fires, packages tied with Christmas ribbon, smiling aunts and uncles, tinsel, crackers, carol singers, and the laughter of friends haunted their minds. Somehow Christmas would make things better. It must, even though the hot sun and cloudless blue sky seemed an affront to the season.

Helen chopped wood and fetched water. Jessie Scholes made cakes and jellies. Amy and one of the Italian nuns made miles of spaghetti. Two turkeys, bred by the nuns and kept out of Simba hands by all manner of subterfuge, came to their predestined end. By a great stroke of good fortune, the three Protestant missionaries in Wamba, Daisy Kingdon and the two younger girls, were allowed to join them.

Every morning the convent rang with joyous music as the nuns rehearsed the great mass they were going to sing on Christmas morning. Helen typed out dozens of song sheets of "Silent Night" in Swahili and "Oh, Come All Ye Faithful" in French, writing a Christmas greeting on every sheet so that Catholic and Protestant could share the festival. For all of them it became more than just a yearly religious occasion. It took on a symbolism which gave it new dimensions for all of them: It renewed their belief that in even their cruel, unjust, and frightening situation God existed and protected them. It revived that most vital ingredient to their survival: hope.

On Christmas Eve the commandant came to deliver a message to the Mother Superior, and she summoned an immediate assembly. The Protestant women gathered around with grave faces, realizing from the Mother Superior's seriousness that something important had happened.

"The Commandant has received orders that one priest and one sister are to go by truck to Mungbere immediately. From there they will go to Aba, three hundred and fifty miles northwards, and then be flown to safety to Juba in the Sudan. If the journey is successful we shall all follow in due course."

There was a long silence. The Sudan meant freedom, yes, but how could they feel excitement? Eyes and lips tightened in distrust. "Only *one* sister and *one* priest?" exclaimed Helen.

"*That* is too dangerous, I agree," said the Mother Superior. "I have decided therefore to go myself, accompanied by four other sisters. I have asked that five priests join us. If we get through safely, then all of the rest of you will follow in similar groups."

"And if we don't hear from you, we shall still all be ordered to leave?"

The Mother Superior nodded. "We must put our trust in God. There is no other way. This area is likely to become a battleground, and if we can move we must."

Helen was doubtful about this course of action.

"When is this going to happen?" she asked.

"Tonight. We have to pack at once and be ready to leave."

She looked around at their glum faces. "We have no alternative. If we don't go voluntarily, we shall be moved by force, and we all know what that might mean."

Amy caught Helen's eye. "General Olenga is at Mungbere," she whispered.

Helen nodded. "Knowing that, I don't fancy anyone's chances much."

"You think we should stay here?" said Amy.

"As long as we can, yes."

General Nicholas Olenga was the man who had issued the order for the slaughter of Stanleyville's white civilians. He was not given to humane or civilized considerations. Another large group of white hostages collected at Mungbere might suit his purposes very well. Delivering them to his authority seemed comparable to sending cattle to the abattoir; Helen wanted no part of such an arrangement.

While the Mother Superior went to prepare for her journey, the Protestants discussed the future. Jessie, Daisy Kingdon, Elaine, and Stebby all felt the same way as Helen. They had survived one nightmare journey from Ibambi to Wamba; they did not want to face another. They decided to postpone leaving as long as possible and be the very last to leave if they could.

The Mother Superior's party left within the hour. Many of the sisters were excited and emotional; they believed this was the great moment, the answer to all their prayers. Helen wished she could share their feelings as she gave her raincoat to one of the nuns to keep out the chilly night air.

The departure inevitably dampened their Christmas spirit. They could not concentrate on either celebration or devotion, knowing that the Mother Superior and four other nuns were somewhere out there, defenseless in the darkness. Christmas morning arrived, and there was still no news. The nuns sang their mass, the children opened their little

presents, the kitchen was busy, but somehow the sparkle of
excitement and anticipation had gone, replaced by uncertainty, fear, and anxiety.

The commandant returned to wish them good fortune,
and Helen seized the opportunity to ask if she could take
the children across to the men's quarters to see the Christmas tree and crèche the priests had built. He agreed. Helen,
followed by a bobbing, delighted trail of children and one
puzzled Simba guard, led them across and managed to talk
briefly to Jack and Brian.

They had already heard rumors of the impending move
but did not really know what was going to happen. It was
only when she returned to the convent and they were sitting
down to lunch that the real news arrived. Trucks were driving in from Mungbere to take them back there in small
batches. The first group was to leave immediately.

Without Mother Superior there to organize, no one knew
quite what to do, but eventually two Belgian women and
their children, five Spanish sisters, and four Italians piled
aboard the truck. They heard also that a second vehicle
had arrived to transport Brian, Jack, and eleven priests to
the same destination. Each person was allowed to take one
suitcase, money, and as much food as he or she could
carry.

This meant the end of Christmas celebrations. They sat
down to the evening meal hardly able to touch the jellies
and cakes prepared so lovingly by Jessie Scholes. Next day,
when Helen was escorted into Wamba to see a sick Greek
man, Mr. Preostos advised her to leave.

"The National Army has advanced thirty miles out of
Paulis," he told her. "They're also at a village only sixty
miles south of here. If they can cut the road between Mungbere and Wamba, they'll have driven a wedge between the
main Simba forces."

This did not make much sense to Helen. "But if they make us all leave the convent, shan't we be more isolated, more vulnerable?"

"You must go," he urged. "You'll be safer at Mungbere."

She had no more time to discuss the situation, and in any case their freedom of action was limited: They did what they were told. On Sunday night the order arrived. "The entire convent will be evacuated. All women must prepare to leave immediately."

Helen clambered aboard the open truck filled with an overwhelming presentiment of evil. Eight Protestant women missionaries and five nuns huddled together, trying to cover themselves with blankets, more to hide the whiteness of their skins than to keep out the cold. Wamba was dark and empty. Patches of mist drifted over the forest road, and the white headlights threw blurred reflections back in their faces. They halted at two deserted road barriers; at the third a surly guard glimpsing a white face struck out angrily with a stick, a blow which caught Elaine on the head and dazed her. Fortunately, the truck was moving, and they accelerated out of range before he could do anything worse.

Helen peered out from her blanket at the stars high in the night sky. She felt sick with apprehension. Why had they been moved so late at night? Practically everyone else had left in daylight. Everyone knew that danger and death skulked in the darkness, that Simba law and order—if it existed at all—certainly did not function at night. In the darkness, ultimate barbarity took over.

They passed through several more roadblocks, and all were deserted. They reached Betongwe at half an hour after midnight, and stopped. A guard came around to the back of the truck. Betongwe was a minute village where very little happened.

"Why have we halted?" she asked. The guard looked

bored. "We spend the night here. Get out, all of you. Come on, move."

Helen clambered down. "But it's only twenty-five miles to Mungbere. Why can't we drive there?" she protested.

She received a prod in the back for her impertinence, and saw then that they were being taken towards a large dark bungalow set back from the roadside.

One of the nuns whispered, "It belonged to the Belgian planter. He was murdered weeks ago."

They were pushed up the veranda steps and into a big room with huge picture windows, furnished with two armchairs and a sofa. Everything else seemed to have been looted. They were ordered to sit on the cement floor, their backs to the wall, and a few seconds later a Simba lieutenant marched in to issue instructions. "We're taking the truck back to Wamba to pick up another batch of prisoners," he snapped. "You'll spend the night here and be moved to Mungbere tomorrow." They heard him shouting orders to the local Simbas as he left.

Helen sat against the wall, her hands clenched, her mouth dry. The room was lit by one hurricane lantern. Other lanterns flickered outside. There seemed to be an almost physical atmosphere of evil and hate in that house.

She realized that the entire episode had been prearranged. It could not be a coincidence that thirteen defenseless women were bustled into a lonely, deserted house by the roadside when in forty-five minutes' easy driving they could have reached Mungbere.

She was right. The Simba attack was systematic and ruthless: They had been brought here to be raped. The door opened. The two Simba guards who had brought them from Wamba came in. They grabbed the first girl sitting by the door, hauled her to her feet, and pulled her out into the corridor. She began to scream. They heard the screams turn to sobs in a nearby room. Helen closed her eyes in sick despair, then, almost without conscious reflection, moved across to take her place. She had lectured Sister Dominique on the principle that by accepting the men's attack, she saved others from the same humiliation. Helen did not dread rape any more; she knew she could endure the shame and humiliation and survive. The act would not destroy her. She had made peace with God and her own heart. She knew what to expect now; perhaps she could save others. Basically she was frightened of intense physical pain, although she was not afraid of death. A quick death would be a merciful release, but the thought of torture, of prolonged physical agony, was a continuing nightmare in her mind.

The door opened again. A figure loomed above Helen. A hand grabbed her shoulder to pull her up. She did not resist being pushed along the corridor and into the bedroom.

Through the next two hours the rapists brutalized them. To resist meant a vicious beating up, possibly death, but certainly no avoidance of the humiliation. It was dangerous to protest. When the Simbas came to take out the young girl sitting next to Jessie Scholes, Jessie cried out angrily, "You'll leave her alone. D'you hear me? You'll not touch this girl!"

The guard said nothing. He reversed his rifle and lifted the butt end high into the air to smash it down on Jessie's skull. The young girl scrambled to her knees, to her feet, throwing herself forward to protect Mrs. Scholes.

"Please don't hit her. Please don't. I'll come with you. I'll come with you."

She was led out, and Jessie Scholes wept. When Elaine de Rusett's turn came and she was taken into the bedroom, she slid gracefully to the floor and sat there, saying in Swahili with a forceful Australian accent that she did not then, or ever, intend to accede to their demands. She was not violent, tearful, or hysterical; only firm and resolute. And amazingly enough, it worked. The men had satiated themselves and could not be bothered with anyone so adamant. Hearing Elaine's story afterwards, Helen felt a great sense of guilt. Perhaps she should have reacted violently, screamed, kicked, scratched, and defended herself until knocked unconscious. But that night there was no time for logical reflection. That was a night beyond all hope of humanity and mercy.

By 2 A.M. the Wamba guards were finished. Before they left to go back to town, they brought in half a small deer they had killed with the truck on the journey from the convent, and contemptuously left it for their captives as a gift. The women now lay in a tight square against the wall, hemmed in by the sofa and an armchair at either end. They heard the cab door slam, the engine rev up, the vehicle grind away into the night. Then all was silent except for stifled sobbing.

Helen lay there holding one of the girls who had been raped. She sobbed in an agony of pain and shock, and Helen could do little to assuage her bitter grief except to hold her tightly in her arms and wait for the dawn. She scarcely knew what to pray for now except that daylight might come soon.

But morning brought only another threatening experience. The news had gone around the village that white women prisoners were held in the house and that no doubt some had been raped. A mob of Africans gathered outside the windows shaking spears and sticks and yelling obscenities. It was like being trapped in a huge fishbowl with predatory creatures menacing them through the glass walls.

Fortunately, the sergeant major in charge of the local garrison was not hostile. Food? There wasn't much food, but he would try to find some rice and peanuts for them. Water? He would get a couple of old men to draw some. Meanwhile, they had better cook the half deer left by the Wamba guards before it putrefied.

At lunchtime another truck arrived from Wamba, carrying seven Belgian women and nine children. They were to be left at Betongwe while the driver returned to Wamba for another load. While the unloading and arguments were taking place, another overloaded truck arrived, carrying eighteen nuns and five men. It took five nuns from Helen's party and two Belgian women and their children when it moved off for Mungbere.

The driver of the first truck insisted that his orders compelled him to return to the convent to pick up the last of the prisoners; he promised, however, that he would be back before nightfall to take them to Mungbere. This news left them tense with apprehension. The thought of another night in the bungalow contending with the Africans howling outside their windows and the designs of the local Simba guards was sickening. "Please," the women pleaded, "please come back and take us to Mungbere."

They were deeply depressed when the driver left, and someone pointed out that there was practically no chance of his returning that night, because he had no lights. Fearfully, those remaining—eight Protestant missionaries, five Belgian women, and six children—watched the coming of darkness. Throughout the afternoon and early evening, the young Simbas and local hooligans continued to shout threats outside the windows, while Helen tried to console little Godeliefe. This time, luckily, the local sergeant major and his men appeared actually prepared to take their guard duties seriously. The sergeant major also produced more rice and peanuts and even a chicken, so they were not hungry.

That evening they arranged their tiny fortress of sofa and two chairs in a square against the wall. They covered themselves with blankets so that it was not possible to distinguish between old and young, woman and child. They made a pact to cling to each other and refuse to let go, a strategy previously used by some of the nuns, who had formed human circles when attacked. They lay motionless under their blankets, each tiny noise causing breath to be held, muscles to contract.

An hour later the attack seemed imminent. They heard shouts and threats outside; fists and sticks banged against their door, feet thumped across the veranda. Two of their guards were forced back into their room, and they leveled their rifles at the intruders while the third guard ran off to fetch the sergeant major. The sergeant returned with his second-in-command. The invaders, three Simbas of his own garrison, demanded the right to be assigned guard duty over the women. What they actually wanted, Helen finally understood, was to rape the women and then destroy them. The intruders charged that the guards who had leveled their rifles and tried to protect the women were traitors; they had refused them their "rights," and therefore had blatantly disobeyed the Simba code. They demanded an immediate tribunal to judge the guards' guilt. The frightened sergeant major agreed to their preposterous demand, and other Simbas who had drifted into the room, alerted by the shouting match, were all in favor of the trial.

The farcical tribunal began literally over their heads as argument, accusation, and counter-accusation were traded. First one and then another took the part of defense counsel, prosecution counsel, judge, and jury, and though it may have seemed ridiculous, its impact was terrifying to the cowering women. The three newcomers maintained that the other guards should be relieved of their duties; they, as loyal upholders of the Simba creed, should be granted responsibility for the prisoners.

Helen clung to Amy and prayed. There was nothing else to do, no other action of which she was capable. So often in those weeks of continuing suspense their lives had seemed to hang on a mood, a whim, a turn of argument, but this situation had reached the limits of human credibility.

Fortunately, the weight of the sergeant major's authority and argument carried conviction; the three loyal guards were given the right of appeal and dismissed to the adjoining room while the altercation continued. Suddenly the debate was interrupted. A strange wailing sound emerged from the next room. Was it tortured human being or animal? Was it human at all or some horrific creature out of the jungle? The sergeant major and his interrogators rushed for the door, and at the same moment the whine of sound was obliterated by roars of laughter.

One of the guards appeared. In his hands he carried a piano accordion. He pumped the bellows backwards and forwards, pantomiming broadly. The murdered Belgian owner could never have known such an appreciative audience; the guards all howled and capered around the player. The notion of rape had gone from their minds. A concert was the thing! Music to delight the heart! They all wanted to try out the instrument.

Helen and Amy, clasped in each other's arms, felt their facial muscles relax, their screwed-up eyes open, their giggles become compulsive as they dissolved into helpless laughter. Tears poured down their cheeks, the temporary relief from tension so overwhelming that their mirth bordered on hysteria. The Simbas happily carried their instrument outside into the night. These chuckling children had a new toy with which to play, and had forgotten the thirst to kill.

A little later their own loyal guards crept back into the

house and closed the door. The women huddled closer together under the blankets. The children slept easily and quietly; the women dozed and moved about fitfully.

None of them dreamed that the first light would lift the curtain on the last act in this bloody arena.

# CHAPTER 11

At 1:30 A.M. on December 31, 54 Commando, under Lieutenant Joe Wepener, left their headquarters at Paulis. Their objective: to rescue a group of white civilians thought to be held prisoner at Mungbere. They were also in radio communication with two Sikorsky helicopters which would rendezvous with them in Mungbere and land to help in any evacuation should that prove possible.

It was pitch dark. The headlights of the leading Ferret Scout car, followed by three armored jeeps and four big trucks, cut white swathes through the darkness. They had not been going for more than an hour when the lead truck, formerly United Nations property, broke down. Since speed and surprise were essential to their enterprise—they expected to encounter a well-defended machine-gun post a few miles farther on—they immediately abandoned the UN vehicle and transferred its ammunition and armament to the other vehicles.

Every vehicle was fully armed: fixed mountings for the Browning machine guns and Ericksons, plus a variety of weapons from captured Russian Kalashnikov AK 47 automatic rifles to Lee Enfields which had seen service since the First World War. A variety of young men manned the vehicles. They had been recruited mainly in South Africa and were an international crew: Rhodesians, British, Germans, Belgians, French, Australians, South Africans, New Zealanders, Poles, and Danes. Practically every man had army experience and had been recruited on a six-month contract at around fifteen pounds a day. They were to earn every penny in the Mungbere operation.

They had picked up one new and useful volunteer in Kurt Van Wilde, a Swiss planter rescued the day before in their foray into Wamba. He had been one of the few remaining prisoners in the convent and was able to tell them that most of the civilians had been evacuated to Mungbere. Since he knew both the road between Paulis and Mungbere and the surrounding district, he offered his services as guide. Lieutenant Wepener accepted his offer gratefully and drove with him in the leading scout car. He was also valuable for having introduced a most colorful tactic into their strategy. The flying column of jeeps and lorries were to operate without lights in the darkness, and for much of the journey would have to contend with dust swirling up from the wheels. In such conditions it was easy for one of the vehicles to lose sight of the car in front. Van Wilde owned a trumpet and made use of it. One blast meant that the leading scout car was proceeding straight ahead, two blasts that it was swinging right, three that the turn was to the left.

The pace slowed as they moved out onto the rough dirt road and headlights were switched off; there was no point in alerting the Simbas to the fact that an enemy convoy was penetrating the area. They had to cover the one hundred and twenty kilometers along a road held by one of the strongest Simba concentrations in Congo, and there were thousands of armed black warriors between them and their objective. The jungle on either side was dark and silent.

After driving for about an hour Van Wilde told them that the village where the first machine-gun post was sited lay about a mile from their present position.

"Okay," replied Joe Wepener. "We'll close to about three

hundred yards and then blast through with headlights blazing and all guns firing."

"They'll hear us before we get there."

"I like to think they'll believe it's a Simba convoy approaching."

"We shall wake them all up," said Van Wilde casually.

"Something like that."

Wepener was a tall, tough, laconic Rhodesian, one of the few mercenaries driven by a deep sense of mission. He believed that Congo in particular and Africa in general should not be allowed to fall under either Russian or Chinese domination. His thin lips and jutting chin, the steady eyes which seemed to look straight through you and out the other side, gave him an air of resolute dependability. He realized that everything was at stake.

During these Congo hostilities you killed or were killed. Prisoners on either side were inevitably tortured and then murdered. Simbas and National Congolese Army committed bestial atrocities against each other's forces as a normal concomitant of warfare.

Van Wilde reacted to some passing landmark. "The village is ahead now."

"Right," snapped Joe Wepener to his gunner. "Prepare to open fire."

The noise of their approach in low gear had obviously been heard by the Simba defense. As headlights were switched on, gears thrust into fast speed, and machine guns opened up, they were met by return fire from half a dozen positions in the village. The mercenaries roared into the village, wheels lifting and bumping over rutted surfaces, machine guns, rifles, and revolvers pouring broadsides from every position. They knocked the flimsy barricades of boxes high into the air and cannoned off ancient cars set up as roadblocks. Incendiary tracer shells sliced through the darkness in brilliant scarlet arcs, their speed and arcs beautiful to watch. They struck thatch, and fire broke out. Dark figures scurrying between the houses and across the road were suddenly silhouetted by flame and toppled to the ground as they were caught in the concentrated stream of bullets. Someone in the last truck was tossing out hand grenades, which burst in a series of spectacular orange-colored explosions.

A truck without lights lumbered down the road towards Wepener's Ferret car. Its windscreen disintegrated under a blast of bullets from Wepener's Browning, and slowly, like some enormous and surprised Neanderthal creature, it fell sideways into a ditch. Headlights were switched on and off to confuse defense. Horns blared; engines raced. Dust churned from spinning wheels, the loud chatter of machine guns was constant, and Van Wilde blew long single blasts on his trumpet. The action could not have lasted for more than two or three minutes, even though it felt like an hour to all the participants. Wepener's men roared on through the village, leaving destruction behind them and suffering no more than a few holes in each vehicle's superstructure. In the next few miles, as the first pale grayness began to filter into the sky, a few sporadic rifle shots were directed at them from the edges of the road. They replied with bursts from the Brownings, and usually there was no return fire.

At the next village, with darkness now steadily fading, Africans raced towards them shouting loudly, and Van Wilde translated their cries as "We are Simbas like you. Don't shoot."

Joe Wepener fired a short burst from the magazine of his Browning. The figures fell.

It was broad daylight now, and they were acutely vulnerable when they reached the outskirts of Mungbere. Like

Wamba, it is a small Belgian colonial settlement with wide earth streets, single-story bungalows, a few administrative buildings, and a line of wooden stores. It had probably been telephoned in from somewhere along their route that an attacking mercenary force was approaching, for the defenses appeared to be alert and shots were directed at them as they passed the first buildings. They charged down the main street returning the fire, swerving around corners, and blasting out windows, with Van Wilde trumpeting loudly to indicate changes of direction.

Any well-organized defense force faced with this vulnerable column of jeeps and lorries would have blown them apart within minutes. As it was, the noise and surprise of the attack scared the Simbas into immediate flight, and the column glimpsed them scuttling to safety through the gardens at the back of the bungalows. The resistance did not crumble completely, however, and the sound of bullets ricocheting off armor plate filled the air. Above the racket, Joe Wepener yelled, "Where the hell are these prisoners supposed to be?"

Van Wilde shouted back, "How do I know?"

"We can't go on driving around and around these streets under fire for ever."

"They're here somewhere."

"Well, we'd better find them quick."

They accelerated down another side street, and Wepener's driver shouted, "I saw a white face at a window back there, Lieutenant."

"Good," returned Wepener, directing a burst in the general direction of a tall building. "Get back. First right and right again."

Their circular route seemed to have cleared a complete section of Simba resistance. They braked to a halt outside a number of large bungalows set back on green lawns. The well-drilled mercenaries slid out of their vehicles, Brownings giving off regular bursts, and with machine pistols ready for action. As they got closer to the bungalows they raced forward to kick down doors. Within seconds they were embraced, hugged, kissed, and wept over by what seemed to be a whole convent full of crying, laughing, joyous nuns, mothers, and children.

When Jack Scholes and Brian Cripps were dispatched to Mungbere three days before Helen, their journey proved uneventful. Eighty male prisoners, priests and civilians of an assortment of nationalities, were locked into three bungalows; the women and children were imprisoned in other bungalows nearby. By this time, every Belgian or American male had been murdered.

The Simba command decision to concentrate its white civilian prisoners at the railhead of Mungbere was based on the fact that they could use this strategic post as a bargaining counter. They let it be known that they planned to take the hostages three hundred and fifty miles northeast to Aba, on the Sudan border, and then fly them to safety. Simba forces were running out of territory. The National Congolese Army with its supporting units of white mercenaries had already captured Paulis. The Simbas had shown at Stanleyville that they regarded the slaughter of civilians as a legitimate military stratagem; a concentration of whites at Mungbere presented similar intimidatory opportunities.

The priests and missionaries were outside the bungalow, sitting around on the lawn, when they first heard the firing. This gunfire sounded like automatic weapons, and it was accompanied by a repetitive trumpet blast.

"Better get back inside the house!" shouted Jack. But they could not get back inside the house. The Simba guards had suddenly become menacing. Rifles were leveled. Bolts snapped into breeches. Fingers curled around triggers. For three heartstopping seconds Brian was certain that this was going to be another Stanleyville: A single order by an officer would have started a fusillade which would have killed him and all his fellow prisoners. But it was seven o'clock in the morning, and there was only confusion among all ranks. Eventually they heard the orders, "Back into the house, everybody. All prisoners inside at once!"

Brian and Jack flattened themselves on the floor beneath the eighteen-inch windowsill. Above the huge window a burst of machine-gun bullets stitched a neat row of pockmarks in the concrete lintel but left the glass unharmed. A voice from one of the back rooms shouted, "The Simbas are running for their lives back into the forest." A few moments later they heard the noise of lorries and jeeps, and English voices shouting orders. The door was kicked open; young men in camouflage jackets and black berets poured through, and Lieutenant Joe Wepener stared down at them. He was abrupt and decisive. "Get moving," he snapped. "My orders are to get you back to Paulis at once. We shot our way through various Simba encampments on the way here. We'll have to do the same going back. So into the trucks—quick!"

They clustered around him. "The women and children?" someone called.

"They're all right. We're calling down our two Sikorsky helicopters onto the football pitch now. They'll take as many as possible. The rest in the trucks!"

"One of the priests is wounded—a bullet in the thigh."

"Right! Load him in the helicopter too."

It was Jack's turn to protest. "But my wife? All our Protestant women. They're held in a house at Betongwe. We can't leave without them. We can't."

Joe Wepener was at once alert. "How d'you know they're still there?"

"We had a truck come through from Wamba only yesterday afternoon. They must be still there."

Wepener glanced up at the huge Sikorsky helicopters overhead. The Simbas in Betongwe, he knew, would have heard the exchange of fire. In such situations they invariably killed their prisoners.

"We *must* try to save them," pleaded Jack. "There are other women and children with them too."

Joe Wepener frowned. "How many?"

"At least eight British. Probably half a dozen Belgian women and children."

"You're certain they're there?"

"Yes, people on the last truck which came through from Wamba saw them. They must be alive," said Jack. "They must be. After all this, they must be."

Joe Wepener stood his ground. "I've got strict orders to rescue all civilians in Mungbere and get straight back to Paulis. Those are my orders." He looked at Jack again. "British, you said? British?" That seemed to make a difference.

"Yes, British missionaries."

The Sikorsky helicopters coming in to land were now drowning the sporadic rattle of gunfire. Wepener turned to Van Wilde and asked, "Mr. Van Wilde, d'you know this Betongwe place?"

"Of course. I've lived in the district for years."

"How far?"

"At our speed, about an hour from here."

"Do we have to retrace our steps—come back this way to get back to Paulis?"

"No, but about twenty miles past Betongwe we can take a right fork and another road to Paulis."

Wepener turned back to Jack Scholes. "Okay. As soon as we've got everybody aboard, we'll try for the ladies."

Within an hour most of the women and children had been crammed into the Sikorsky helicopters, leaving eighty men and twenty-five women and children to be carried by the three trucks, which were incredibly overloaded. No luggage could be taken. The tailboards had to be let down to find room for the last few, and Brian and Jack Scholes hung on there.

Joe Wepener kept engines roaring and machine guns firing as they churned relentlessly forward, spraying patches of grass or jungle at the side of the road where Simbas might be lurking. He hoped, by so doing, to terrify the life out of them.

Ten miles from Mungbere they were waved to a halt by a group of pathetic Greeks, who stood at the roadside outside their store surrounded by enough suitcases, boxes, and bales to fill the three trucks twice over. They had heard the helicopters and prayed the rescuers would come their way.

"No luggage," ordered Wepener sternly. "Not a single suitcase. Just get aboard quickly."

The procession continued and Van Wilde said, "I pray to God we'll be in time."

Brian glanced at Jack's tense face. His prayers were concentrated on the same hope.

For Helen and the others, the night passed peacefully enough. As usual, daylight woke them, and they heard the guards quarreling among themselves again. It ended in a fight, blows being exchanged, and in a few minutes the women knew the worst. Their old guards had lost; the new contingent marched in to take over, and their aggressiveness presaged immediate danger. Suddenly, from somewhere high in the sky above the forest, they heard the sound of aircraft engines and wondered what could be going on. The Simbas went mad with rage. The women were pushed, pummeled, and kicked back into the big room. Doors and windows were slammed shut.

One of the new guards screamed at them.

"If the planes begin to bomb us, we'll kill you. If the bombs don't do it, then we shall. D'you understand? If necessary, we shall all die together, but you will die first."

Helen glanced around at the hunted-looking faces of the other twelve women and six children. Little Godeliefe sat huddled in her mother's arms, her eyes bleak. Helen knew that they were expendable. Their use as prisoners, as hostages or simply as women available for sex, had ended. Their only remaining value was as objects on which the Simbas could vent their hatred and barbarism.

They heard the distant sound of explosions in Mungbere —how were they to know that the mercenaries were blowing up Simba ammunition dumps? It sounded exactly like bombing, and enraged their guards. The door banged open. The sergeant major, as angry as the other Simbas now, headed this party. They struck out with rifle butts and boots and drove the women from the big room into the smaller one.

One of the guards, unable to fathom that the helicopters were following the Mungbere-Wamba road as a reliable geographical guideline, had decided that they must have been summoned by radio signal. Therefore, he concluded, one of the women must have a radio transmitting apparatus with her.

The new guard commander, the thick cords of his neck straining, screamed, "We know how you brought the planes here to bomb us! One of you has a radio which transmits signals. Who sent this signal? We demand to know, and she will be punished."

Daisy Kingdon spoke up. "It's ridiculous to think—" she began, but was unable to complete her protest because the nearest guard lifted his rifle butt and smashed it down against her head. Blood streamed from the wound. The act of violence triggered off another vicious wave of hysterical anger against all the women and children. They were attacked indiscriminately. If you talked you were struck; if you kept silent you were hit just the same. And above the angry shouts the guard commander's hysterical voice continued: "Where is the radio transmitter? Who has the instrument? We shall find it, understand that. You will be searched."

Helen shouted, "We've been searched before, dozens of times. Our clothes, baggage, everything. We've nothing to hide."

"You're lying. We know you're lying. You will be searched in couples. Everyone will be searched." He prodded two terrified Belgian women. "You two first." The weeping women were jostled back into the big room and ordered to point out their baggage. It was torn open, the contents scattered. Then their clothes were torn off in this ludicrous excuse of a further search. Practically naked, the two Belgians were prodded back into the inner room. The next two women were selected. To move, speak, or make any gesture now invited a torrent of abuse and a series of vicious blows. Daisy Kingdon sat bowed, her hands clasped over her head, blood welling between her fingers.

Helen sensed rather than saw Stebby's sudden terrible apprehension.

"Stebby, what's the matter?" she whispered.

"My hearing aid," mumbled Stebby in confused agony. "My hearing aid."

"What about it?"

"It's in my suitcase, here." With a slight nod of her head, she indicated her feet.

"But?"

"They'll think it's a radio transmitter."

"Oh Stebby!" She realized that Stebby was right. It would make no difference to these men if they explained that the device had been shown to the commandant at Wamba, who understood what it was.

"I'll take it in and show it to them," Stebby whispered bravely. "I'll try and explain, convince them what it really is . . ."

Helen nodded hesitantly. It was the only sensible thing to do. If the rebels found it when they searched her baggage, all the women might be killed. If Stebby owned up, then they might have a chance.

She watched Stebby fumble in the small suitcase and produce the small, boxlike amplifier with its length of wire and earpiece. As she went towards the door, the second pair of Belgian women who had been searched were pushed back through the door past her, clutching the torn remnants of their clothing and weeping hysterically. The guard shouted at her angrily. Then he saw what she was holding, and he shouted excitedly to his comrades.

Helen heard the triumphant screech of anger as soon as they saw what Stebby carried in her hand. They struck her across the face repeatedly; the hearing aid was snatched from her.

So this was the apparatus she had used to signal the enemy planes! Right, she would be executed. The others who were obviously part of the plot would also be executed. The guard commander struck her across the head and face again and again.

"You will go before a firing squad, but first you'll confess. How did you signal the National Army with this machine?"

"I didn't signal," cried Stebby. "It's for my deafness. It's a medical device."

"You're a liar. We shall shoot you. But there are worse things for you before that happens. Explain how you signal with this machine."

Now the entire house was full of maddened Simbas, shouting and attacking in a frenzy of violence. They pushed and kicked the women and tore their clothes. The news excited them: The Protestant women had signaled the enemy planes. They were going to be executed. A blood lust that was almost tangible filled the air.

Children huddled against their mothers, crying. The women clung together. Stebby was jerked to her feet, to be led off the veranda to be shot. Then she was pushed down again. A quick death was too good for such a crime. The scene was lunatic, full of noise, confusion, and violence. It seemed plain now to Helen that their prayers had gone unanswered. This was the end God had obviously chosen for them. They must face this with whatever reserves of courage they could find. But how difficult it was. Terror caught at the heart, stopped the breath.

Then another sound! In the distance, a strange staccato stuttering . . . a rhythmic, spine-prickling tattoo that seemed to freeze the screams and threats.

Somebody gasped. "A machine gun! It's a machine gun." The guards' reactions were maniacal. Those being searched and interrogated in the big room were driven back into the smaller one with curses and blows. But this was their last stand. The Simbas were frightened. Now self-preservation took over. They fled in panic, falling over one another to leave the house.

Abandoned and bewildered, the women could hear the gunfire getting closer. In their inner room there was only one small window, set high up in the wall. But the walls were made of thin matchboarding. Bullets would slice through as if they were muslin. "Down on the floor," shouted Helen. "Quick! Down on the floor." A volley of bullets—one long burst from a machine gun—might kill them all.

The noise outside was chaotic: Simbas yelling contradictory orders, running feet, rifles firing. And droning closer all the time the sound of powerful engines.

Helen's mind was confused. Lorry engines? Jeep engines? Surely it couldn't—at long last—be the sound of their rescuers? It was not possible. No, it couldn't be possible . . . yet why else would the Simbas run for their lives? But even if that were the case, the rescuers *wouldn't know* they were here. They would think this was only a Simba roadblock. This inconspicuous bungalow near the roadside would mean nothing to them.

They would hurtle past, and as soon as they were gone the Simbas would be back to murder them all. Helen was hysterical with frustration.

"They'll miss us," she screamed. "They won't know we're here." She leaped for the window, but it was too high for her and she couldn't see out.

"Amy," she cried desperately. "Lift me. Lift me. Oh, lift me so they can see a white face. Quick, quick!"

Amy scrambled to her feet. She grabbed Helen around the waist, trying to push her up. Desperately Helen grabbed at the windowsill and tried to push her face against the glass. Her spectacles fell off. She could feel the glass, but she couldn't get high enough to see through it. Oh God, somehow they had to see a white face!

Then they heard the noise of heavy boots outside. Their door was kicked in—by white men.

Helen slid down from Amy's hands and slumped to a sitting position on the edge of a chair. This was beyond belief. It couldn't be rescue. Not at this last minute . . . it couldn't happen that way. She felt the tears running down her face. She was aware of the screaming, crying, and laughing of women and children around her, celebrating their joy and relief. Helen was weeping as if her heart would break. The relief was as unbearable as the agony.

Through blurred eyes she saw the young soldiers throwing their shirts so that some of the Belgian girls could cover their nakedness. One of the young soldiers put his hand on Helen's shoulder. He said, "We're glad, miss. We really are so glad. You're the first British women we've managed to save. We've always found the English girls murdered. Sometimes we've been only a few minutes—seconds almost—too late. We're so glad."

Helen had never seen a mercenary before. The word had previously had a distasteful connotation for her, but it never would again. In the future, whenever she heard the word "mercenary" she would remember Joe Wepener and his twenty-four brave soldiers who came to their rescue.

Wepener gave orders, and his words started her moving. "Ladies, you can't take any luggage. You can't take anything."

"Not even a briefcase?" somebody asked.

"Yes, a briefcase, okay, but no luggage. We haven't got room and we must hurry."

Helen went out into the sunlight. Little Godeliefe was walking back towards the house, crying bitterly, and Helen stopped to pick her up.

"Godeliefe? What's the matter? We're rescued. We're all going home."

"Daddy's not in the trucks. Mummy's been to look for him, but he's not there."

Helen's feeling of euphoria was instantly dispelled. This moment of such happiness was shattered by a bitter note of truth. Of course there were no daddies for any of the Belgian children; they had been murdered long ago. Everyone had known, of course, but Helen had forgotten that the

Belgian girls had refused to accept it. Now they had to acknowledge this finality and surmount that most agonizing heartache of the human condition: grief. Helen embraced the despairing child, weeping with her and trying to comfort her.

"There, darling, there. It'll be all right. You're going home. It'll be all right."

She knew it wouldn't be all right. But what else could she say?

Godeliefe's mother, a lonely, inconsolable figure, was standing next to one of the trucks, her forehead pressed against the wooden side, weeping with bitter and silent intensity. She had endured all those endless terrible nights at the Wamba hotel supported by one flimsy hope. She had felt that she could endure almost anything if that grain of hope was real. They had promised they would let her husband stay alive, they would not murder him; if she allowed them to use her body, they would save him. The Simbas would have raped her anyway, but that promise had made her more compliant.

Helen hurried towards the trucks, carrying Godeliefe in her arms. Everywhere people were crying. Jack Scholes had leaped down from the lorry to gather Jessie into his arms. The two "gray hairs" who had done so much to help Helen in all her troubles wept unashamedly together. Joe Wepener started everyone moving.

"We must get back to Paulis before nightfall," he insisted. "It's a hundred miles. We must get back before it's dark. All aboard, please. Quickly!"

A mercenary helped Helen to hand little Godeliefe back into the interior of one of the trucks. She climbed up after and found a place on Brian's knees. He grinned and said, "Hallo, Helen."

She felt lightheaded. The physical sensation of relief was

still inside her. It was so good to feel the lorry move off, so wonderful to be among friends. She could not feel safe yet; at that moment she doubted that she would ever feel safe again. But to be moving away from that dreadful bungalow and those terrible memories made her feel that she was starting life anew.

The armored jeeps raced ahead of the convoy, their wheels churning up the red dust. It covered their faces and clothes. The leading jeeps kept up a constant pattern of firing. A two- or three-second burst was aimed into any patch of jungle which might provide cover for an ambush. They met no resistance, however, and drove into Paulis at six o'clock, just before dark. The little town Helen remembered as a gay and bustling place was deserted, its very silence sinister and sad. The streets were empty; windows were smashed or boarded up. The war had left Paulis a ghost town.

The mercenaries had set up their headquarters in the modern brewery, and the convoy stopped here to unload Helen and six other women. The building was crowded with a number of young and high-spirited soldiers, who reacted to the sight of female missionaries in various stages of undress with a chorus of wolf whistles. Steely-eyed Joe Wepener, who knew the emotional state of his charges, would have none of this. He halted the procession. With arms folded across his chest, he turned to glare at his younger subordinates. There was immediate silence, an embarrassed shuffling of feet, a few hesitant coughs. The procession moved on inside without further comment.

A warm-hearted friendship grew swiftly between Helen, her colleagues, and the young mercenaries. Their main task had been to stiffen and bolster the morale of the National Congolese Army, but during the past few weeks this duty had basically been accomplished. Their function had altered and they had recently taken on the role of a rescue force. And this in itself had worked a philosophical change in the men.

They had joined for any number of reasons: They were young and wanted adventure, they needed the money, they were tired of their life at home, they thought that the experience of danger and violence set against the background of tropical Congo might provide them with the material to write a best-seller. Few of their motives had had anything to do with philosophical or Christian values, though some probably had thoughts of "saving civilization in Africa." Basically, however, they were just mercenaries. Their work as a rescue force, saving many self-less people who had labored for a lifetime under the hot Congo sun, had given them a new and unexpected experience. The twenty-five of them had fought thousands of armed Simba warriors to save the lives of people they did not know, and this deed had given their whole profession dignity and purpose. Helen later wrote in her diary, "They were deeply touched by our gratefulness and also by our obvious overflowing joy . . . our hearts are too full for words."

That night they all collected in the great brewery hall at a long table formed by pushing a series of trestle tables together. Soldiers and missionaries sat down to a simple meal and joined in a community thanksgiving, which was very moving. They had come through the fire. They had survived, and they gave thanks. The soldiers sang their songs, suitably bowdlerized for the occasion. A New Zealander performed a Maori war dance. Helen and the others sang the doxology. The hostages spent the next morning scrubbing their clothes and bathing. As Helen blithely admitted: "Some of us hadn't really washed for weeks, and I have an idea we must have smelled and looked like it."

Just before dashing toward the entrance to the huge,

open-ended C.130 U.S. transport plane, Helen posed for a picture with Lieutenant Joe Wepener. As she went off, he stood on the tarmac waving. Many months later, Helen heard that he had been killed only a few weeks after this leave-taking.

The plane roared through the night to Leopoldville. The American ambassador and a group of missionaries stationed there met them at the airport. It was New Year's Eve, and there were only two newspapermen to meet them: a man from Reuters and another from the *Daily Telegraph*. Both were kind and considerate. For the first time, Helen and the others heard of the murders of many of their close friends and colleagues, and they wept together.

The next day they flew on to Amsterdam and then to London, but they still could not really orientate themselves. Helen was silent: She simply could not forget or diminish her overwhelming sense of fear. It had grown inside her like a cancer; it lurked in the recesses of her mind; it stayed on the periphery of sight like some dreadful apparition, always there, never tangible. Oh yes, she opened her mouth and words came out; she moved her lips and formed laughter; she was even ready with clever comments for the newspapers. When a reporter asked Helen if she would ever go back to Congo, she laughed and answered glibly, "When you've just escaped from the lion's cage at dinnertime, you don't go back to offer yourself as dessert."

But inside, she was frozen up. Perhaps a spring thaw would come eventually and bring back sanity and awareness into her life, but she could not believe this. When she arrived at her mother's home, she did not cry. She was quite controlled and just wanted to sleep. With a certain dry academic detachment, she wrote in an epilogue to a slender published edition of letters she had sent to her mother, "The situation in Congo is so disturbed and fraught with danger from inside and outside, that it is almost impossible to predict at all what the future may hold."

Many other people felt the same way. A team of *Reader's Digest* editors doing a story on the Congo disaster reached the conclusion that "the Europeans won't go back for a long time, if ever."

Helen agreed with that sentiment. She was never going back. Nothing in the whole wide world would ever make her go back.

For Lady Roseveare, her mother, Helen's reappearance was little short of a miracle. She not only loved her eldest daughter very dearly but also admired her. She had read weeks previously the report of Helen's death: a picture on the front page of a newspaper and the headline "Doctor Killed in Ibambi." Lady Roseveare, unaware that another physician, Dr. Swertz, had been the victim, had prayed silently and tried to keep a tiny flicker of hope alive in her mind. The local minister had visited her and said that he supposed they should hold a memorial service for Helen, but he was uneasy about the whole matter. Perhaps they should wait and hope for the best.

On December 31, she received an invitation to a New Year's Eve party from a close friend, but declined it because she knew she could make no pretense of enjoying herself at a time like this. Later that evening an acquaintance rang her to tell her that the BBC had reported the rescue of a group of missionaries from the northeastern province of Congo.

Lady Roseveare's sister, who had been a missionary in China for twenty years, was staying with her over the holidays, and both of them waited up anxiously for the BBC's late-night news. They were joyful as they listened to the announcer read a list of names of missionary survivors, all of whom were colleagues of Helen's: Jack and Jessie

Scholes, Florence Stebbing, Amy Grant, Elaine de Rusett, Brian Cripps . . . eight names in all. Then the announcer stopped. But where was Helen's name? He must have made a mistake and left her out. He'd correct himself at once, say, "And Dr. Helen Roseveare." Instead, he paused and, turning to a different subject, went on reading the news.

The two sisters sat silently in their living room. They did not speak. They were old and wise enough not to buoy themselves up with vain hopes any longer; the headline about the doctor killed in Ibambi must have referred to Helen after all. It was certain that if she was not with this final group of personal friends, then she must be lost. At last Lady Roseveare said quietly, "I think I'll go to bed."

As she climbed the stairs, the bells of thousands of suburban Victorian churches and the ancient chimes of many more hundreds of tiny village churches throughout the English shires began to peal out the message that it was midnight. Nineteen sixty-five had arrived, and the bells proclaimed good will to all men; God was in His Heaven, all was well with the world. Lady Roseveare lay back against the pillow and stared into the darkness. Helen, her first-born daughter, was dead. She had to live with that fact; she had to bear it. When the sudden ringing of the telephone beside her bed startled her, she wondered how she could possibly answer some kind friend's greeting at this moment. Hesitantly she lifted the receiver and managed a muffled "Hallo."

A voice from the other end of the world said: "Lady Roseveare? This is Leopoldville. We have news for you."

She couldn't answer. What was there to say?

"This is the *Daily Telegraph* representative. We have good news. Your daughter Helen is alive and well. She will fly home tomorrow."

Lady Roseveare began to cry. She was so overcome that

she replaced the receiver in its cradle without even thanking the man for his kind thoughtfulness. There were tears on her cheeks as she slipped out of bed and hurried along to her sister's bedroom. She knew from her sister's look that she expected the phone call had been a confirmation of the very worst. Lady Roseveare was barely able to get out the words "She's safe, she's safe."

Two elderly ladies on New Year's Eve, 1964, sat side by side on a bed weeping as if their world had come to an end, when actually it had just started again. Then they dried their eyes, and Lady Roseveare said she just couldn't keep this news to herself; she was going to ring up her friend who was giving the party, because she was bound to be up.

A male voice backed by the sound of a very jolly party answered the phone. Lady Roseveare, suddenly a little confused and nervous, said, "Oh, I wonder if you'd mind passing a message to your hostess saying that Helen is safe."

The man paused as if taking in the news and then burst out: "Why, that's marvelous. That's great!" She heard him shout into another room, "Listen, everybody. Helen's safe. Helen Roseveare's safe."

Lady Roseveare heard the sudden cheers, the marvelous clamor of people at a gathering who loved her daughter and whose hearts had lifted at the news. And she didn't even think to wonder—while tears were pouring down her cheeks—when she had ever been so happy.

PART FIVE 🌿

# CHAPTER 12

Palm Sunday morning a week before Easter, and the tiny stone-built Cornish church was crowded. Bunches of yellow daffodils filled the vases near the altar; pale spring sunlight filtered through the thin Gothic windows. In the deep lanes which led to the church, primroses blossomed along the sheltered banks, and the dark blue sea stretched below the lanes and out to the horizon, restless and flecked with foam.

To Helen, the voices of the children in the front rows, trilling clearly with such beautiful innocence, were very moving. They were upsetting in a way, too, for they sang the same hymns that the children would be singing back in the church at Nebobongo. She was hardly aware of the first tear to run down her cheek and splash on her prayer book. She looked at it with some surprise, never guessing that this was the breakdown point, the release of all her pent-up emotion. Suddenly tears were flowing, and her sobs must have been audible to everyone, especially to her mother, standing next to her in the pew. She tried to stop, tried to control herself, but every time a hymn started she was off again. The entire service seemed designed to churn up her emotions; it brought back so many memories. The vicar brought all the children seated in the front rows into the service; he made them aware of their part in the ancient, loving Christian ritual. A small girl shyly read a story about Christ's entry into Jerusalem on a donkey. The vicar took up this theme, extending the thought and saying that all of them should be creatures willing to be led by the Lord. And Helen wept openly and eventually unashamedly through it all. No matter how she tried to staunch the tears, they kept coming. She wept in the car driving back through the lanes to the cottage; she wept as she prepared lunch; she went on crying for the next two days, and her wise mother did not interfere. Helen had no idea why her bottled-up emotion should come to the surface at this particular time so long after all danger was pàst. Perhaps it had something to do with the fact that she was never going back to Congo; she had to consider a new sort of life, for she had made up her mind what she was going to do in the future: probably a three-year training course, another degree, perhaps; then some sort of post at a university if she was lucky.

She found that she was a very popular speaker during the next three months. She traveled all over the country and often spoke twice a day. That August she went to a youth camp near Anglesey run by the British leader of WEC, Len Moules, a man she much admired. She did not care much for camps, and felt depressed as she forced herself to talk to dozens of noisy, unruly girls. No news of Ibambi or Nebobongo had reached Helen or the Scholes since they left, though the newspapers gave daily reports of fighting and general unrest.

When Helen found a letter in her tent bearing a Congo stamp and addressed in John Mangadima's handwriting, she tore it open eagerly. The first miraculous news was that Ibambi and Nebobongo had been liberated by mercenaries only a week before John had written this letter, and they were free. John was filled with joy to learn that she and all the others were still alive. He had heard—and later reports had confirmed—that they had been murdered. Then the mercenaries had brought him the stupendous news that they

were safe. He was so overwhelmed that he found it hard
even to think of the words to write. They had no stationery
or pencils at Nebobongo, but a mercenary soldier had given
him this piece of paper he wrote on, with a pencil and an
envelope, and had promised to post the letter for him.

It was very important, he wrote, that Helen know that
as a Congolese he was ashamed that countrymen of his
could act in such a manner. He apologized for all the
dreadful things she had gone through in Congo. She had
given herself entirely and unselfishly to his people—given
all her love and affection, all her skills, all her hard work—
only to be repaid by violence and imprisonment. He hoped
that she would find it in her heart to forgive him personally
and Congo in general. He knew she would never return
after such treatment—there was no point in even mention-
ing the subject—but would she try to remember that many
people there still loved her? Things were very bad at Nebo.
They had nothing left: no food, clothes, money, utensils,
drugs, or medicines. It was, he supposed, like Congo before
the first missionaries arrived. They would have to start again
from the beginning. But with God's help they would perse-
vere and succeed.

There was no self-pity in his words, only a deep affection and understanding. Helen carefully folded the letter
and returned it to its envelope. It had been raining, and
she squelched across the muddy grass to the tent occupied
by Len Moules. He had been a pioneer missionary on the
Tibetan border; his film about that experience, entitled
Three Miles High, had thrilled Helen in her university days
and had turned her spirit towards WEC. She pushed back
the flap, walked in, and asked quietly, "Have you got the
group arranged yet for the return to Congo?"

Len Moules, tall, good-humored, and graying, looked up
from the table where he was writing. His face creased into

a smile. He began to laugh. When Helen was silent and he saw the look on her face, he stopped. "Sorry. I thought it was a joke!"

"No joke," she said firmly.

He rose from the table and pushed forward another chair so she could sit down. "Helen," he said. "You had a very hard time. D'you know what you're saying?"

"Yes. I want to go back to Congo."

Len sat down again and tapped the table with his pencil. "There's still fighting in the northeast province. The Simbas still hold huge territories there. The mercenaries and National Congolese Army are having a rough time."

"I know."

"Winnie Davies is still held by the Simbas. We haven't given up hope for her, but . . ." He raised his eyes and shrugged his shoulders.

"I know," Helen repeated.

Len Moules stared at her solemnly. He knew Helen well enough.

"All right," he said after a pause. "I know Jack Scholes has something similar in his mind. I'll write to him."

The return letter told him that Jack and Jessie Scholes also wanted to go home. Their lives, their hopes, their work, their dreams—even the place where they would eventually die—waited in that clearing in the tropical rain forest for their return. They were too young to retire but too old to change now. They knew that missionary work in northeast Congo was back at its beginnings, but they wished to help in that second beginning. There were no teachers or doctors. They *had* to go back, and they agreed with Len's suggestion that Helen return, if not with them, then as soon as possible afterwards. Jack Scholes and Frank Cripps would go out first and push up through military-occupied territory to see if they could reach Nebo and Ibambi; they would cable back as soon as it was possible for Helen and the two wives to join them.

Jack and Frank flew to Leopoldville in January and began to hitchhike their way north in army planes and convoys. Their letters described the misery and destruction. They reiterated that when the women came out they must bring everything with them: food, clothes, supplies, medicines. The shops were empty; there was nothing left. And eventually the final letter arrived: Although there were large areas where fighting was still going on, they had obtained the necessary permits for the three women to enter Congo.

Helen realized that, for better or worse, the rebellion had altered her; she had changed physically, mentally, philosophically, and spiritually, and she expected everyone else who had been through that rebellion to have changed also. They had not.

She tried to define her new feelings in the lectures she delivered during the months when they were waiting for Jack and Frank to give them the all-clear. The first period of her life in Congo, she felt, had coincided with the end of the colonial era, in which the Europeans had treated the Congolese as small children. Independence had ushered in adolescence. Now she would be returning to a situation where an adult friendship would exist between black and white. The blacks would need the financial, teaching, training, and intellectual skills of the whites, but they would work as partners, side by side. When she arrived back in Congo, of course, she realized that her theory had been far too oversimplified. Life was never as straightforward as that. Friction and frustration, disappointment and heartache were the norm in this world, far more common than the joys of friendship, understanding, tolerance, and love.

In March—fifteen months after leaving—Helen arrived back on the Ugandan border of Congo. Jessie Scholes and

Mrs. Cripps were her passengers in her brand-new Land-Rover, bought by subscriptions from a thousand well-wishers. Helen drove with a self-satisfied feeling of having, at last, a vehicle to do the job she required of it. With a trailer hitched to the Land-Rover, she began the long climb from the level of the Nile up the steep escarpment which separates Uganda from Congo.

On a particularly bad stretch of road with no room for two vehicles to pass, they met a descending bus. The bus driver shouted impolitely at Helen, instructing her to reverse. In barbed Swahili she pointed out she had never in her life reversed a Land-Rover hauling a trailer and she did not intend to risk her precious vehicle. She had not brought her beautiful Land-Rover all the way from England to lose both it and herself over a precipice. The argument reached boiling point. Her Swahili was as good if not better than the bus driver's, her shrug of the shoulders equally disdainful. The tactic of their exchange was to be offensive without actually becoming crude. Mrs. Cripps and Mrs. Scholes got out and pretended to admire the scenery. All the passengers in the bus got out and listened, totally enthralled, to the slanging match. Helen put her hands on her hips and reiterated her position. She would, if necessary, stay put for the rest of the week; she would not reverse her Land-Rover and trailer one inch down the mountainside.

Her dramatic if slightly un-Christian confrontation won the argument. The bus driver reversed. They continued and reached the point in the escarpment at the Congolese border where customs officers stopped them. Soldiers looked them over suspiciously. The customs officers were away getting drunk and had to be fetched. Everyone was surly and unhelpful, but they were allowed through. Helen engaged the gear lever and accelerated away, realizing that her throat was dry, her nerves on edge. Those soldiers! That roadblock! Simba roadblocks had been exactly the same. Here she was imagining things were going to be different, and now she had to accept the fact that nothing had changed. With a terrible, sinking feeling, she understood that she had probably made the biggest mistake in her life by even *thinking* she could come back to Congo.

They spent the night at the mission station at Rethi. Jack Scholes and Frank Cripps were there to meet them. It lay eight thousand feet up in wide, sprawling grasslands. That night the stars were high and clear and it was cold enough for a fire. Helen slept fitfully and was tormented by nightmares. Tall, spear-carrying African watchmen patrolled in the darkness; the cadence of the wind in the eaves was sometimes a soft whistle and occasionally a shriek. Helen tossed and turned; she talked in her sleep and screamed aloud as she relived the rebellion. How did she begin to tell all of them that it was no good . . . she could not go through with it? The terrible fear had seeped into the marrow of her bones; she was like a shell-shock victim, and this return to the battlefield was unendurable.

Next day, in the pouring rain, with windscreen wipers that didn't work, they reached Nyankunde, a place which was then only a comparatively small mission station. Helen tried to be polite to everyone, and tried to push away into the dark of her subconscious the awful realization that she wasn't going to be able to cope any more.

The following day, the rain was still driving down. They toiled up a steep hill over a track cut into deep gullies by the pouring torrents. Helen had to make instant decisions as to where to direct the wheels to maintain momentum. Suddenly, the trailer dropped into a gully, skidded out again, slid sideways, jackknifed, and jammed across the road.

Fortunately, the leading vehicle had been stopped by a

roadblock at the top of the hill. The women yelled for assistance, and Frank Cripps and a group of Congolese soldiers came down to get them moving again. Back on the road and pointing in the right direction, Helen felt a little better, but the endless roadblocks—about one every thirty miles—revived all her old fears. The situation was frightening to Helen: The soldiers were invariably drunk, they were rude, and she was never quite certain which one was going to hit her. She was positive now that she was not going to be able to stick it out. The farther she got into Congo, the more she wanted to leave. She had not realized she was quite so mentally unprepared, and was bewildered by the extent of her unpreparedness.

After another night's journey, they drove along the straight, red-gravel road between palms which led to Ibambi. By a strange coincidence, it was Palm Sunday morning, just a year since she had wept through that service in the tiny Cornish church.

The noise of their arrival came through the open windows of the great brick church, where a congregation of three thousand were singing a hymn. The congregation came pouring out: There was a great stream of people laughing, crying, singing, and clapping. Helen, Jessie, and Mrs. Cripps were hugged, kissed, and swept back into the church in a wave of enormous emotional exaltation. The patients in the leprosy camp heard the news and came carrying flowers, and bowls of eggs and fruit. The depths of its emotionalism, the ecstasy of reunion, were unbelievable. They sang and they sang and they sang in joyful cadences of harmony. After her initial emotionalism had subsided a bit, Helen became aware of things she had not observed at first. Before the rebellion the congregation had all owned clothes; now all they wore were a few rags and cloth made from beaten tree bark. They sang the hymns by heart because they had no hymn books. They were older, they were scarred, and she could see the suffering in their faces. And they were so poor. Of course, they had always been poor, but now things were indescribably worse.

One thing, however, was just the same. As they sang the hymns over and over again with soaring voices, they were uplifted; whatever the rebels had taken from them—and they had stolen or destroyed practically everything these people possessed—they had not taken their faith.

At Nebobongo a thinner, older, but equally overjoyed John Mangadima clasped her in his arms. He explained how the Simbas had occupied Nebobongo, using it as a military center. He explained with pride how he had saved the drugs. "I divided them up into ten parcels, each containing aspirins, antibiotics, anti-malarials. Then, one at a time, I called in each male nurse and said, 'Take this parcel away and hide it in the forest where no one can find it. Don't tell anybody. But when I ask, you must bring it back.' "

"And it worked?"

"The Simbas never got a thing."

Helen realized that there *had* been a doctor at Nebobongo during the year and a half she had been away. John had replaced her.

The village was badly damaged: There were bullet holes in roofs, walls, and doors. Her own house had also suffered, but attempts had been made to repair the damage; one wall had been completely rebuilt, and even though the office, bedroom, and bathroom were stripped, one place had been restored in preparation for Helen's arrival. The women made a great fuss, giggling delightedly, as they turned the key of the guest room. Within stood a bed with an interior-sprung mattress neatly spread with sheets and blankets; there were curtains at the window, a jam jar of flowers on the table. Impoverished though they were, they had managed this for her!

That night she lay in her bed and looked up at the ceiling. She was thrilled by their welcome; boundlessly touched by their joy at her return. But the inner doubt still remained. Was she a fool to come back? Could she summon enough strength to continue? Anxiety oppressed her. If she was to be honest with herself, she knew she would not be able to stand it.

There were at once so many things to assess, repair and restart—and to forget. First of all, Helen had to look at her own capabilities; to admit to *herself* that the rebellion had altered her. Reluctantly she accepted that working eighteen hours a day was too much; she would have to settle for sixteen.

As usual, the problems at Nebobongo were never-ending. Where and how did she start? Nobody had any money; she was faced with a refugee problem, a housing problem, a clothing problem, a feeding problem. In the primary school the teachers hadn't even a blackboard, a piece of chalk, a sheet of paper, or a pencil. Her heart was torn in a dozen different ways. Whom did she help first?

But her main consideration was survival: How to stay in Congo? Her internal conflict of indecision might only be a needless expenditure of emotional energy: The authorities might throw her out anyway! All five missionaries had come in on visitors' visas, which allowed three months' residence; the days were running out quickly. When Helen journeyed to Paulis to make inquiries about new passports, the authorities were totally unsympathetic. They made it clear that whites were not welcome. Without whites there would have been no rebellion, would there? Why, therefore, had they chosen to come back?

Helen did not bother to point out that the Belgian colonial regime had been ousted some four years before, and *they* had been the hated whites in question. The recent rebellion had concerned a black, so-called People's Liberation Army fighting a legally constituted black republican government. Obviously, nothing could be accomplished here in town. Permits were needed for nearly every activity: road permits, identification permits. Each form was to be approved and stamped by at least three government departments. When she went to Leopoldville on another attempt to get their passports renewed and to talk about having her medical school recognized by the government, she made her feelings quite clear.

"You don't know what's been happening up in our northeastern province. You've had it all right down here in the seat of government, no great battles, no scorched earth; you've been comparatively comfortable. And now you're making all sorts of unreasonable laws. It's no use telling us that children over the age of fourteen can't go to secondary schools, because where I come from all the children over the age of fourteen are dead. They were collected by the Simbas in lorry loads and taken off to the battle front near Bunia, where the National Congolese Army mowed them down with machine-gun fire."

But she could not really find the correct government department to complain to. She could only walk from office to office for hour after hour and wait in queues and end up talking to some bored and indifferent civil servant. She did manage to get her own passport extended; the other four had to go in person before theirs could be issued. She also managed to get five tons of goods: blankets and food, pencils and paper, clothes and utensils to distribute back at Ibambi and Nebo.

Long before independence, Helen's fundamental objective had been government accreditation of her medical school. This would give her the right to train students, to set examinations, and to issue diplomas with which they could get jobs in government hospitals or in any branch of medical work. She had had no idea of the years of trial which lay ahead when she began her work, inspired by the appearance of John Mangadima.

She remembered a certain traumatic day back in 1963. She was busy cleaning the carburetor of her car and hardly noticed a second car draw up alongside. She did, however, recognize one of the three white men getting out of it as Dr. DeGott, the local government doctor at Paulis. Wiping her oily hands on a bit of rag, she walked across for him to introduce her to the others.

"This is Dr. Trieste, a government doctor from Leopoldville, and this is Mr. Jenkins from the World Health Organization," he said.

Helen shook hands and invited them into the house. All the time a nagging little worry disturbed her. What did they want? Surely this couldn't be the crucial inspection that would decide whether accreditation was to be granted? No, it wasn't possible. After all, she'd been waiting nine years for the important event, and they were bound to give her notice about such a matter.

Dr. DeGott glanced at his watch. "We haven't got much time if we're going to inspect the entire hospital," he announced, thereby shattering her equanimity.

Helen passed her hand across her brow.

"Inspect the entire hospital? Oh yes," she said. The idea was preposterous, the time inconvenient, and the outcome too hideous to envisage. This was undoubtedly the government group that would decide on her qualification and right to run a medical training school and who would either recommend her or destroy any hope she had of recognition. But why had they not warned her they were coming? She had been waiting so long for this visit. She did not know how to react. Should she protest and say this went beyond a joke, that really it wasn't very gentlemanly not to have given notice? (It was not until the next day that the telegram they had dispatched a week earlier arrived; they had thought she was quite prepared for their visit.)

She said instead, "But of course there's time for coffee."

Helen knew that somehow she had to delay them. Half an hour would undoubtedly do it, but twenty minutes were an absolute necessity.

"You must have coffee," she insisted again. "It won't take a second."

Dr. DeGott was philosophical. "All right then, as long as it's quick, but remember, we have to make several other calls."

Benjamin, her houseboy, was already at the door awaiting instructions. "Coffee, Benjamin, please," said Helen in a voice she hardly recognized. Then as he turned to leave she followed him for a few steps. "Tell John Mangadima at once," she ordered. "At once! Tell him Plan X. Plan X."

Benjamin stared at her with wide, uncomprehending eyes, then nodded. He was used to his mistress's customary madness.

Five minutes later she poured the coffee with a hand she hoped was not trembling visibly and began asking a series of ridiculous delaying questions.

"How was the weather in Leopoldville? Were the plane services between the capital and Paulis functioning all right? Now that independence has brought Congolese government supervision to all medical services, do you gentlemen think they can train sufficient staff?"

She prattled on, each time-wasted minute passing like an hour, her guests becoming increasingly impatient.

"We're really only allowed one hour for the inspection," said Dr. DeGott. "I really do think we ought to be starting."

"You've plenty of time," insisted Helen, busily refilling another coffee cup. "After all, the school's only fifty yards from here. Another biscuit, Dr. Trieste?"

But Dr. Trieste was already on his feet. "Thank you very

much, Dr. Roseveare, but no. I agree with Dr. DeGott, we must start the inspection at once."

Helen plodded across the hospital compound, her heart pounding, the gravel crunching beneath her feet. Slowly they passed through the women's ward, the men's ward, the office, the outpatients, the operating theater.

The beds were superb, their bedspreads spotless. Every patient was either lying in bed or sitting up, neatly tucked-in, washed, combed, immaculate. None was limping about, smoking, or sprawled on another's bed as was usually the case. All had up-to-date charts hanging at the foot of their beds. Every nurse or student nurse wore his very best uniform; John Mangadima in his white overall coat and trousers would have done credit to the Mayo Clinic.

Helen's heart was full. She had never seen a hospital like it. She had certainly never seen *her* hospital like it. All the female staff at maternity were drawn up in two lines outside the door as if waiting for an inspection by royalty. Their faces shone, their uniforms were impeccable. All the mothers were in bed, all the babies in their cots. The ward was spotless. Helen began to glow with pride for her team.

Plan X had been devised for precisely such an emergency. John and Helen had worked it out and rehearsed it with the regularity of a fire drill. The bedspreads and uniforms had been laundered and relaundered for so long that it was surprising they were not worn out. The staff had been trained with military efficiency. Nothing had gone wrong. After the inspection party had left, John grinned at her.

"What kept you so long?" he joked. "We were ready for you in eighteen minutes and thirty seconds flat!"

Helen could have kissed him. "It was the longest twenty minutes I've ever spent in my life," she admitted.

But their success did them no good at all. The report

commended them for uniforms, general turnout, presentation of facts, and high morale, but unfortunately their hospital buildings were not up to the standard required by the government—which was hardly surprising, since Helen had employed local labor to construct them from mud and thatch. The number of students under training was also criticized; there were not sufficient patients to warrant such a number.

Helen had actually expected this reaction. Every mission hospital in the northeastern province had failed to qualify. It did not mean they would have to shut down or stop training medical students, although in the long run this was the government's objective. It did mean, however, that their students would not receive the much sought-after accreditation which would qualify them for jobs anywhere in Congo.

Some two hundred miles away from Nebobongo, the Africa Inland Mission at Oicha ran a hospital and training school along the same lines as her own. Dr. Carl Becker, a much-respected veteran American surgeon whose mission hospital had also failed to qualify, was in charge. Dr. Becker, a tall, spare, graying, scholarly man whom Helen knew and admired, had spent forty years toiling patiently and tirelessly. He was a first-class surgeon and physician who would have graced the staff of any major American hospital, but he sought neither fame nor personal advancement. Helen was certain that in his quietly effective manner he had done more to help Africa than a dozen "big wheels" operating in the various international agencies. He was a godly man, and they were friends. Behind his glasses his eyes shone benevolently as Helen repeated the story of Plan X. Both of them knew that independence spelled the end of the small mission hospitals and one doctor trying to cope with all the problems such a situation entailed.

All the mission hospitals had in their time and way performed miracles. They had also provided medical services where none existed before. But the newly independent and ambitious Congolese government wanted better things, higher standards, a twentieth-century medical service, not primitive techniques out of Dr. Livingstone's handbook.

Dr. Becker and Helen agreed emphatically with the government's goals, but both wanted to preserve in their medical service the Christian ethic and ideal. Their plans began to take shape. For many years the enormous northeastern territories of Congo had been divided into spheres of influence by the five Protestant missionary organizations working there. No one organization had enough money, equipment, or medical staff to fulfill government requirements. Alone they were powerless, but together they might succeed. Dr. Becker and Helen had been exploring the idea of such a merger when the rebellion broke out. They envisaged one all-embracing medical center with a large hospital whose maternity and outpatients wards would be staffed by European and American doctors and highly qualified nurses. The medical teaching school would be directed by Helen; Dr. Becker would run the hospital and be overall director, since no one else possessed the seniority, experience, and qualifications necessary for the job. They drew up plans for a flying doctor service. Small airstrips would be hacked out of the rain forest at places like Nebobongo where the flying doctors would spend a week on rota duty. They had even chosen their building site: Nyankunde, which was four thousand feet up in the grasslands above the rain forest. To the west lay the great mountain ranges bordering Uganda. It was remote, but it was healthy.

This was an ambitious plan, and in June, as soon as Helen had solved most of the problems she found at Nebobongo, she went up to the border station at Rethi, where Dr. Becker was working. It was the first time they had met for more than two years. He had not changed at all, Helen decided, although she knew that now he was over seventy. He was still the lean, kindly, fatherly figure, intensely dedicated to his task of advancing Congo's medical progress. Work did not stop because of Helen's visit; he simply recruited her to act as his assistant surgeon, and she found it an enlightening experience. Indeed, as she stood beside him at the operating table, she couldn't help reflecting how much better it would have been for her if she could have spent a year under Carl Becker's guidance when she had first arrived in Congo. He was so much more experienced and skillful than she was; under his tuition she would certainly have lost much of the fear which inhibited her surgical progress for so many years.

He was far advanced with plans for Nyankunde. "We've got the site for your medical school arranged," he explained. "I'll drive you down there tomorrow and you can see it. Nice piece of ground about two hundred yards square. My hospital foundations are already under way."

Helen asked him, "You've abandoned the possibility of taking over a government hospital now that most of the Belgians have left?"

"Absolutely. The government is adamant—and who can blame them?—that in their own hospitals they'll be responsible for the recruitment, training, advancement, and dismissal of staff."

"Which means Christian influence and teaching will play no part at all in that training?"

"None at all. It's their country; they can call the tune. So, as arranged, we're going ahead with our own Evangelical Medical Center at Nyankunde."

He smiled at her, "What about your students? Where are you going to get them from? When will you be ready to start?"

Helen had considered her plans, even though she was

surprised to find Dr. Becker so far advanced in his. "I'll obviously bring some of my own from Nebobongo. I've sent details by radio and letter and word of mouth to all the secondary schools in the northeast asking for students to take our examination and be ready to start in August."

Dr. Becker's eyebrows lifted. "I hate to mention it, but what about the school buildings?"

She laughed. "I hope they won't run back home when I confront them with the fact that they've got to build their own classrooms before I can start to teach them."

"Knowing you," said Dr. Becker, "I expect you'll manage."

Helen deeply regretted having to leave Nebobongo after so many years, but the government's decision made this inevitable, and she would, of course, as WEC's medical director, still be in charge there. Nebo would still continue as a small hospital and medical center, and with luck and some cooperation from WEC, she hoped that John Mangadima would eventually be ready to take over as medical director there.

Between 1966 and 1967, two problems deeply concerned Helen. Winnie Davies, her friend and colleague, whom she had visited so many times at Opienge, was still a captive. Winnie had lived in Congo for twenty years; she had worked at Nebobongo before Helen took over, when it was only a small leprosy settlement and maternity center.

When the Simbas captured Opienge it was thought at first that Winnie had been killed, and many months passed before news was received that she was a captive of the Simbas in the rain forest. Rumors that she was still alive reached British authorities; it was Helen who received the first letter, from an African pastor at Opienge, giving accurate information. Winnie had been marched through the forest, with a Dutch priest named Father Strijbosch, always a few miles ahead of the approaching National Congolese troops.

Helen felt strongly that an attempt to rescue her must be made. Accordingly, she visited the lieutenant in charge of the Nationalist Army in Bunia, explaining that she knew the treacherous road through the forest to Opienge very well; after all, she had made many night stops there. It was obvious that a full-scale army attack through this sort of territory would never succeed, but she had another idea.

"The Simbas must be by now lulled into a false sense of security. They know that you can't mount an attack along such a road, so why not surprise them? A small, resolute force could take them unawares. Just a small force . . . I know the district very well."

The lieutenant listened politely. Plainly, the idea of a commando raid led by Dr. Helen Roseveare did not appeal to him at all.

"Dr. Roseveare," he replied, "the colonel in charge of the operation is in Stanleyville. He has given orders that the Stanleyville road is to be opened within a month and the area cleared of rebels. I believe that a . . ." He fumbled for words, in an attempt to avoid using "foolhardy," "idiotic," "insane," and "suicidal." ". . . An expedition such as you suggest would clash with these plans and not meet with his approval."

"But if you wait it'll be too late," Helen protested. He shook his head, and after more argument she departed, thoroughly depressed. Winnie's life, she felt, was desperately at risk.

In June, 1967 the news she dreaded was confirmed. Father Strijbosch had been rescued, and he told their story. For thirty-four months Winnie had been held captive by the Simbas, driven on long, exhausting escape marches as the National Congolese Army closed in. But, even weakened and ill from lack of food and from living in the jungle, she had nursed the sick Simba women and continued to preach to the Christians among them.

With the final National Army encirclement, the insurgents made a chaotic rush for safety. Father Strijbosch, forced on ahead of Winnie by his Simba guard, realized when he saw Winnie resting by the side of the path ahead of him that in the general panic they must have circled on their tracks.

He limped closer. "I thought she was resting," he wrote, "but as I approached I realized she was dead, lying there in her faded green dress. She must have been dead for about fifteen minutes. There were knife wounds on her head and throat, with blood on her mouth."

He had staggered on for another few hundred yards, and suddenly been confronted by three armed men. He crossed himself and waited for the bullets. Then a voice shouted, "We are the National Congolese Army. We are here to rescue you." Father Strijbosch broke down. His companion had been so close to the safety he now knew. This time, like so many times in the past, the rescuers had arrived a few minutes too late.

Helen grieved deeply for Winnie. To have gone through so much and then succumbed was such a bitter irony. But she knew that Winnie would have made her peace with God and would have wished them all to go on working to save the living. A year earlier, in May, 1966, Helen had done just that; she had accepted a rather dangerous mission when approached by a desperate commanding officer in her area.

He appealed to her for help. He expected that his forces would flush the enemy out of Wamba within the next two or three weeks. They would then press on in pursuit. But the news that Wamba was free would reach those hiding in the rain forest and the exodus would begin. Refugees who

had been hiding there for as long as two years would see
the sunlight again. He expected there would be thousands
of them, and he knew that they would be in a terrible state.
Could she help? Could she mount an immediate relief operation and give the Army and the Congolese authorities a
breathing space?

Helen knew she had no alternative. The school at Nyankunde, affairs at Nebobongo, everything would have to
wait. There was no one but herself equipped medically to
do the job, and this was an emergency.

Above all else she would need supplies and willing helpers. Obviously, she could recruit church workers when she
arrived in Wamba, but she wanted two or three experienced
Europeans to help supervise the operation. She decided she
would appeal to Colin and Ina Buckley, two WEC missionaries recently returned to Paulis. She also learned, to
her great joy, that Agnes Chansler, her lovely American
"auntie" who had worked in WEC for thirty years, had just
returned to Congo.

In all her time in Congo Helen had always admired her
two "aunties," Agnes Chansler and Marjory Cheverton. She
had known and loved them since her first arrival in Africa.
Two spinster missionary ladies with hearts of purest gold,
their Christianity was compounded of the essential virtues:
compassion, love, and pity. To be with them, for even a
short time, helped to renew one's hope in humanity.

She remembered 1961 after that first year of independence when her health had broken down; a solid twelve
months with no other doctor within a hundred miles,
generally working an eighteen-hour day had worn her
down completely. Had her "aunties" not carried her
off to their mission station, away from the wards and
responsibilities at Nebo, when she collapsed with acute
malaria and physical and mental exhaustion, she would
probably have died. Without a moment's hesitation they had

taken her to Egbita, some sixty kilometers away, and for ten weeks nursed her back to health and sanity. Helen was pale, skinny, and very depressed, and they gave her their mutual and undivided attention; they fussed over her, mothered her, and spoon-fed her. These two fine missionaries were happiest when they were out "visiting." "Visiting" meant loading up their old car (in the old days it had been a journey either on foot or on bicycle) and driving off into the rain forest. They would seek out the loneliest paths and the poorest villages and there they would carry out the mission which had brought them to Africa in the first place: They would tell the story of the Christian miracle. For thirty years they had ventured into places in the dark, mysterious rain forest, full of snakes and wild animals, with a wonderful cheerfulness, oblivious to everything but the job at hand.

In the villages they would introduce themselves to the headman or chief, admire the babies, chat with the mothers, and make notes of the more obvious illnesses, which later they brought to Helen's attention. In the evenings they sat by the fire and discussed the crops and, more philosophically, the trials of mankind. Gradually they moved towards the purpose of their visit, to tell the most important story of the man called Jesus Christ who promised forgiveness of our sins and life everlasting. Sometimes in Swahili, often in the local Bangala dialect, the tall elegant Englishwoman and the shorter American told the story and went about their business with humor and laughter, a capacity for friendship, a sense of belief, and that inner serenity which is linked with the very roots of their faith.

When Helen asked Agnes if she would, therefore, go with her on the relief expedition to Wamba, she was not in the least surprised when the older woman accepted immediately—when did they start?

The logistic headaches of the Wamba operation were awful. Helen knew it would have to be accomplished in one week; by the end of that period their supplies would be exhausted—if she could get any supplies at all, that is. She could not steal back her hard-won drugs from Nebo; they were so scanty that they would be used up in two or three hours anyway. Better to leave them for the needy at Nebo and Ibambi and endeavor to get new supplies elsewhere. This meant a journey to Stanleyville to plead with and cajole every source she could find.

She arrived at Stanleyville on the morning of July 5. Two hours later she met Big Bill, the American in charge of air transport in that area. He listened carefully to her appeal. Certainly he would do all he could to help.

At once radio messages began to flash back and forth between Stanleyville and Leopoldville and from them to Army HQ in Bunia and Wamba. Helen began her search in the war-torn city of Stanleyville and appealed to every medical source she could find. "I raided everybody. I showed no mercy to anybody. Greeks in their shop, relief organizations . . . I went to the big hospital at Stanleyville and saw the marvelous Spanish doctor who ran it and said, 'If you've got two hundred flacons of penicillin I want one hundred!' Everybody who'd got any drugs I confronted and said, 'I want half of them.' "

The Protestant and Roman Catholic relief missions gave generously. They delivered corn, oats, wheat, milk, soyabean flour, clothing, and blankets. In Paulis, a few days later, she received a wonderful donation from Dr. de Ville, the Belgian physician in charge of the hospital there. He handed over penicillin for at least five thousand injections. Helen could hardly have started her relief work in Wamba without this generous gift.

On Helen's behalf, Big Bill buzzed across the Congolese

radio waves and demanded air transport, lorries, government permits. All drugs and supplies were to be flown to
Paulis and then trucked into Wamba. The government medical supply officers in Leopoldville were stunned by the
enormity of Helen's demands. Distressed radio replies confirmed that the matter had been taken directly to General
Mobutu himself, and over a crackling radio line Helen had
a slightly incoherent conversation with the military dictator
of the land, now engaged in bringing law and order back to
his troubled country. The interview was inconclusive, but
she understood everything was being done to help, though
as usual red tape and inefficiency held up the progress of
her work. One huge transport plane arrived from Leopoldville reportedly filled with foodstuffs and supplies. As it
droned to a halt at its dispersal point, the great doors were
winched open. Big Bill and Helen hurried forward—to find
the holds completely empty.

Towards the end of her hurried search for supplies, she
had to break off and return to Nyankunde. It was vital to
her first school year that she mark examination papers
there. The future of her hospital depended on the nurses
who were to take over there, after all.

To travel from Stanleyville to Nyankunde and back to
Nebobongo was an ordeal in itself. She wasted day after
day at various small airports trying to hitch a lift by military aircraft, hoping that when she landed she could get
another lift by road. Dr. Becker met her at Bunia and
drove her to Nyankunde. She spent eight hours selecting
forty-eight students from several hundred applicants, and
returned to Nebo hoping that those she had selected were
strong, willing lads who would not object to a pre-course
three-month chore as building laborers. Before they could
start learning, they were going to put their school together.

She left almost immediately for Paulis. The road between

Ibambi and Paulis had survived Simba destruction fairly well. Every hundred yards or so an elephant trap—a huge hole dug in the road, mined, and covered with palm fronds —had been roughly filled in. Two lorries were stuck in one steep muddy hill with a deep water gully on either side. Helen had no idea how she was going to maneuver the Land-Rover through the narrow gap. Fortunately, one truck driver, a very determined man, volunteered to pilot the Land-Rover through. He accomplished this with great skill and then gallantly insisted on driving them all the way into Paulis.

Next day the expedition, reinforced by Colin and Ina Buckley and Agnes, transferred to a large lorry and headed for Wamba. As they neared the town they saw the devastation caused by the fighting: deserted villages, burnt-out houses, schools overgrown and empty. In one village they found their first group of refugees building flimsy leaf huts against the impending torrential monsoon rains. There was mud everywhere. The refugees had no clothes. They were living on leaves and grubs, tiny animals, anything they could scavenge. Helen explained the object of her journey. "We've come to help you," she announced. "We're setting up at the Protestant mission in Wamba and in forty-eight hours' time we'll be ready to start our distribution. Tell anybody you meet the missionaries are back. Tell them to come to Wamba."

CHAPTER 13

Driving into Wamba was like driving into a graveyard. The center, government offices, post office, and shops were gutted; only the prison remained untouched. Some repairs had been made in one main street, and they stopped at the first store which showed signs of occupation. Inside, Mr. Mitsingas, Helen's old Greek friend, was chatting with two mercenary officers. Mitsingas saw her and stopped in midsentence. His mouth hung open for a long moment. Then, recovering, he rushed to embrace her.

Hugging her, he said excitedly, "Dr. Roseveare! It can't be true. You're in England! You're not in Congo! You're in England . . ."

Helen was already expertly appraising the selection of goods he had on display—items she was going to need very badly in the next few days.

"Why come back to Congo?" he continued. "You must be—" He swallowed the word "mad" and, hardly pausing, babbled on. "And Wamba of all places! You were in prison here. All those dreadful things happened here." He was obviously quite unable to comprehend her actions or motives.

"*You're* back, Mr. Mitsingas," she said pointedly. He released her from his embrace so that he could use both hands to make his point clear. "But we've got nowhere else to go. Everything we have is tied up here. Shops, houses, money—"

She interrupted him. "I've heard that there are thousands of refugees all around Wamba."

"We've still got trouble," he admitted, although he did not seem greatly interested in that problem. He indicated the smiling mercenary officers. "You can see we've still got trouble. There's fighting less than fifty miles from here. This place is not far behind the front lines."

"But it will soon be ended," she insisted. "And we must start to get things organized." It was plain, however, that Mitsingas still didn't understand. He turned back to the two mercenary officers.

"She didn't have to come back," he murmured wonderingly. "She didn't have to come back at all."

"Oh, yes, I did," replied Helen, promptly directing the conversation back into its proper path. "We shall need buckets, tables, cups, axes, soap, matches, all sorts of things."

But even the thought of these sales did not really excite Mr. Mitsingas. "Your mission station's in a terrible mess," he confided. "The Simbas used it as their headquarters. A dozen homeless families are squatting in it now."

"We shall clear it up," Helen countered briskly. "We shall enlist every church worker we can find as a volunteer. We understand there's a great need."

"Ah yes," echoed Mitsingas, "a great need." It seemed to be his cue to return to his role as a businessman. "All these things you want, I can supply them for you." The shrewd glance and the tone of his voice took her straight back to the old days of percentage discounts for cash, short supply, a cousin who might use a little influence, and the question of whom should he charge the account to.

She stared straight back into his eyes. Helen knew the kind of price gouging that had been going on. No African in that district had so much as smoked a cigarette for nearly two years, but the newly arrived traders had rushed in supplies and were prepared to sell a single cigarette at the outrageous price of one shilling *each!* The traders had arrived behind the advancing troops, stocking their shops with every conceivable item which made life a little easier. They were now overcharging, with the assurance that their goods were unobtainable elsewhere.

Helen had already made up her mind that this was going to be Mr. Mitsingas's day of brotherly love and Christian charity. She was not going to pay him one single cent. She had decided he would donate the supplies she needed for the starving children, and the hungry, desperate, and sick at heart. It was, she reasoned, for the good of his soul and the benefit of the community. Although they did not continue the negotiation, Helen was reasonably certain she would get her way when the time came to discuss it. As they left she said, "Thank you, Mr. Mitsingas. We'll send around tomorrow to collect all the things we need."

Helen had anticipated that the mission center would be damaged and filthy. As their deadline to begin distribution was only forty-eight hours away, they had to move quickly, cleaning, scrubbing, and collecting volunteers. On Saturday night the sound of the talking drums went rolling across the countryside. When the first stopped you could hear, far away, their message taken up by other distant drums. The news was relayed over an area some eighty miles in radius. "The missionaries have come back . . . it is safe to come out . . . they have brought things to help us . . . they will be giving these things away in two days' time . . . come to Wamba . . . come to Wamba!"

From the darkness of the rain forest, the Africans came out of leaf shelters they had erected, and out of holes they had dug between jutting, angular roots of trees. They came out and stood in the darkness listening to the muted throb of the hollowed tree-trunk drums competing with the sharp *chirp-chirp-chirp* of the night birds, the shrill cicadas, the grunt of the leopards, the occasional distant squeal of elephant. For two years they had managed to survive, not knowing if they would ever return to their villages or if they were destined to die in the forest. Now they went back into their hiding places, took up the tiny bundles of possessions, the children, the sick, the old, even the dying, and began to walk through the night towards Wamba. That evening Helen faced her audience of fifty-six church workers; they had assembled as soon as they heard she needed them. Many had only recently come out of the forest and were thin and undernourished too. But they wanted to work, they wanted to help; this was the therapy of which they were most in need.

"The church will be the distribution center," she explained. "And we must keep a numbered record card of every single case. We must know what we've done and what we've got to do. There must be a continuity of treatment, especially with the penicillin injections and any special feeding that is necessary, and there will be much that is necessary."

Most churches in the northeastern provinces of Congo are immense. Materials and labor are cheap, congregations are large. The church at Wamba was built of gray cement blocks, in simple but cathedral-like proportions, with wide-open spaces for windows which admitted air and light. It held fifteen hundred worshippers. All the benches had been stolen or burned by the Simbas. The floor had never been finished, because the money had run out. There was an area of raised concrete around the baptistry which Helen knew would be useful as a platform.

"We'll admit them through the big doors at the end of the church," she went on. "We'll erect four lines of bamboo stakes so that we can get them into four queues and control the flow."

One of the senior church workers told her, "the army commander has said he will send us soldiers to keep order. The army is afraid of riots when the food distribution starts."

Helen said thoughtfully, "We may need soldiers, but I hope not. Tell him to have a couple standing by just in case." She returned to her briefing. "Now, we're not going to issue the clothing until later in the week. If we start issuing *that* straight away, there might well be a riot. We all know that most of them would probably sooner be clothed than fed. It's status. If you've got a shirt on your back to cover your nakedness, you're respectable again. No one can see an empty stomach, therefore you can put up with it." She and her coworkers started getting ready for the first arrivals.

That Sunday evening they labored late into the night to get things ready, and they used headlights of the lorry shining into the church so that they could see. As Helen had intended, they divided the length of the building into four aisles separated by rows of bamboo stakes. They placed tables and chairs near the main doors and arranged piles of differently colored cards ready for their identification processes. They prepared syringes and medicines, great bowls of oatmeal, and gallons of milk. They went to bed late and very tired, unaware that the next day would be one they would remember for the rest of their lives.

Helen woke conscious of a faint, almost inaudible noise, a persistent sound which she had never heard before, and went to the door to peer out. The pre-dawn mist was thick and drenching; she could barely make out the outlines of the church. As the light grew, the noise increased, a sort of rustling, like trees shaking in the wind, yet this was a deeper sound, closer to soft surf rolling on a distant reef. Then she realized that it was a human sound: It was the murmur of thousands of human beings moving and gathering together.

For the first time Helen began to understand exactly what this war had done to an Africa of bewildered primitive people. Their tribal systems had been destroyed, their faith distorted, their value as human beings made superfluous. The fury of men driven by different faiths and beliefs had destroyed them. Now the black child with the swollen belly, the emaciated mother with the hungry eyes and her outstretched skeletal hand, were the pitiful residue of that anger.

Helen went out into the half-light and watched them straggling in towards the church. She began to form them into lines, to push them gently into place, to tell them that they had to be patient. At 8 A.M. the church doors were opened and the lines pressed forward.

At that precise moment a Congolese lieutenant and three soldiers drove up in a jeep and perfect order was restored. The people queued up in silence and misery and poverty. All of them were nearly naked, and physically bent with suffering and sorrow and near-starvation.

Helen took the cards for the medical cases. She wrote out every card herself as she went slowly down the line; each card indicated what treatment that individual should receive when he reached the front of the queue. As the light grew she saw that the line of people stretched from the church, across the football field, past the mission station, past the sentry boxes, and away into Wamba itself. As the sun rose, almost everyone on line stood with a hand shielding his eyes. They had been hiding in the forest for two years, and the light was too much for them. Most were suffering from eye disease. Many were in the final, irreversible stages of malnutrition: skin stretched over bone, hair cream-colored, even the irises of their eyes depigmented. Some had flesh which was bloated and rotting, peeling off their bodies. Helen separated the very sick into a small compound near the church, giving them special cards and immediate attention. Many of the children were in a desperate state, and Agnes took charge of them. Helen showed her how to feed them by making up the milk powder into a thick cream and feeding each child with half a teaspoonful every half hour. Many of the children died there at the church. Even small corpses were brought in by desperate mothers who thought that somehow, perhaps, the breath of life could be blown back into the child. Agnes was quite undone by it all. She did not stop working, and she hardly ever stopped weeping, for the plight of some of the children was heartbreaking. But as long as there was a child to feed, she continued her work.

Helen discovered two of her old students waiting in the queue for attention. Immediately she hauled them out and made them part of the medical team. "You're trained and you know what to do," she told them. Their recovery, which took place within hours, was remarkable. Two teams of young men with limited medical knowledge gave the penicillin injections: One did nothing but clean and boil syringes, a second drew the penicillin from the phials, a third handed the syringe to the boy who injected, a fourth checked cards, a fifth prepared the patient. Others put ointment in eyes, others treated ulcers, others issued food. The cycle went on endlessly from sunup until late in the day. By the end of that first day two thousand six hundred people had been treated and fed.

Late that afternoon Helen received a message that she was urgently needed at Wamba hospital. There she found one African head nurse gravely concerned over the condition of a pregnant woman. A quick examination revealed that an immediate Caesarian operation was needed. Tired, but now working with an automatic determination, without gown, mask, general anesthetic, uterine or delivery forceps, using the only scalpel she could find, which was blunt, Helen delivered the baby. Mother and child did well. Helen's mind flew back momentarily to that first traumatic Caesarian on the Pygmy mother so long ago.

On Tuesday, five thousand one hundred and seventy-six people passed through the church for attention. Wednesday's total was six thousand eight hundred and sixty-eight. Now word had gone around the district that the missionaries really meant what they said, and the queues stretched out of sight.

Every night, with lorry headlights flooding into the church, they worked until every patient had received attention. Helen ate very little; the starving condition of so many of the refugees completely shattered her. She had never bothered much about food; now she could not eat, knowing that so many outside were hungry. On Friday morning Ina Buckley carried two sandwiches and a cup of coffee out to where Helen stood attending to the patients. "Now come on, Helen," she urged, "drink this and get these down, else you'll be no use to anybody."

Obediently Helen took a bite of her sandwich. A second later it was snatched from her hand. A small boy of about five stood below her in his place in the queue. He had crammed the whole sandwich into his mouth and gulped it down like a starving animal. His eyes were huge and sick with hunger. With a terrible inner despair he looked up at the second half of the sandwich, on the plate beyond his reach. Helen stared back at him. Then quietly she handed it over. It vanished instantly. She went on working.

They distributed the porridge, multivitamin tablets, iron

tablets, and milk. The soya-bean flour, the corn, everything they had. They made it a rule that the milk and tablets had to be swallowed as soon as the recipient received them. They entrusted most of the mothers with a supply of milk to last a fortnight, teaching them how to make the mixture and what dosage to give the children. By eleven o'clock on Friday morning they had used up everything: every flake of oats, every tablet, every drop of milk, the penicillin and ointment. The difference in their patients was spectacular, and some of their "cures" bordered on the miraculous.

By Friday they had clothed ten thousand people, and Helen had photographs to prove what an astounding difference a garment makes to morale and happiness. Every one of the ten thousand was given a piece of soap as well. They had also issued half a ton of grain for planting and a hundred hoes to till the soil. The horde had been fed and doctored, and most of them no longer needed to shade their eyes from the sun. Helen knew that it was only a beginning, but at least these people would not go back to the forest, and that was the main thing. The army would take over now and feed them a small ration. They would be put to work clearing the debris, rebuilding the broken houses, and starting again. Helen knew it would be a year before they were really back on their feet, and even in that time their subsistence would be borderline. They could harvest a crop of ground nuts within three months of planting, but sweet potatoes took ten months to swell, so in between times they would have to forage. But they would survive.

Helen lectured her church workers on the importance of continuity. They must lead; morale must be maintained; there must be no backsliding. The white missionaries would be back as soon as it was possible, but the African church workers must see that the patches of land were dug and

hoed and planted with seed. Everyone must throw off
despondency and despair. The schools had to start again.
Helen personally would see that there were exercise books,
blackboards, chalk, and pencils. They had recovered some
of their self-respect. Now they must keep going forward,
and she would send them all the help she could.

Finally, she made a call on Mr. Mitsingas. She explained
that unfortunately she was not in a position to pay anything at all for the goods he had so kindly provided. He
smiled and nodded and said no doubt she would do *him*
a favor some time. And as she drove away Helen had a
strange feeling that the old rascal had known from the
very beginning that she had no intention of paying.

Helen looked around at her flock, the twenty-two
eighteen-year-olds gathered around her in the wilderness.

"Now," she said authoritatively, "this is our first meeting.
You've all been found a place to sleep. You've each been
given a blanket, plate, mug, spoon, and last night you had
an evening meal."

She felt she was sounding like a camp counselor, but the
sooner these young men realized that they were not starting an academic career at Cambridge, Heidelberg, Harvard,
or the Sorbonne, so much the better. This was Congo after
years of bitter civil war.

One of the better-dressed students stepped forward, a
look of perplexity on his face. He came, Helen knew, from
Blukwa, was certainly better educated than some of the
others, and probably already saw himself, white-coated and
benign, discovering a cure for cancer or healing like the
Curies, whom he had read about in some popular magazine.

"Madam," he began politely, "we have passed our
entrance examinations and come here to study at a medical school. Where is the medical school?"

Helen nodded understandingly. "Ah," she said, "now you have put your finger on the problem. As a matter of fact, you are in the medical school."

Twenty-two pairs of mystified eyes rolled around to observe the waist-high grass, the brambles, the thick bushes; their eyes moved upwards to the distant green mountains. They passed over the foundations of Dr. Becker's new hospital, the brick walls now three feet high, standing some three hundred yards away, and came back to rest on Helen. No doubt this small white lady in the spectacles was playing a joke on them and at the proper moment would surprise them all with the truth. Helen, however, took the "joke" a step further.

"I have to tell you," she said, "that before I can start to teach you about medicine, we have to build the school." Ignoring their startled reaction, she continued rapidly.

"But for the Simba rebellion, the school would certainly be completed and functioning properly by this time. Because of the troubles, the vast damage to property, the lack of money and building materials, as you can see for yourselves, there is, as yet, no school."

The look of mystification on their faces had now changed to one of utter and total disbelief. "But, madam——" began the bright student from Blukwa.

Helen continued, "We have to build the entire school: lecture rooms and laboratories. We have to build the student village, dormitories, kitchens, married quarters, and all the things that go with them. We'll need cement and bricks, doors and windows eventually, but to start with we have to cut timbers from the forest, build the walls, thatch the roofs. In fact, I'd say getting ourselves basically started will take about three months."

The voice of the young student from Blukwa was a long wail of protest. "But, madam, we do not know how to build.

We are students who have just passed our entrance examinations."

"Very creditable," she retorted firmly. "But don't worry. I shall teach you. First we shall build and when we have completed the first classrooms we shall open the medical school and your real studies will begin." The young man from Blukwa, silent and defeated, withdrew from the unequal confrontation.

Helen looked boldly into as many pairs of eyes as she could. "No doubt you will want time to consider this proposal of mine and discuss it among yourselves. Therefore, I suggest we all meet again tomorrow at the same time in the same place and you will then tell me of your decision."

She felt it necessary to add a note of encouragement. "But please remember, we are building this medical school for Congo. Not only will you benefit yourselves, but also the generations of students who will follow after you." She paused and smiled at them. "So that's my offer. You work. I'll teach."

They went away, a stunned and silent group, and that afternoon Helen found it difficult to concentrate. Huge problems remained from the period after the rioting and mutiny which followed independence in 1960 and intervention by the armed force of the United Nations. The Simba rebellion of 1964* had added to these problems. These civil wars in such an enormous country had left bad roads, poor communications, and a civil service and local government organization which scarcely existed.

Nineteen sixty-six, the year Helen was planning her medical school, was an inauspicious time to start anything in Congo. Everyday news of riots and mutinies was heard on the radio. Apparently, the latest concerned a mutiny by

---

* Pockets of Simba resistance still continued even in the seventies.

Katanganese and mercenary soldiers stationed near Stanleyville against the central government in Leopoldville, which had not paid them. Rumor suggested that they were proposing to march back to Katanga, and it seemed likely that the whole process of coup and counter-coup would start all over again. There were other disturbing reports that hundreds of Simba prisoners had been released from jail. It was all terribly depressing. The shops of the Greek, Cypriot, Portuguese, and Indian traders in their area had been looted by Katanganese deserters, and no plane services had operated for weeks. Due to this uncertainty and lack of travel facilities, half her students had failed to reach Nyankunde by the start of the term, and the best she could expect was that the rest of them would appear by ones and twos during the month to come. (Sixteen extra students from Paulis and six from Stanleyville eventually turned up. Two from Stanleyville took one look at the building work in which they were expected to involve themselves and immediately departed for home.)

"Well, have you made up your minds?" she asked her potential students the morning after her ultimatum.

The earnest faces stared at her solemnly. The boy from Blukwa stepped forward. "Yes, we have talked it over, madam," he said and smiled. With that smile Helen knew she had won. "All of us have decided to accept your offer."

"Good," said Helen. "Very good indeed. Now we shall start work immediately."

Her first preoccupation was to find lodgings for her students. Nyankunde, chosen as the site of the new medical center, had functioned for many years as a simple mission station. The primary-school children were on holiday temporarily, so she obtained permission to bed her boys down in the classrooms. Three girl students were immediately demoted to supervise the cooking and shopping. In those first few weeks their meals were spartan: morning coffee, midday coffee, and a large dinner in the evening. They ate in the open air, using planks set up on bricks as benches, while Helen expounded some intricacy of the builder's craft. Her own knowledge had been acquired from field courses taught by Jack Scholes at Ibambi plus years of trial and error at Nebobongo. She discovered that 99 percent of her students knew nothing whatsoever about the craft of building, or indeed about the hard labor such work entailed. To ask the average student to wield an axe to cut down a young sapling was dangerous: He risked amputation of a limb. Nevertheless, Helen persevered, and slowly their skills improved. At a reasonable price, she had obtained permission from a local chief to cut support poles for roofs and walls from his reforestation plantation, and each morning at dawn she set off in a lorry with a party of chosen students to cut the essential timber.

She went out with them, felling and hauling young trees, clearing the site, measuring out buildings for the student village, erecting suitable poles, fixing roofing saplings, and thatching. There were a dozen and one skills needed for African house building. It was not all work, though. From her earliest days in Congo she had decided with true British spirit that athletic games should play a large part in any school curriculum. As far as she was concerned, there was very little difference between the rules of hockey and soccer, and she refereed the football matches from the playing position of either left-back or, if she was very tired, goalkeeper. Everyone was always exhausted and feeling fine when they went to bed.

Nevertheless, there were many frustrations. The Belgian colonial administration had bequeathed to the new regime a legacy of red tape complicated enough to strangle it at birth. The Congolese *fonctionnaires* followed the same pat-

tern with zeal and determination. Helen's upbringing and
dedication made it absolutely impossible for her to bribe
anyone, even though she knew it was a matter of course in
Congo. Consequently, she found that on numerous occasions there would suddenly be no timber for the roofing, or
no nails for the timber when the timber appeared, or no
window frames available when the wall supports were in.
Petrol was scarce, and it was even difficult to change
money at the bank in Bunia. The bank never knew what
the exchange rates were supposed to be, and usually had to
refer to the bank in Leopoldville, a thousand miles away.

Although Dr. Becker's hospital was not finished, he and
his small team of medical workers were already attending
to fifteen hundred outpatients and one hundred bed patients,
and a long list of operative cases was steadily building up.
For the first time in Congo, Helen had real professional
help. There had usually been two or three white coworkers
at Nebo but nevertheless it had been a lonely life. Now she
lived in a small community, mainly American, and although
there were occasions of petty irritation, trials, and jealousies,
there was a great deal of friendship and assistance.

Richard Dix, for example, was in overall charge of
design and building at Nyankunde. His wife, Ruth, was a
doctor working with Dr. Becker's team. One of his first
jobs was to fix a tap in Helen's school compound which
gave them a constant supply of pure water from a high
mountain spring. Helen wrote to her mother: "We've never
been so spoiled in our whole lives." Later, when she built
her own thatched-roof bungalow on a hill overlooking the
school compound, Richard installed a toilet which actually
flushed. Helen could not believe her good fortune. This
was a phenomenon unknown in the rain forest.

Good-natured leg-pulling and teasing were natural between
British and Americans, and one such incident took Helen a

long time to live down. One morning she cut her thumb
while opening a tin of sardines. Deciding it was rather silly
to get the wound full of mud on the building site, she
decided to drop in at the hospital to have a strip of plaster
stuck on it. She bent her fingers back to stem the blood
and got over to the operating room. The young male nurse
on duty was eager to help. As she was the lady doctor, he
obviously felt it not quite the thing merely to stick a bit of
plaster over the wound. He procured a sterile towel, a bowl,
disinfectant, and bandages, and sat her down to perform an
expert job. He took her hand and opened the fingers gently,
and blood gushed out. Helen took one look at the crimson
flood and swooned in a full-blown syncopal attack which
left her prostrate on the floor.

The horrified male nurse tried to take her pulse but
could not feel any; he tried to take her blood pressure, but
there wasn't any. What had he done? In his care the lady
doctor had died! Deborah, a student assisting in the theater,
came in at that moment, and he screamed his panic at her.
"The lady doctor has died! Go fetch help! The lady doctor
has died!"

There were two wards in use at that time. Dr. Becker
was working in one, Dr. Herb Atkinson, a young American, in the other. To make certain everyone got the news
as quickly as possible, Deborah rushed through both wards
screaming that the lady doctor had died in the operating
room. Herb Atkinson beat Dr. Becker to Helen's side by a
few seconds, realized at once what had happened, and
brought her back to life by the undignified but necessary
procedure of pushing her head between her knees.

By October 30 the school village of three dormitories and
homes for twenty-one married students was ready for occupation. The mud walls hadn't properly dried out, they
weren't completely whitewashed, but the walls were up, the

roof was on, and they could move in. And the mission lent them a hall as a classroom for the time being.

Helen knew that a building program lasting many years still stretched ahead of her, but she was satisfied merely to stick to her first promise. "You work, I'll teach," she had said, and three months from the commencement of that work she faced her students in her classroom, ready to begin to impart the fantastic story of the blood rivers that run from the heart, the great winds which course through the lungs, the miracle of livers and spleens, bowels and bladders, and the enormous and unfathomable mystery of that mighty work of creation, the brain.

In Congo nothing was ever easy and nothing ever stood still. Besides the constant conflict with the educational authorities in Leopoldville to get them to accredit her medical school, she struggled with the ceaseless job of attempting to educate, inform, coerce, and discipline some forty boisterous, noisy eighteen-year-olds bursting with pride at their secondary-school achievements. They came from fourteen different tribal areas and spoke fourteen different languages—their *lingua franca* was Swahili and the official school language was French—but Helen overcame these difficulties and managed other projects as well. She was a member of the Christian brotherhood of doctors dedicated to bringing medicine in that great province of Congo into the twentieth century. Helen, of course, was providing Dr. Becker's wards with a succession of willing trainees, and this helped progress toward their goal. One of the most important innovations, though, depended on air transport. Helen's pet idea began to see the light.

As a small rural medical center, Nebobongo was bound to benefit from having Nyankunde with its expert staff and technical facilities available, but to facilitate this, a landing strip had to be built so that the light planes flown by the

Missionary Aviation Fellowship could move patients, drugs, and doctors in and out. Helen encouraged the Nebo team to persuade the local chiefs to provide labor for a runway eight hundred and fifty yards long and not less than fifty yards wide on terrain which had to be cleared of vast ironwoods and mahogany with roots driven deep in the earth and tangled undergrowth. Five local chiefs were each supposed to provide two hundred workmen, and for three months this somewhat unwilling labor force worked intermittently between rainstorms and holidays. Fortunately, the soil proved to be gravel, and when the site was finally cleared, a Land-Rover dragging a large tree trunk behind it was able to harrow the ground fairly level.

When the first light, five-seater plane droned in over the high trees and bumped along the runway to settle like a contented queen bee among a swarm of delighted Africans, Helen realized that a new medical future had begun for the whole region.

Indeed, all through the late sixties and early seventies their ability to cope with medical problems in the area improved enormously. Four medical centers were established in a huge circle around Nyankunde, as well as the original one at Nebobongo. Each center also supported between ten and fifteen smaller rural hospitals.

Every Monday on a weekly rota a doctor from Nyankunde flew in to one of the centers carrying a supply of drugs sufficient to last the center and its ancillary hospitals for a month. The plane then returned to Nyankunde, ready for any emergency work. The flying doctor commenced operations immediately; there were usually thirty to forty surgical cases to cope with in those five days. At Nebobongo the surgeons were most ably assisted by John Mangadima, whose enormous skill was improving daily.

In his week's duty the doctor operated and examined all

medical cases. He assisted the center with its bookkeeping and drug orders, and generally boosted the morale of the European and Congolese workers. On Saturday the plane flew in from Nyankunde to pick him up and ferry him back for a week's stint there before flying another doctor to another medical center for the next week. Radio links kept Nyankunde in touch with every center, and every day a local roundup of news, requirements, and emergencies was relayed between all stations.

Helen's twenty-year-old dream of clinics scattered throughout the territory was a dream no longer. She and Dr. Becker had been able to make reality of their identical vision and had provided a network of medical facilities beyond all of Helen's hopes.

# CHAPTER 14

March 19, 1971. As they circled above the dirt airstrip, Helen glimpsed the corrugated-iron roof of her old house at Nebobongo, almost hidden among the trees, and the thatched huts of the leprosy village directly below. They leveled out and dropped down towards the narrow corridor cut between the trees. Their wheels bounced on the sun-baked earth, the propellor of the light aircraft shrieking as they came in for a landing. On either side the rain forest towered to what seemed an enormous height. It was on these trips back to Nebo that Helen first began to understand how the forest isolated you from the rest of the world, and magnified both your problems and your loneliness. It was only when you soared off the ground again, saw the trees and branches whipping past at incredible speed, and you emerged high up in the sunlight and the wide blue sky with a view of the mountains and a distant horizon that you realized any other world existed.

They swirled around in a cloud of dust at the end of the runway, and the young American pilot from the Missionary Aviation Fellowship switched off the engine. Helen knew she was home. She unfastened her seat belt as he opened the door, and there waiting were all her friends.

At once the atmosphere was different. The sun was hotter, the shade deeper, the colors brighter, the earth baked as hard as ancient terra cotta. The welcome was marvelous. She was drowned in a sea of laughter, kisses and hugs. It had been so many months since she had been to see them, having been in England on holiday since her last visit. They were so pleased when they heard she was back and working at Nyankunde once more. Was everything at the school all right?

Yes, said Helen, although she kept back the whole truth. She could have told them about her feelings of depression during that holiday in Britain over the fact that no one in authority seemed to think that accreditation was important. She was absolutely determined not to quit but to return and start again. Her battle with the educational authorities was not finished yet. She had received a message through the usual grapevine that all was not well at Nebobongo, and as medical director of WEC it was her duty to look into it. Before she arrived she had guessed the source of the trouble. Two veteran British nurses worked at Nebobongo, and they were marvelous women, experienced, hard-working, and warm-hearted. But John Mangadima was the assistant surgeon who operated with Herb Atkinson and the other highly qualified American surgeons when they did their duty rota at Nebo. Who, therefore, was in charge? Who was senior? Helen saw the root of the trouble at once. So many workers, teachers, nurses, helpers of all sorts in every African missionary organization could not rid themselves of their parental outlook: The African was a child and could not be allowed to take responsibility. In vain Helen had reiterated that they must step out of the nineteenth century and into the twentieth. The African had the right to run his own affairs, and they would have to appreciate that fact.

At Nebobongo John greeted her with warmth and affection. Then he said quite simply that he and his fellow African medical workers would like to talk to her confidentially. As John went off to collect his staff, the senior of the British nurses said that perhaps she should also attend the meeting.

"No, dear," Helen replied. "They have asked for a private talk with me, not a general discussion, so let me have first go."

There were half a dozen African male nurses assembled in the room with John. They were quiet, courteous, and gracious. They had told Helen fourteen months previously of their grievances, at a medical conference held at Nebo, and she had promised to try and deal with them. At the moment they were compelled to work under the overall direction of two British nurses. This was not good enough. John's capabilities and skills made this situation absurd. The atmosphere affected all of them; they could not work to their maximum potential under such conditions. They had been patient for fourteen months, waiting for Helen to change things, and she had not done so.

"Are you or are you not," asked one of the senior medical workers, "the head of WEC's medical service in Congo?"

Helen tried to explain. While theoretically, in terms of the Congo government, she was leader of the WEC medical team, WEC itself did not really appoint such directors. Jack Scholes was leader of the mission at Ibambi and therefore Helen's boss.

The medical workers looked at her. Obviously, this did not satisfy them, and they wanted her to take responsibility. They answered: "Dr. Roseveare, if you *are* in charge, will you please make changes. If you are not in charge, we intend, as a group, to leave Nebobongo."

Helen looked across at John. He had scarcely spoken. But by his face she could tell that he agreed with their sentiments.

"Please think it over," she said.

"We have thought it over for fourteen months."

"If John and you, this team, leave, Nebobongo will close down as a medical center."

"No, no, others will come and replace us."

"But we've built Nebo. We are Nebo. If we go, Nebo goes, and the people of the forest will have no one to help them."

She looked at John and knew she had scored, perhaps unfairly. That thought upset him.

There was a tap on the door. It was the senior British nurse. She hated to interfere, but a patient with a strangulated hernia had just come in from the forest. Without an immediate operation, he would die very quickly.

The middle-aged African crouched on the veranda outside was an abject figure, pained and bewildered. As Helen examined him with the others standing around, one of the great inspirational moments of her life occurred.

"We must operate at once," she said.

"I thought so," said the senior British nurse. "I'll prepare the theater."

There was a moment's pause; then Helen said firmly, "John will operate. I shall act as his assistant." The effect on the small audience gathered around her in the heat of that March morning was dumbfounding. Dr. Helen Roseveare was handing over the responsibility for a highly complex major operation to an unskilled and unqualified African male nurse. The senior British nurse tried to pass it off as a joke in rather poor taste.

"Yes, Helen, but of course you'll be in charge."

"No," she said. "John will be in charge. I shall be his assistant. Is that all right, John?"

John was staring at her with those intense dark eyes of his. She knew that look well, and smiled as he nodded.

Twenty minutes later, masked and gowned, they stood beside the operating table, the two senior British nurses similarly dressed, ready to assist. Helen knew that whatever private feelings distressed them, it would not influence their actions one iota. They would be as professional as ever.

It was one of the most astonishing experiences in her medical life. John was brilliant. He'd worked under Dr. Becker, Dr. Wilkie, Dick Ulrich, Herb Atkinson, all highly qualified surgeons educated in the best medical schools in the U.S.A. He had assimilated their techniques. He loved surgery, while Helen hated it. She remembered when, as a boy hardly out of his teens, he had nagged her to do more surgery so that he could assist and learn. Now his fingers were deft and practiced; his technique amazed her. Some of the time she did not know what he was doing. At one point she said, "But John, where are we now?"

His eyes above the mask did not move from his task. "Dr. Ulrich showed me that if the bladder gets involved in one of these difficult hernias, it's a good idea to evaginate the peritoneum. D'you see?"

She watched him in sheer amazement. She could see what he was doing, and he did it beautifully. Everything he did was carefully thought out and performed with minute accuracy. There was no panic, no haste; there were difficult moments, but he saw his way through them and overcame them. She was so thrilled, she could feel herself smiling behind her mask. That John, her very first student, was capable of such a performance excited and thrilled her.

At the end of it she thanked him politely for allowing her to assist, and he nodded and smiled, and between them was such a conspiratorial joy that neither could speak.

She went back to her old house of so many memories to have lunch with the two British nurses, a visitor, and the young American pilot. The two British nurses were cool and distant. Helen had betrayed them.

Helen understood how they felt and wanted to comfort them. They were old comrades in arms, and they had toiled and laughed and suffered together for many years; the fact that now they could not let go, could not comprehend what she was trying to do, saddened her immeasurably. Helen knew that John's qualifications were in a sense better than theirs for the particular job to be done; perhaps they felt an inferiority because of that; perhaps they were jealous of him and even jealous of her relationship with him. Perhaps they clung to the feeling that Nebo was really theirs, and they were frightened they might lose their positions or that people would not respect them if they worked under an African. Perhaps it was because they simply could not bring themselves to believe that he could do the job properly.

Of course, Helen had a special relationship with John. They had struggled together for seventeen years, and had seen the place grow from absolutely nothing. Without equipment, drugs, or laboratories—only an endless succession of patients needing help and their skill—they had supported each other, often at times when everything seemed against them. At any time John could have found a job with the government hospital service which would have paid him about three times what the mission gave him, but he stayed at Nebo and had married and brought up his children there, because he believed that God had called him to serve at Nebobongo. So she had to be on John's side no matter what the others thought.

Lunch ended and they went outside into the sunshine to board the Land-Rover to take them to Ibambi, where they would spend the night before flying on to Wamba.

One of the orderlies brought the news: Another villager had just staggered in suffering from the same ailment as the one earlier— a strangulated hernia. Death would be only hours away unless an operation was performed immediately.

John Mangadima was already examining the man on the veranda when they walked across. Helen's visitor asked, "Is this just a coincidence or is a strangulated hernia commonplace in this area?"

"Common enough," Helen replied, "though I've never had two in one day before. It's something to do with their diet."

Helen had already decided that this was not coincidence or luck, it was God. He had put this final, crucial opportunity into her hands, and she intended to use it.

"John," she said. "You can do this operation by yourself." She glanced at the two British nurses. "You have two very able assistants. If you need me I shall be at Ibambi, which is only seven miles away. I'll come back tomorrow morning to have a look at both patients."

As they drove along the familiar, red, rutted road past the rubber estate which Helen knew so well, she had fears about the outcome of her decision. The right moment had arrived to resolve the situation at Nebo, and she had seized it. And she had things to say at Ibambi. The meeting with Jack Scholes and the committee that night lasted three hours, and Helen emerged from it tired from arguing, reasoning, and persuading. Next morning when they returned to Nebo she walked straight into John Mangadima's house. "Sit down, John," she said as he approached her. "I've got some news. It's worked out. You're officially going to be made director of the hospital, with the right to do emergency operations. We shall have to clear it all with WEC back in England and with Nyankunde, but we've done it, John, we've done it!"

He stared at her. Then he got up and flung his arms around her and hugged her, the tears running down his face, and she wept too. All the years of waiting, praying, believing, and trusting had resolved themselves so wonderfully. Helen could not resist, a minute later, giving him a little Christian homily on the future, because the situation seemed to call for it. "Hold tight to a testament of humility and graciousness," she said. "Every operation you do, you must ask God to do it with you. The day will come when you'll have the tragedy of a death on the operating table, and it will be very hard to bear. You must understand this and be ready to meet it."

She examined the two hernia patients with him. Both were doing well. Then she went back to the house to pick up the rest of the party for the flight to Wamba. One of the younger mission girls told her, "Oh, they've been on the radio circuit from Nyankunde for you, Helen. They wanted to pass on the message that they've received an official government acknowledgment that the school is accredited. They said you'd want to know that."

Helen, still overcome from her session with John, was in no fit state to take it in. March 20, 1971, was a day to remember. And, by an odd coincidence, the people of Wamba also decided to seize their opportunity to make something of the day.

The small party flew out of the jungle airstrip at Nebobongo and landed at Wamba some twenty minutes later. Daisy Kingdon met them with a Land-Rover and as they jolted towards her mission, Helen smiled as she heard the noise of the talking drums in the distance. They were saying, "Our doctor's here!"

"That's a fine welcome," she said to Daisy.

"I think," Daisy responded, "they have something arranged for after lunch."

They drove first to the grounds of the old convent. Helen had not revisited the place since her traumatic departure in 1964. It was quiet and almost deserted. Eventually they found an African nun who took them to the one priest in residence. He was a tall, pale Dutch father who spoke good English. No, the nuns had not returned, and he thought it very unlikely that they would ever do so. The Mother Superior, Marie Frances, and the other Belgian nuns could be found in convents in their native country; Sister Dominique and the Italians were in northern Italy. Perhaps one day other sisters would return. He did not know. He thought it sad, of course, since this was such a wonderful place for a convent: It was so quiet and peaceful here.

Helen walked along the corridors and stared out over the sunlit expanse of countryside. It seemed impossible that the events of 1964 and the terror she remembered so clearly could ever have existed. Wamba still showed signs of its war damage, but its citizens had certainly recovered their resilience. In the distance they heard the drums begin to beat, the bugles and trumpets begin to sound. Slowly the enormous procession of schoolchildren and adults came into sight, marching in line abreast and singing. It looked as if every school in Wamba had been closed for the afternoon and they were performing in honor of "our doctor's visit."

They marched, the drums beat, the flags flew, and the bugles sounded. The children lined up in ranks outside the mission, several hundred of them—the entire child population of Wamba, so it seemed—and sang more songs.

The senior headmaster stood up to make his speech of welcome, apologizing for its brevity because it had been only three hours before that he had heard of Helen's coming. His speech lasted half an hour, and he chided Helen on a number of counts. Why did she think only of the west bank of the Nepoko river, where they had a huge hospital at Nebobongo? What was she doing for Wamba and the east bank, where all they had was a dispensary? Why did she not open a leprosy clinic for them? Why did she consider them poor cousins? The harangue was long and his questions were searching.

"It is not possible to forget you," Helen replied after the children had sung another song. "After all, the National Army helped to rescue us from here in the time of the

troubles, and I shall never forget the kindness and consideration of the people of Wamba during all the years I've
known them. But you must remember that a newborn baby
has to crawl before it walks, and walk before it runs."
There was no point in being less than direct, as they had
been. She continued, "You've just reached the crawling
stage. You have a dispensary, and next year we'll open a
maternity ward." Now she turned to the things *they* had to
do. "But the airstrip is not really long enough for Nyankunde's planes, and you'll have to lengthen it so that your
hospital can go on the rota of visiting doctors. And remember, most of these things depend on you. You need trained
medical personnel to run your dispensaries, clinics, and
hospitals. Therefore, you must send us your sons and
daughters to train as nurses and doctors. Send them to us
and we'll return them ready to be of service to the community."

They all cheered after that, formed up with military pre-
cision, and marched and sang their way back to town.
Helen smiled and waved them good-bye. There was something so wonderfully down-to-earth about these Congolese
occasions. They turned out to greet you with flags, trumpets,
and bugles as a returning heroine, but seized the occasion to
remind you of the deficiencies you were continuing to
struggle with.

She went back into the mission, where Daisy Kingdon
was preparing tea for everyone. What a great day it had
been! Accreditation for Nyankunde, promotion for John
Mangadima. Helen was probably more pleased about what
had happened to John than anything else that had happened
to her in Congo. It was an event comparable with the success of those first students—of whom John had been one—
nearly twenty years ago. This promotion ushered in a new
era; an African was the medical director at Nebo. She

knew that she would now go back to England in the autumn of 1973, well pleased, knowing that the medical school at Nyankunde was fully established, that others could take on her managerial position, and that John could cope perfectly at Nebobongo. Whether she would return to Congo, whether WEC would have a new assignment for her attention, she did not know. She did not really care; the future could take care of itself.

A few months later John was officially confirmed in his appointment. There was a celebration, and he was presented with a new motor bicycle. It was a beautiful machine, sparkling with chrome and enamel, which would enable him to visit Nebo's widespread clinics with speed and regularity.

As he swung his leg across the saddle on that glorious day, he caught Helen's eye and smiled. She smiled back. Their triumph, like their love and affection, was shared. They had come a long way together, the black man from the rain forest and the white woman from England.